Sweigey

In Good Company

In Good Company

Company

THE CHURCH AS POLIS

by *Stanley Hauerwas*

University of Notre Dame Press
Notre Dame and London

Library of Congress Cataloging-in-Publication Data

Hauerwas, Stanley, 1940–
    In good company : the Church as polis / Stanley Hauerwas.
        p.   cm.
    Includes bibliographical references and index.
    ISBN 0-268-01172-9 (alk. paper)
    1. Church   2. Christian ethics—Methodist authors.   I. Title.
BV600.2.H364   1995   94-40578
262—dc20   CIP

The aesthetics of cricket demand first that you master the game, and, preferably, have played it, if not well, at least in good company. And that is not the easy acquisition outsiders think it to be.

C. L. R. James

To
Paula Gilbert
For making me part of her
good company

Contents

Acknowledgments

The author and publisher are grateful to the following for permission to reprint:

The Scottish Journal of Theology for "What Could It Mean for the Church to Be Christ's Body? A Question Without a Clear Answer," reprinted from vol. 47, 1 (Winter 1994): 1–21.

Abingdon Press, publishers of *Theology Without Foundations: Religious Practice and the Future of Theological Truth*, edited by Stanley Hauerwas, Nancey Murphy, and Mark Nation, 1994, for "The Church's One Foundation Is Jesus Christ Her Lord or In a World Without Foundations All We Have Is the Church."

Missiology: An International Review for "Why *Resident Aliens* Struck a Chord," reprinted from vol. XIX, 4 (October 1991): 419–29.

Brethren Life and Thought for "Whose Church? Which Future? Whither the Anabaptist Vision," reprinted from vol. 39, 3 (Summer 1994): 141–52.

South Atlantic Quarterly for "A Homage to Mary and to the University Called Notre Dame," reprinted from vol. 93, 3 (Summer 1994): 717–26.

First Things for "The Importance of Being Catholic: A Protestant View," reprinted from vol. 1 (March 1990): 21–30.

University Press of America, publishers of *Co-Creation and Capitalism*, edited by John Houck and Oliver Williams, 1983, for "Work As Co-Creation: A Remarkably Bad Idea."

Theology for "In Praise of *Centesimus Annus*," reprinted from vol. XCV, 768 (November/December 1992): 416–32.

First Things for "Living in Truth," reprinted from vol. 39 (January 1994): 21–23.

Theology Today for "The Chief End of All Flesh," reprinted from vol. XLIX, 2 (July 1992): 196–208.

De Paul Law Review for "The Kingship of Christ: Why Freedom of Belief Is Not Enough," reprinted from vol. 42, 1 (Fall 1992): 107–27.

Preface

Christianity is connections. Connections often have a bad press, implying that through connections we can get things done in an underhanded fashion. Yet the connections that constitute Christianity, while certainly letting us get things done that would be otherwise impossible, are not hidden. To be a Christian is to be joined, to be put in connection with others so that our stories cannot be told without somehow also telling their stories. Through such telling and retellings we believe that God makes us part of God's story.

One of the remarkable things that I have discovered through writing are connections with others quite different from me and often at great distances. My life has been enriched by Catholics and Protestants around the world—in Australia, in Italy, in Ireland, in Germany, in the Netherlands, in South Africa, in Russia, and even in the United States—who have claimed me by taking my work seriously. To be so claimed is at once gratifying and frightening, but it is also a source of hope that in spite of everything God has not given up on the church. For being so connected I at least know I am made more than I could ever try to be.

One of those connections, Dr. Arne Rasmusson, a Swede, is partly responsible for this book. I first met Arne in England, where he told me he was planning to write a book on Moltmann and me for his doctorate at Lund University. I confess that I was skeptical, not of Arne's abilities but whether I was a fit subject for that kind of serious attention. Once his book was done, coupled with the University of Notre Dame Press decision to publish it, it occurred to me this book might make a kind of companion volume. There are others, such as

Reinhard Hütter, whose work have influenced the direction taken in this book, but I call attention to Arne's book as an example of the kind of connection so important for all of us trying to do theology for the church.

I am indebted to my old "connections" for helping make this book possible. I hope my footnotes indicate some of those debts to the living and the dead, to those I actually know and those I know only through books, to enemies and friends. I have been told that I footnote too much, but I think of footnotes as a way to name the connections that sustain me. I hope that my ongoing debt is obvious to those "connections" called David Burrell, C.S.C., James McClendon, Jean Bethke Elshtain, Robert Wilken, Alasdair MacIntyre, Nicholas Lash, John Howard Yoder. Less obvious, but no less important, is the influence of past and present graduate students who are determined to educate me.

Four of the chapters in this book have been co-authored. William Willimon is a good friend who first suggested that we should try to write something together. We have now done a number of essays and two books. Will said that he was going to make me famous and I will be damned if he has not come close to doing that—at least as famous as any theologian deserves. David Burrell, C.S.C., is one of my oldest friends. We have previously written together and I hope we shall find occasion to do so in the future. We are not members of the same church, nor do we any longer teach at the same university, but happily we continue to discover that we share judgments that make it not only possible but imperative for us from time to time to write together.

Dr. John Berkman, now of Sacred Heart University, is a former graduate student. He forced me to confront my unexamined assumptions about animals and much else. He is, however, wrong to think the American League is superior to the National League. Michael Baxter, C.S.C., I have known almost as long as Burrell. He was originally a student at the University of Notre Dame and is now completing his Ph.D in theology at Duke. I am indebted to John and Michael for risking their futures with me. I am unsure how well I am playing the game, but I am sure I would not play it nearly so well if my life were not graced by such company.

This book feels like a homecoming because for me it is a kind of homecoming. I am again being published by the University of Notre

Dame Press. Notre Dame Press took the risk of publishing me when the emphasis on the virtues seemed quaint and the stress on the church anachronistic. There is still risk, though I suspect of a different kind, in publishing this book. Yet to be published again by Notre Dame seems right, but given the subject of this book it is rightly published by Notre Dame.

I am now, of course, at Duke University. I am indebted to the many friends and colleagues at Duke from whom I not only learn but are a source of delight. Mrs. Wanda Dunn remains the one most needing thanks. She not only tells me when and where I am supposed to be, when I need to write what I had forgotten I had ever promised to write, but she also does all the correspondence that all those connections require. Without her this book would not be. Dr. Jim Fodor, a post-doctoral student from Canada, has not only been an invaluable conversation partner but has also improved the style of these essays. I am indebted to him for the index, which readers of my past work will note is far superior to any I have done.

Paula and I have been married six years. I am not sure which books I have published since we have been together, but I have long wanted to dedicate one to her. I wanted it to be the right one. I hope there will be others equally appropriate, but I believe that this book is about what she cares about. I did not, however, follow her advice for the title of this book. "Mary and Me" is a good title, but somehow it just did not seem "me." That Paula has chosen me as the one with whom she is willing to share her solitude, her humor, and her love of God, all of which I suspect are closely connected, is an extraordinary gift. I thank God for her company.

Introduction

I. Church Matters[1]

In his novel *The Brothers K*, James David Duncan deals only with matters that matter, that is, God and baseball.[2] The novel tells the story of the family Chance's struggle to survive capitalism, war, and the sixties. They have two important resources for survival—Hugh Chance's skill and love of baseball and Laura Chance's fanatical commitment to the Seventh-Day Adventist Church. Just as baseball and Christianity do not always mix well, Hugh and Laura's marriage is filled with conflict. Yet the acquired skills necessary to play baseball and worship God finally conspire to enable them and their children, Everett, Peter, Irwin, and Kincaid and the twins, Bet and Freddy, to save Irwin from being "erased" by the United States military.

The part of the story I want to tell involves Everett's sermon in 1971 at the First Adventist Church of Washougal, Washington. It was an extraordinary sermon, since Everett did not believe in God. His youthful "atheism" resulted in him being virtually disowned by his mother. He had "grown up" to be a student "leader" in the anti-Vietnam War movement at the University of Washington. He finally had to escape to Canada to avoid the draft. Coming back to deliver the sermon meant he would certainly go to jail.

Yet he came back because he thought that it was the only way he had to free his brother Irwin from the "care" he was receiving at a military hospital because he had allegedly gone crazy in Vietnam. Irwin's "craziness" was due to his inability to do as his brothers had done, that is, lose his faith. Irwin never doubted that God was to be found at the

1

First Adventist Church of Washougal. Irwin not only held the church's consecutive Bible Memory Verse record, but also the consecutive attendance record. The latter cost him dearly, because to achieve it he had to miss every ball game Hugh Chance pitched on the Sabbath. Even as he killed, Irwin could not forget, "Thou shalt not kill."

Irwin's trouble began when the Army captain, to whom he was assigned as an aide-de-camp, ordered that a young Vietnamese boy who had been taken prisoner be shot. The boy had probably killed a GI with a booby trap. Yet Irwin recognized that even though this "enemy" was a killer he was still just a boy. Such recognition forced, as Everett describes in his sermon, a reversion in Irwin from being a U.S. soldier to a Christian soldier. Accordingly, Irwin chose to attack his captain with a tube of toothpaste, a Gleem attack, which resulted in some damage to the captain's teeth. In return, Irwin received two concussions and a skull fracture from a rifle butt. The real problem began after the beating, when Irwin kept singing and praying in the brig. The Army decided that they wanted him silenced since his faith seemed recriminatory, which, as Everett points out, it was. After all, Irwin's faith entailed that one "Do good to those who hate you."

The Army, in the person of a psychiatrist, a Major Keyes, diagnosed Irwin as psychotic because he continued to babble about Jesus. According to the Major, Irwin's only hope was electric shock treatment and drugs. Even Hugh Chance, who went so far as to interrupt the baseball season to attend to Irwin's situation, could not persuade the Major that Irwin's "religious speech" was his attempt to hold on to the only thing that he thought could give him sanity in an insane world. The failure of Hugh Chance to deliver Irwin created a hopelessness in the family that finally resulted in Everett's sermon.

Having driven all night from Canada, Everett burst into the service just as Elder Kim Joon, a convert from the Adventist Korean Mission, was about to preach. His interruption was tolerated because his mother, overcoming her alienation from Everett, in a voice quavering with conviction and fear, intervened: "That's my oldest. That's Everett. And he's not an Adventist anymore, or even a Christian maybe. But he came here to tell you something I tried to tell but couldn't. So he's brave, I know that much. And he loves his brother. I know that now too. My family is a good family. We're not a bunch of crazies. But Irwin, what's happening to Irwin, it's making us all—Well *look* at us." Unleashed, Everett began:

The reason my heart, all our hearts, are hurtin' so bad is that the numbskulled heart of our family, the one who always managed to love *all* of us, no matter what we thought or said or believed, is in terrible trouble. And the reason I came here, to Irwin's God's House, is that his trouble started here. I'm not trying to place blame by saying that. This whole situation is a compliment to the staying power of what gets taught here, really. Irwin, after he left here, kept on keeping your faith right up till the day he was unfairly drafted.[3] And every letter we got from him, even from 'Nam, was a Christian letter—the letter of a man who couldn't begin to reconcile *Thou shalt not kill* or *Love thy neighbor* with the duties of a soldier. He's still yours, Winnie is. That's the crux of all I'm saying. He still loves this place, still believes every blame thing he ever learned here, and still tells me I'm nuts when I try to tamper with those beliefs.[4]

Everett then told the congregation what Irwin had done and what the Army was doing to him—namely, trying to erase his faith by erasing Irwin through massive doses of sedatives and EST "treatments." Such treatment is called "therapy," but, Everett observes, "it is the songs you sing here, the scriptures you read here, it's his belief in *this* House and its God that they are out to destroy. It may be hard for you to believe that red-blooded U.S. Army doctors consider your faith a form of madness. But I tell you, Winnie—he's trying to hold himself together by singing little Sabbath School ditties down there, and saying Memory Verses and prayers, right through those terrible sedatives."

Like any good preacher Everett offered an imaginative alternative— "You know, you folks have your *own* doctors and shrinks. There's a med school in Loma Linda, very close to where Irwin's staying. And if some of you contacted those people by phone, or better, drove down and did it in person, I'll bet you could arrange for a *Christian* examination, by doctors who could see Irwin's faith for what it is." Everett, feeling the resistance in the congregation on being asked to act, paused, and changed his tact:

Unlike Irwin, or Bet, or Mama, I don't even believe in God. It's a little odd, for that reason, that I'd have strong feelings about His House. But I do. I feel—because I love Irwin very much—that it's crucial for me to at least *try* to address the One whose House Irwin believes this to be. Since I don't believe in Him, I'm not sure my words qualify as prayer. But I feel I must say directly to You—Irwin's dear God—that if somebody in this House doesn't hear our family's cry, if somebody isn't moved, not by me, but by You, to sacrifice some time and thought and energy for Irwin's sake, then his mind, his love for You, his belief in this House, are going to be destroyed. It's that simple, I think. Which puts the ball in Your court. Not a hopeful place to leave it, to my mind. But it's right where Irwin would want it. And for the first time in my life, I hope it's Irwin, not me, who's right about this place.[5]

This book I hope embodies Everett's hope in Irwin. It is a book about God and God's house. It is a book about salvation from a world that would "cure" Christians of our oddness. It is a book about the politics and practices that constitute that salvation made possible by God through the church. It is a book that believes that God is present even in churches as patriarchal, conservative, moralistic, self-righteous as the First Adventist Church of Washougal. It is a book written by an Everett who has been made more than he could ever hope by being graced by the good company of people like Irwin.

I am known as well as criticized because I have argued so strenuously that the church matters not only for how we live as Christians but how we do theology and ethics. For many, to claim such significance for the church appears dangerously "triumphalistic" and/or as a "withdrawal" from the Christian responsibility to serve all people, regardless of whether they are Christian or not. Moreover, to make the church the center of Christian life and thought seems either hopelessly idealistic or naive, given the "empirical realities" of most churches, particularly in America.

I am not unaware of the highly compromised nature of the church. I am, after all, a Methodist. I have seen the worst, since I attend Annual Conference, as would any obedient spouse of a Methodist minister. I am happy to be present at Conference as a spouse, but I am seldom happily there. The religious and theological vacuity is stifling. How a people who worship a crucified God could become so uninteresting is, as religious people like to say, a "mystery." More importantly, I hope it is a judgment of God.

Current "church-growth" strategies seem intent on proving that you can get people to come to church whether or not God exists.[6] No doubt they will be successful for a time, but the "churches" that result from such strategies are nothing more than paganism in Christian disguise. Indeed, such a description may be far too complementary, since paganism in the past was more substantive than the "religion" associated with the church growth movement. With the "triumph" of

Christianity under Constantine, pagans became so much more inter-esting, since to be a pagan required conviction. I do not expect the pagans that come "After Christendom" to be nearly so interesting.

Below, in chapter 10, I report on the basic course in Christian ethics I teach at Duke's Divinity School which is structured around the church's liturgy. I sometimes suggest that after teaching such a course for twenty-five years I hope to have half the Methodist ministers of the Carolinas feeling guilty for not celebrating the eucharist every Sunday. I know that they will not be doing it; I just want them to feel guilty for not doing so. Such guilt, after all, would be a small sign of hope.

I know that serving the eucharist every Sunday will not necessarily make the church more faithful, but at least God in 1 Corinthians 11 promised to kill us if we do it unworthily. I assume that as long as the church (at least "mainstream Protestantism") is dying, we might as well die for the right reasons. If members of the church are sick or dying for celebrating unworthily, it might at least indicate that God is still using us for God's salvation. When everything is said and done everything the church says and does is done because God matters. Moreover God, I believe, insists on using the church even in our unfaithfulness.

For example, the church, as far as I know, is the only community that is constituted by the practice of confession of sin. Such confes-sion cannot be genuine if it is assumed to be an explanation for sin or why the church is unfaithful. Sin, after all, should not be used as an explanation for anything, though it often is, particularly by theo-logians who think sin might "explain" the human condition. Rather, sin is a description, that is, sin is a "logically primitive" notion, which we only learn to use rightly by extensive training in confession. That confession is often used as an "excuse" is no doubt true, but the very fact that prayers of confession occur in worship means the church has a resource not available to the world.

That is the conviction that I hope animates the essays in this book. They are my attempt to assemble reminders to help us see that God has not abandoned God's church even, or especially, if God's presence means judgment. For I know that God continues to produce Irwins from churches that have done everything possible to hide the fact that God matters. As Everett noted in his sermon, Irwin's problems in Vietnam started in the First Adventist Church of Washougal. Such churches, almost beyond belief, produce ordinary people who do extraordinary things that make no sense if the church does not matter.

II. The Church as *Polis*

I have taken the subtitle of this book from Arne Rasmusson's wonderful book *The Church as Polis: From Political Theology to Theological Politics as Exemplified by Jürgen Moltmann and Stanley Hauerwas.*[7] Rasmusson observes that political theology, though it has quite different forms, was in general "an attempt to positively meet the challenges of modernity, characterized by industrialization, urbanization, science, technology, market economy and a growing state and its various ideological backbones in liberalism and socialism, with their common beliefs in progress and in politics as a means for consciously forming the future."[8] Political theology sought to mediate the Christian tradition in an apologetic fashion to the modern world. Rasmusson observes that political theology has increasingly been undermined by tensions not only between the Christian story and modernity but by the contradictions inherent in the modern project itself, now described as "post-modernism."[9]

  Rasmusson uses my work (which he characterizes as a "theological politics") to provide a contrast to political theology. According to Rasmusson, a theological politics understands the church as an alternative *polis* or *civitas*, which is constituted "by the new reality of the kingdom of God as seen in the life and destiny of Jesus. [Hauerwas] therefore understands the politics of the world, and relates to it, in the light of this new politics."[10] In contrast to political theology, which makes the political struggle for emancipation the horizon in which the church's theology and practice is interpreted, a theological politics makes the church's story the "counter story" that interprets the world's politics. Rasmusson notes that making the church the primary locus of politics not only changes the political horizon, but also requires a different understanding of the nature of politics.[11]

  The attempt to exhibit such a politics is what this book is about. Of course, much of my past work has had the same intent, but too often I have relied on abstract characterizations of politics rather than exhibits. Politics is certainly about the conversation necessary for a people across time to discover goods that they have in common, but what is needed is the actual display of the material practices that constitute that conversation. I have tried to do that by calling attention to practices so common to Christians that we hardly notice their significance. That we fail to do so is not necessarily a problem unless, as I think is often the case today, our failure to attend to these material practices results in their being made part of quite foreign narratives and/or lost altogether.

The C. L. R. James quote which is the epigraph of this book—"The aesthetics of cricket demand first that you master the game, and, preferably, have played it, if not well, at least in good company. And that is not the easy acquisition outsiders think it to be"[12]—suggests the kind of politics intrinsic to the salvation made available through the church. God's salvation made present in and through the church requires at the very least acquisition of skills as complex as those required to play cricket. Though such skills require great effort, it is a joyous effort exactly because through such effort we are made part of a common endeavor called worship.

James loved cricket first and foremost because it is such an engrossingly elegant game. He also loved cricket because it provided a liberation from the power of race and class. He was aware, of course, that racism was in cricket.[13] Yet by the very nature of cricket racism ought not to be. By learning to play cricket, by learning to watch cricket,[14] by learning to write about cricket, he tells us that he was plunged into politics long before he was aware of it. Moreover, when he did turn to politics he confesses that he did not have much to learn.[15] In like manner I assume that when Christians turn from our embeddedness in that politics called church we should not have much to learn.

Of course, the difficulty is that cricket for James (or baseball for many of us) seems more "real" than church. That such is the case is no doubt partly due to the fact that baseball asks more of us and is accordingly more fun. That baseball asks much of those who play and watch is the reason the game is open to construals of significance that seem as appropriate as they are surprising. For example consider these reflections from *The Brothers K*:

I cherish a theory I once heard propounded by G. Q. Durham that professional baseball is inherently antiwar. The most overlooked cause of war, his theory runs, is that it is so damned interesting. It takes hard effort, skill, love and a little luck to make times of peace consistently interesting. About all it takes to make war interesting is a life. The appeal of trying to kill others without being killed yourself is that it brings

suspense, terror, honor, disgrace, rage, tragedy, treachery and oc-
casionally even heroism within range of guys who, in times of peace,
might lead lives of unmitigated blandness. But baseball is one activity
that is able to generate suspense and excitement on a national scale, just
like war. And baseball can only be played in peace. Hence G.Q.'s thesis
that pro ballplayers—little as some of them want to hear it—are basically
just a bunch of unusually well-coordinated guys working hard and artfully
to prevent wars, by making peace more interesting.[16]

My strategy is to try to help us recover the everyday practices that
constitute that *polis* called church that are every bit as interesting and
exciting as baseball. What we Christians have lost is just how radical
our practices are, since they are meant to free us from the excitement
of war and the lies so characteristic of the world. The difficulty is that
the church, for some quite understandable reasons, is constantly
tempted to imitate the false politics of the world for its own life. Such
politics, based as they are on fear and envy, undermine the joy that
Christians should find in the difficult but rewarding task of being
church.

I should not hide the fact that informing this account of the church
is a quite different understanding of salvation than is assumed by
many Christians today. I have little use for the current fascination
with individual salvation in either its conservative or liberal guises.
Such accounts of salvation assume that God has done something for
each person which may find expression in the church. I do not assume
that salvation is first and foremost about my life having "meaning" or
insuring "my" eternal destiny. Rather, salvation is being engrafted
into practices that save us from those powers that would rule our lives
making it impossible for us to truly worship God.

Rev. Joe Dinoia, O.P., observes that Christian soteriological
doctrines must be set into the whole pattern of the Christian life.
Accordingly, any description of salvation must suggest how "the
dispositions to attain and enjoy the true aim of life develop over the
course of a lifetime of divinely engendered and sustained 'cultivation.'
Christian salvation means, finally, becoming a certain kind of person, one who can enjoy the end of life that the Christian community
commends. It makes no difference to the specificity of this aim that
Christians believe it to be identical with the aim all human beings
should seek."[17] The church's politics is our salvation.

III. In Good Company

Yet we cannot forget that essential to that politics, particularly for those of us who, as James puts it, play, but "not well," it is crucial we play in good company. James does not define what he means by "good company," but rather displays what a good company entails through his depiction of people who created in him a love for cricket and writing. Some of that company, such as Constantine, the great West Indian cricketer, he knew well. Yet James equally counted W. G. Grace, the great Victorian cricket player who transformed the game, part of the company that formed him. He makes Grace as vivid for us as he was for James by providing an extraordinary account of Grace and the contribution he made to cricket.[18]

Christianity is the name given that company across the generations that have learned from one another the skills necessary for the worship of the God made known in Jesus Christ. Of course, worship itself is a skill distinguishable only by the centrality and purpose it gives to all that Christians do. Like cricket, or baseball, the worship of God to be appropriately "appreciated" requires mastery that comes from "playing" well, but such mastery requires masters located within the company. So the skills required to worship well are not separable from the company itself. That is why theology, even one that is strictly "orthodox," proves insufficient for the care of the tradition, since it lacks the company necessary for it to do its work for the upbuilding of the community.[19]

Christians confess that we "believe in the Holy Spirit, the holy catholic church, the communion of saints, the forgiveness of sins, the resurrection of the body, and life everlasting." Such a confession seems odd, since why should we confess belief in what seems so apparent? Does not "church" simply name those diverse groups that gather on Sundays that, in spite of their differences, still claim some identity as Christian? Yet at least in some of those gatherings those gathered rightly confess their belief in the church. They do so since confession is the practice necessary for Christians to remember that the church is God's creation, not our own.[20] God has given and will continue to give us company so that we will know how rightly to worship. Those who have gone before, like W. G. Grace, made and continue to make our faithful living possible through that skill called memory. Such a memory is not "in the head," but rather in the material habits that make us what we are.

Of course, the church calls some, who today are often called historians, to engage in a systematic fashion in the discipline of remembering those who have gone before as part of the exercise of faithful living. Yet Christians do not believe in an ecclesial golden age which we must constantly try to repristinate.[21] We are tempted to think that our forebears were more faithful than we are as, no doubt, they often were. Yet to be faithful to them and, more importantly, to God, we cannot try to make their accomplishments an achievement that can free us from being as courageous as they were.

For example, it took extraordinary courage for the church to create the canon, to make the Old Testament forever part of the Christian story, to make the church's story unintelligible apart from our ongoing relation with Judaism. We cannot remain church if we ever abandon those decisions, but such "decisions" are not "back there," done forever, but rather require the same courageous skills of our forebears if we are to be capable of the "innovations" faithfulness requires. Such skills are appropriately called political, since they require Christians as God's company of people to maintain the life of the church so that the gifts of those who have made us what we are will not be lost.

These essays fall into that area of theology called ecclesiology, but I do not pretend to deal adequately with the scriptural, historical, and systematic issues usually thought necessary to "do" ecclesiology.[22] Such work is indispensable and much of what I have done in this book I hope indicates how much I have learned from those who do more "traditional" ecclesiological studies. In truth, I am not sure how to characterize the genre of essays in this book other than to suggest they are my attempt to tell others what I have learned from those Christians—Catholic, Protestant, and Anabaptist—who have claimed me as part of their company. I should like to think what I have done here might make some contribution to the ecumenical task, but I am aware that my views are too "homeless" to represent "a church."[23] If these essays are "ecumenical" they are so because of the various "good companies" that have claimed me.

As will be clear from the essays in this book, I do not have a clear ecclesial stance. I do not know whether I am Protestant or Catholic, which is not surprising since I am a Methodist. Methodism, or at least Methodism as construed by Albert Outler, Robert Cushman, Thomas Langford, and Geoffrey Wainwright, among others, is that form of "practical divinity" that has both Catholic and Protestant motifs.[24] It is no doubt true that most Methodists in America would be surprised to learn they are members of a "perfectionist sect," but some of us continue to count ourselves Methodists because we cannot deny that God, through this company, as accommodated as it may be, put us on the road toward perfection.[25]

I have not tried to hide the ambiguous character of my ecclesial stance, but rather I have tried to turn it into a resource for service for Protestant and Catholic alike. God knows what God is doing by making some of us ecclesially homeless, but at least my homelessness has made it possible as well as necessary for me to learn from other Christians.[26] You do not spend fourteen years with the Catholics at Notre Dame without being marked by that experience. Nor is it easy to ignore the Anabaptists when you have been as deeply influenced as I have by John Howard Yoder and James McClendon.[27] Yet I am aware that I remain a person primarily shaped, for good and ill, by the practices of mainstream American Protestantism. I do not pretend that the ecclesial position developed here is finally coherent, but only that I have tried to do justice to what that good company of people have taught me.

Some of these essays may appear far too "personal" to be considered "serious" theology. For example I actually "name" people, such as Charlie Sheedy, C.S.C., who for me was "Catholicism." I am aware, of course, that there is more to Catholicism than Charlie, but that is also a lesson I learned from him. One of the essays, moreover, is in honor of the life and work of James McClendon. It is not "about" Jim, but I hope it at least elicits the "Catholicity" of this Baptist.[28] That essay also includes the most personal piece in this book—a sermon I preached at my father's funeral. I was hesitant to "use" the sermon in an essay, but I finally thought it appropriate in an essay honoring McClendon. He and my father not only share being Southern but an extraordinarily hard gentleness. I have included the sermon because it is the only way I have of naming the importance of my father's company for helping me master, in whatever small way I have, the skills and practices of being Christian.

IV. Do We Need "Yet Another Book from Hauerwas"[29]

Some have observed that I write (and publish) much—indeed, far too much. I confess that I am not quite sure what to make of this criticism.

I feel a bit like one of my former colleagues at Notre Dame, a philosopher and a Catholic, who was once told by a person concerned with what was then called the "population explosion," that he had too many children. It seems he was over the appropriate limit by three and a half children. He was puzzled by how to have "a half," but even more he wanted to know which ones he should have left out. I do not want to be told that I write too much. Tell me what you want left out and why.

There are two standard criticisms against those who write a great deal: (1) we are repetitious, or (2) we are not careful. I am not sympathetic with either of these criticisms in the abstract and, in particular, applied to my work. I do not believe that repetition is a fault, but only repetition that is boring can be faulted. It is not for me to decide whether my work is boring, but I can say one of the things I most despise is boredom and I am not bored by my writing. Writing often exhausts me because it is hard work but enjoyable precisely for the same reason. Of course, it is not just the writing that is hard, it is the thinking that is inseparable from the writing that is hard. Yet the hardness of the writing as well as what I write about means that I am seldom bored by what I do.

I confess that I neither have nor do I intend to read back through what I have written to see if I am repeating myself. I do sometimes have the occasion to reread something I have written, but I do so not in order to avoid saying something again, but to recapture what I once thought. For what I once thought may be better thought than I currently think. Of course, it is also true that some of the ways I currently have learned to think are more adequate than what I once thought. Which is but a way to remind myself and the reader that we are in this thing together to the extent that readers may read better than I write (or think). As a result, I am often pushed to write by new readings by myself and others about what I have written in the past.

I do not write because I am interested in trying to develop another "position" to populate the academic landscape. I am trying to foment a modest revolution by forcing Christians to take themselves seriously as Christians. Such an ambition means that I am not simply trying to give new answers to old questions, but I am trying to change the questions. That forces me to develop new, or at least different, ways of putting matters that are not easily learned—particularly by me. To change the questions involves nothing less than learning to speak differently.[30] To learn a language, as anyone knows who teaches or has learned a second language, requires repetition. I find that if I do not go over the same ground I forget what I believe and care about.

Repetition is not foreign to the most common of Christian activities. For example, we go to church Sunday after Sunday where we, hopefully, do pretty much the same thing. We rightly do not tire of such repetition because it is ever new. Moreover, through repetition we discover that we are empowered with resources to resist those powers that would have us forget what God has done to us through our baptism—baptisms we must learn to remember since our baptism cannot be repeated. Yet just as repetition is never the "same," simply because it is impossible for it to be such, so I hope readers who are good enough to read my work will find changes that are surprising and enlivening.[31]

To the charge that my work cannot be "careful" because no one can write as much as I do and be careful, I have no response. Since the criticism is true by definition, no reply can be sufficient. I do not believe, however, that my work is "careless," though I know what I am trying is risky and the risk is increased by my "contrarian" or polemical style.[32] The risks I take are of the academic sort and, therefore, not all that "risky." I know that I recklessly cross academic lines, which makes me vulnerable to those who know "more," but given the task before theology I cannot conceive of any alternative. Such risks are minor given the challenges before the church.

Polemics are also risky, since they invite retaliation. That is fair and good, but it also results in my writing more. I do try to respond to criticism, as I often learn even from criticisms that I think are flat out mistaken. I cannot help but be sympathetic even with what I think are misshapen criticisms, because they are to be expected when you are trying to change the questions. I confess, however, that I have now been writing over twenty years without remarkable success in changing the questions.[33] So all I can do is keep writing in the hope the exercise of writing and reading will make a difference to me and, hopefully, to that good company called church.[34]

It is nonetheless true that I do not try to write "the last word" about anything. That is partly because I do not believe in the last word about anything, but also because I find the politics of such scholarship offensive. "Perfection" kills community. To try to write to anticipate all possible criticism, to qualify all strong claims in the name of "scholarship," protects authors but too often produces work that serves to defeat the necessity of community. That it does so is not surprising, since that is exactly what it is meant to do. In contrast, I assume the point is to write in a manner that invites others to care about what I care about because they sense there is so much to do given the incompleteness of what I have done.[35]

I have not tried to arrange the essays in this book to make a cumulative argument. The essays in the first section, "In Protestant Company," are "Protestant" primarily because they are not Catholic. The first chapter is in many ways the most theoretical but I thought it necessary to begin with it, even though it was one of the last written, since it sets the agenda for the rest of the book. Through the writing of that essay I discovered better how to read my earlier essays regarding the church's importance for ethics. I hope the readers of this book will discover something similar. Chapter Two was an essay written to honor James McClendon, but its most unusual feature is my use of sermons to "make" the argument. What better way to argue for the significance of practices such as preaching than to preach? Of course, once sermons appear as "text" they may lose their character as sermons, but I nonetheless hope they "work."

The term "Resident Aliens" in the title of the next chapter refers to the book by that title which I wrote with Will Willimon.[36] That book has now sold over 50,000 copies. I think our reflections about why the book has "struck" a chord are illuminating for no other reason than for what they suggest about the character of contemporary Protestantism. The next essay may seem far too specific to the Anabaptist context for some readers, especially those who have never heard of Harold Bender. All I can say is that it is time for mainstream Protestants and Catholics to learn who he was and, more importantly, about those people who produced him and continue to argue about his significance for their lives.

The essays "In Catholic Company," excepting the first one, are more strictly concerned with "ethics" and, in particular, the Catholic social encyclicals. Yet the first essay, I hope, helps "set the scene" for the more formal reflections on moral theology and the encyclicals, particularly for the non-Catholic reader. Catholicism is a world in which I was privileged to live and work for fourteen years. The first two essays are my attempt to give something back to that world by saving it from people like me.[37]

I have included the essay on *Laborem Exercens* even though in the next essay on *Centesimus Annus* I take back some of the criticism I made about the former encyclical. I still think, however, that the primary argument I make against *Laborem Exercens* is correct — namely, that the understanding of work in the encyclical does not appropriately suggest how work is at once distorted by sin and yet the means God gives us to serve one another.[38] Yet the power of *Centesimus Annus* and *Veritatis Splendor* are a remarkable testimony to the theological and moral discourse that Catholicism is capable of producing. I know of no other tradition so capable of providing such a telling and critical stance on our world.

I confess that I have wondered if it was quite fair to make Václav Havel an ally of the Pope, but the recent speech he gave when he received the Liberty Medal makes me think I may be right to do so.[39] In that speech, which I suspect came as a surprise to some of those who gave Havel the Liberty Medal, Havel notes that the ideas that shape the politics of the "Euro-American" sphere, such as the notion of rights, were based on an Enlightenment view of man. The notion of "inalienable human rights grew out of the typically modern notion that man — as a being capable of knowing nature and the world — was the pinnacle of creation and the lord of the world." This modern anthropocentrism, Havel argues, inevitably meant that the Creator, who had allegedly endowed us with dignity, was "gradually pushed into a sphere of privacy of sorts, if not directly into a sphere of private fancy — that is, to a place where public obligations no longer apply." Havel suggests that when "rights and freedom" are no longer seen as integral parts of a meaningful world order they cannot help but appear, as many today suggest they are, as fantasies.

Havel quotes "a modern philosopher": "Only a God can save us now" to suggest that only someone who submits to the authority of the universal order and values their participation in the created order "can genuinely value himself and his neighbor, and thus honor their rights as well." Havel calls this recognition of our creatureliness "transcendence," which is our only "real alternative to extinction." He concludes, "The Declaration of Independence, adopted 218 years ago in this building, states that the Creator gave man the right to liberty. It seems man can realize that liberty only if he does not forget the one who endowed him with it."[40]

Havel's appeal to transcendence is an attempt to save the liberal project from self-destruction. Such an appeal is not only philosophically incoherent, but "transcendence" cannot save us. By criticizing

Havel I do not mean to suggest, as is obvious from my use of him below, that he has nothing to teach us. Havel has to make vague appeals to transcendence because he does not have a church; at least, he does not have a church as president of the Czech Republic receiving the Liberty Medal. But Christians do have a church, whose task is not to save the liberal project but to be the church.

Of course, I am not trying to save the liberal project, I am trying to save the church from the liberal project. If that can be done then the church may actually be able to make a contribution to the world that comes "after liberalism." I certainly hope that will be the case. If any church has the resources for surviving liberalism as well as helping us see alternatives to liberalism, Catholicism does. My reflections on the encyclicals are shaped by that judgment.

The last section of the book, "Ecclesial Ethics," contains essays that are more strictly "ethical." Each is meant to illumine my conten-tion that the "ethics" done by Christians makes no sense abstracted from the practices of the church. The first essay in this section describes how I teach Christians ethics structured by the liturgy. By submitting the very way I organize a course to the discipline of worship, I hope to show that the argument of this book is not just another "idea."[41] The following essay on casuistry is meant to display how such an understanding of ethics makes a difference for concrete adjudication of cases. The next chapter on the status of animals, I hope exhibits the kind of casuistry I tried to defend in the preceding chapter. That essay, moreover, develops some of the more strictly "theological" arguments running through the other essays.

The chapter on "freedom of religion" seems a fitting climax to the book. To challenge the pieties shared equally by religious and secular people—namely, those that undergird the celebration of "freedom of religion" in America—means you will surely need a church to protect you.[42] Moreover the focus on the feast of Christ the King is a reminder that what keeps the state limited is not a constitution, but a people who are formed by worshipful practices that can produce people like Irwin Chance and his family.

PART I

In Protestant Company

What Could It Mean for
the Church to Be Christ's Body?
A Question without a
Clear Answer

I. Why Some Remnants of "Constantinianism" Are, after All, Not Such a Bad Idea[1]

We were on our honeymoon. Theological questions were not high on our agenda as we toured Ireland in 1988. We drove innocently into Sneem, a village on the ring of Kerry, identified as the "tidy town of Ireland." It was certainly that. The houses that surrounded the central square were as immaculate as they were colorful.

We decided to stop and shop at one of the stores selling Irish sweaters. We were enjoying the large and beautiful selection the shop offered when, suddenly, the young man who seemed to be the proprietor announced that he had to close up shop in order to go to Mass. It was eleven o'clock on a Thursday. So I asked what was going on that might make an enterprising young man close his store just as the tourists were showing up.

He explained that it was the feast of the Ascension and also the traditional day marked for first communion. Suddenly little boys and girls appeared from everywhere fitted with white suits and white dresses. Then they all marched together into the church for Mass. After Mass, we were told, they all came out of the church, circled the fountain in the center of the square, while everyone in the town cheered and clapped. This was confirmed in every little town we

This paper was prepared for the Society for the Study of Theology meeting at Winchester College, Oxford (April 1994).

passed through that day in west Ireland. Little girls and boys dressed in white were everywhere celebrating their first communion.

I confess that I have suspicions about what it means to dress up young girls to become brides of Christ. I even have deeper questions about the very idea of "first communion," believing that if you baptize infants there is no reason not to commune them. Yet I could not suppress the thought: "If this is Constantinianism, I rather like it."[2]

That, of course, is not a thought I am supposed to have. I have, after all, been labeled a "sectarian, fideistic tribalist" who is calling for the church to beat a retreat from the world.[3] George Hunsinger and William Placher, in a note introducing a particular essay by Hans Frei observe that the essay

> is valuable for understanding Frei because of the way it addresses political themes. An interest in progressive politics was an important part of his life but something he wrote about only rarely. Many of those often placed in the same theological camp as Frei seem to propose that the Christian community focus on its own internal identity, arguing that it serves the larger society best when it witnesses to the possibility of a different kind of community formed by a different language. Stanley Hauerwas maintains such a stance most forcefully, but it also sometimes appears in the works of George Lindbeck.[4]

This puts me in a particularly difficult position, not only with regard to explaining why I find Sneem on the feast of the Ascension so attractive, but also in fulfilling the mandate that came with the kind invitation to address this conference. As Dr. Logan put it in his letter to me, "The overall theme for the 1994 Conference is taken appropriately from the famous letter of Bonhoeffer of 30 April 1944: 'Who is Jesus Christ for Us Today?' We therefore invite you to give the final paper on the topic: 'The Church as the Body of Christ', drawing out the ecclesiological-ethical implications of the more 'theoretical' discussions explored in the earlier papers (respectively, 'Biblical Criticism and Christology', 'Divine Agency in History and the Question of Universality', 'Spirit of Christ? Trinitarian Theology and Christology' and 'Christ, Contingency and Gender: The Ontology of Human Being')." I appreciate the quotes around the word "theoretical," but I still fear, as one identified with "ethics," that I am supposed to be the one who spells out the "practical implications" of the more straightforward theological claims. If the "ecclesiological-ethical implications" still need to be "drawn out" then I worry that the "theology" is embedded in a politics I have long tried to resist by admittedly inadequate means, that is, by refusing to distinguish between theology and ethics.

Yet ironically that refusal is the reason some would argue I should not, on my own account, be able to say what kind of social ethic is appropriate for the church understood as the body of Christ. And if I wish to remain true to my view—in particular, if I am serious in my oft-made claim that the first task of the church is not to make the world just, but to make the world the world—then I cannot "draw out the implications" since the implications are embedded in my theology. What I will try to do, however, is to show why it is necessary to make such a claim about the church's first task if we are to appreciate appropriately what it means, particularly under the conditions of modernity, for the church to be the body of Christ. By doing so I hope to suggest why Placher's and Hunsinger's characterization of my position as proposing that the Christian community focus on its own identity is a misunderstanding. It is, however, a misunderstanding that is understandable and it is important to understand why it is so.

Even if I am successful in countering the claim that my stress on the importance of the church commits me to an apolitical account of the Gospel, I fear that I still will not have written the paper that was desired for this conference. For in truth I fear that part of the problem is the very presumption that theology constitutes "thought" which then must seek embodiment. Once theology becomes "thought" the church has already accepted modernity's disembodiment of the Gospel. Why that is the case, therefore, becomes part of the burden of this paper.

In a letter to Eberhard Bethge in 1940, Dietrich Bonhoeffer raised what I take to be the challenge before us. He was reflecting on the Kirchenkampf of the previous decade, but I think his words are as relevant today as they were then:

> The question is whether, after the separation from papal and from secular authority in the church, an ecclesiastical authority can be established which is grounded solely in Scripture and confession. If no such authority is possible, then the last possibility of an Evangelical Church is dead; then there is only return to Rome or under the state church, or the path of individualization, of the 'protest' of Protestantism against false authorities.[5]

The problem is, quite simply, that we can talk all we want about the church as the body of Christ, but in fact such talk is more than likely to be just that—i.e., talk. We have no means of knowing if the Holy Spirit has abandoned the church because we have no means of knowing what it would mean for the spirit to matter as matter.[6] In short, we have few ways to resist what seems unavoidable everywhere but in Sneem; namely, the "spiritualization" of the church.

II. Why the "Body of Christ" Is Not an "Image"

These last remarks are not meant to disparage the importance of Christological and ecclesiological analysis. Rather they are meant to remind us that theological reflection never occurs in a vacuum—a point easily made and usually eliciting universal assent but whose implications are seldom appreciated. For example, it surely makes some difference that I write as a Christian schooled by the habits of American academe. What I say about the church as the body of Christ cannot help but be shaped by that context.[7]

My claim "that the church does not *have* a social ethic, but rather *is* a social ethic" cannot help but sound, in some contexts, like a call for group narcissism. Yet I make such a claim in the hope of reminding Christians in America that we too are an imperialistic polity that must challenge the imperialistic pretensions of that entity called "The United States of America." The question for me, then, is how does the description "the body of Christ," help Christians better understand what we must be in order to face the challenges of being the Church in the United States. That much is clear. What I remain unclear about, however, is how much actually hangs on which particular "image" of the church is thought of as primary.

I can illustrate my unclarity on this point by recalling some of the debates that surrounded the drafting of *Lumen Gentium* at Vatican II. At the time I was a seminarian and Catholicism for me was, at best, a theoretical idea. I did, however, have the advantage at the time of taking classes with George Lindbeck. The issue, as presented by Lindbeck, was whether the primary image for the church was to be "the body of Christ" or "the people of God." The former was said to be associated with hierarchal and authoritarian forms of the church; the latter was said to indicate a more open and democratic understanding of the church.[8] At the time, of course, I was on the side of the "people of God" image, since I just assumed that any right-thinking person was against hierarchy.

What seems odd to me now is the assumption that an "image" entails a sociology. I have no doubt that the presumption that "the body of Christ" *is* an image is produced by a certain sociology and politics—a sociology and politics that I wish to counter. What I am unclear about is why the choice comes down to one between "the body of Christ" or "the people of God," and why either one of these images, in and of itself, determines an ecclesiology. As Paul Minear suggested in his book *Images of the Church in the New Testament*, a book that was said to have a profound influence on the participants at the Council, there are well over fifty images for the church in the New Testament.[9]

I think there can be little doubt that "the body of Christ" is, as Minear argues, one of the major descriptions of the church, particularly for Paul.[10] Moreover, if the image does in fact entail some hierarchic account of the church, then I am for it. As *Lumen Gentium* puts it,

> Having become the model of a man loving his wife as his own body, Christ loves the Church as His bride (Eph. 5:25–28). For her part, the Church is subject to her Head (Eph. 5:22–33). "For in him dwells all the fullness of the Godhead bodily" (Col. 2:9). He fills the Church, which is His Body and His fullness, with His divine gifts (Eph. 1:22–23) so that she may grow and reach all the fullness of God (Eph. 3:19).
>
> Christ, the one Mediator, established and ceaselessly sustains here on earth His holy Church, the community of faith, hope and charity, as a visible structure. Through her He communicates truth and grace to all. But the society furnished with hierarchical agencies and the Mystical Body of Christ are not to be considered as two realities, nor are the visible assembly and the spiritual community, nor the earthly Church and the Church enriched with heavenly things. Rather they form one interlocked reality which is comprised of a divine and a human element. For this reason, by an excellent analogy, this reality is compared to the mystery of the incarnate Word. Just as the assumed nature inseparably united to the divine Word serves Him as a living instrument of salvation, so, in a similar way, does the communal structure of the Church serve Christ's Spirit, who vivifies it by way of building up the body (Eph. 4:16).[11]

Of course, the question must then be asked whether the hierarchy of Christ as head of the church must take the form, as *Lumen Gentium* later suggests, of the hierarchy of bishops ordered to the office of Peter. Yet what I take to be significant about *Lumen Gentium* is that we at least have a definite politics associated with the "image." For it is no longer simply an "image" for "self-understanding," even on the part of the church, but a question of who has authority over bodies. *Lumen Gentium* quite rightly assumes that questions about the status of the church as "the body of Christ" are inseparable from questions of government.

Such a practice is necessary for a reading of the Pauline stress on the body if we are to avoid the ontology of the body so characteristic of liberal societies—i.e., that my "body" is an instrument for the expression of my "true self." That is why I suspect that nothing is more gnostic than the celebration of the "body" in liberal societies. The "body" so celebrated turns out to be the body created by the presumption that there is an "I" that *has* a body. Nowhere is such a view of the body better seen than in the assumption, enshrined in modern medicine, that there is no limit to what we can and should do to overcome the limits of the body. Thus the difficulty of distinguishing torture from some forms of medical practice.[12]

The body politics of liberalism can make no sense of passages like 1 Corinthians 6:12–20. Paul did not think that we, as baptized believers, ought to view our bodies *as if* we were one with one another through Christ, but rather that our bodies are quite literally not our "own" because we have been made (as well as given) a new body by the Spirit.[13] What is crucial, therefore, is not whether the Church is primarily understood as "the body of Christ" or "the people of God," but whether the practices exist through which we learn that our bodies are not "ours."

Such practices require community disciplines through which the story of our baptism is embodied in all that we do and are. We require practices through which we learn that we do not know who we are, or what our bodies can and cannot do, until we are told what and who we are by a more determinative "body." In this respect, the saints are reminders of the character of what it means for us all to be members of Christ's body. For the saints cannot know who they are until we, that is, the communion of saints, tell them who they are.[14] In like manner, we are only known to the extent we are known by God and by God's church. To learn to live our lives on the basis of such a "knowing" requires, I am sure, a lifetime constituted by many disciplines. White suits and dresses at the feast of Ascension is surely a small and insufficient step in such disciplines, but something like that practice must surely be part of the process.[15]

III. Why the "Body of Christ" Is Not a "Community"

I use the word "community," as well as the example of Sneem, with trepidation. The use of the word "community" soon earns one the label of being a "communitarian," and examples like Sneem are usually dismissed as hopeless and naively romantic. The latter designation usually carries with it a strong condemnation for one's failure to see the ugly underside of Sneemlike villages where male patriarchy and Roman Catholic oppressiveness continue to rule. All I will say about the latter criticism is that, given the alternatives, I would rather deal with the problems presented by a Sneem. At least in Sneem you have practices in place that give you a basis for making non-arbitrary judgments.

I must be more emphatic in my rejection of the description of being a communitarian.[16] Community is far too weak a description for that body we call church. As Alasdair MacIntyre has pointed out, contemporary communitarians usually advance their proposals as a contribution to the politics of the nation-state. Liberals want government to remain neutral between rival conceptions of the human good. Communitarians want government to give expression to some shared vision of the human good that will define some type of community.

> Where liberals have characteristically urged that it is in the activities of subordinate voluntary associations, such as those constituted by religious groups, that shared visions of the good should be articulated, communitarians have insisted that the nation itself through the institutions of the nation-state ought to be constituted to some significant degree as a community. In the United States this has become a debate within the Democratic Party, a debate in which from my own point of view communitarians have attacked liberals on one issue on which liberals have been consistently in the right.[17]

What must be resisted, according to MacIntyre, is the identification of the Romantic vision of nations as potential communities, whose unity can be expressed through the institutions of the state, with the Aristotelian conception of the *polis*. Unfortunately, an idealization of the latter, combined with the Romantic vision, has led some thinkers, particularly in Germany, to view the nation-state as an all-embracing community. And that combination, as we know only too well, certainly can generate totalitarian expressions. Yet, according to MacIntyre, the practice-based forms of Aristotelian community generated in the modern world are small-scale and local. (Of course, if smallness is made an end in itself, these Aristotelian forms of community can also become another form of romanticism.)

Liberals mistakenly think that the evils they associate with authoritarianism and/or totalitarianism arise from any form of political community which embodies practical agreements based on a strong conception of the human good. In contrast I assume, with MacIntyre, that such evils arise from the character of the modern nation-state. As MacIntyre puts it,

> The modern nation-state, in whatever guise, is a dangerous and unmanageable institution, presenting itself on the one hand as a bureaucratic supplier of goods and services, which is always about to, but never actually does, give its clients value for money, and on the other as a repository of sacred values, which from time to time invites one to lay down one's life on its behalf. As I have remarked elsewhere ('Poetry as Political Philosophy: Notes on Burke and Yeats', in *On Modern Poetry: Essays Presented to Donald Davie*, ed. V. Bell and L. Lerner, Nashville, 1988, p. 149), it is like being asked to die for the telephone company.[18]

I seek, therefore, not for the church to be a community, but rather to be a body constituted by disciplines that create the capacity to resist the disciplines of the body associated with the modern nation-state and, in particular, the economic habits that support that state.[19] For the church to *be* a social ethic, rather than to *have* a social ethic, means the church must be (is) a body polity. The crucial question is how the church can be such without resorting to mirroring the nation-state and/or being tempted to use the nation-state for the disciplining it so desires and needs. The latter temptation is almost irresistible in modernity once the church has been forced to become a "voluntary association."

IV. Why the "Body of Christ" Is between Rome and Ephesus

Which brings us back to the question posed above by Bonhoeffer and, in particular, whether our only alternative is to return to Rome. It is not clear, however, what such a "return" would mean, since it is not clear that Rome *is* Rome. As Karl Barth observes at the beginning of the *Church Dogmatics*,

> We are faced with the fact of Roman Catholicism, in the form which it gave itself in the 16th century in the struggle with the Reformation. And within the organized unities of the Evangelical Churches we are faced with the fact of pietistic-rationalistic Modernism, with its roots in medieval mysticism and the humanist Renaissance. The fact of the modern "denial of revelation," etc., is entirely uninteresting compared with this double fact. For at this point, in its opposition to Roman Catholicism and to Protestant Modernism, evangelical faith is in conflict with itself.[20]

The situation is even more complex than Barth suggests if we remember that Catholicism is not only what it is because of the Reformation, but Catholicism is what it is because it has also been produced in reaction to modernity. In this respect, I am thinking of the concentration of administrative power that seemed necessary to counter the rise of the modern nation-state. I often observe that it is unclear whether Texas politicians first started looking like Southern Baptist pastors or Southern Baptist pastors started looking like Texas politicians. Whatever the order, what is clear is that the church is always tempted to imitate the habits of those in power. I assume that Rome has no built-in immunity to such processes.

I have no wisdom to offer in this respect other than to suggest that whatever a "return to Rome" might involve, it will also require Rome to do some "returning." Actually I think the image of "return" may be misleading, since it is not a matter of return, but rather one of how Protestants and Catholics alike must learn how to go forward so that once again the church might discover that we are Christ's body. In effect, we must ask what is required to sustain a Sneem. It is at least reasonable to suggest that Rome has something to do with that.

Reinhard Hütter rightly argues that,

> the church is not just another instantiation of the overarching genus "polis." It is, rather, a public in its own right. One way to show that the

church is a public in its own right in distinction from the "polis" is to draw upon the "other" of the antique polis, namely the *oikos* or household. Eph. 2:19 shows wonderfully how the church can be understood as something similar to a *polis* and to an *oikos*, though not identical with either one: So then you are no longer strangers (*xenoi*) aliens (*paroikoi*), but you are citizens (*sympolitai*) with the saints and also members of the household (*oikeioi*) of God. If we take this sentence in all its radicality we have to conclude that the *ekklesia* explodes the framework of antique politics which is precisely built on the strict dichotomy between *polis* and *oikos*.[21]

But then the question becomes what politics or sociology is necessary to sustain such an account of church?

V. Why the "Body of Christ" Does Not "Exist" Except as Jewish and Eucharistic

I am aware that the account of the church as the body of Christ toward which I have gestured here and elsewhere seems at once insufficiently theological and sociological. I fear that, given my understanding of Christian practice, particularly in modernity, there is a sense in which I can never be sufficiently theological or sociologically concrete. The problem is how to give an account of the church as Christ's body that makes clear that we are neither a "theology" nor a "sociology."

For example, Georges Florovsky, rightly I think, suggests:

> Christianity entered history as a new social order, or rather a new social dimension. From the very beginning Christianity was not primarily a "doctrine," but exactly a "community." There was not only a "Message" to be proclaimed and delivered, and "Good News" to be declared. There was precisely a New Community, distinct and peculiar, in the process of growth and formation, to which members were called and recruited. Indeed, "fellowship" (*koinonia*) was the basic category of Christian existence. Primitive Christians felt themselves to be closely knit and bound together in a unity which radically transcended all human boundaries — of race, of culture, of social rank, and indeed the whole dimension of "this world." They were brethren to each other, members of "One Body," even of the "Body of Christ." This glorious phrase of St. Paul admirably summarizes the common experience of the faithful. In spite of the radical

novelty of Christian experience, basic categories of interpretation were taken over from the Old Testament, of which the New Covenant was conceived to be the fulfillment and consummation. Christians were indeed "a chosen race, a royal priesthood, a holy nation, a people set apart" (I Peter 2:9). They were the New Israel, the "Little Flock," that is, that faithful "Remnant" to which it was God's good pleasure to give the Kingdom (Luke 12:32). Scattered sheep had to be brought together into "one fold," and assembled. The Church was exactly this "Assembly," *ekklesia tou Theou*, — a permanent Assembly of the new "Chosen People" of God, never to be adjourned.[22]

This seems just right to me. My problem is, given our current conceptual resources, knowing how to depict such a "new community." John Milbank, I think, is struggling with the same problem in his response to the essays in *New Blackfriars* on his *Theology and Social Theory*. There he notes that the purpose of his book was not to imagine the Church as Utopia nor to discover in the past some single ideal exemplar. According to Milbank, that would be to see the church in spatial terms — that is, as another place which we might arrive at or as an identifiable site which we can still inhabit. He asks, how could such a place or site characterize the church which exists, not in time, but as time in the mode of gift and promise? The church can exist, he maintains, only as gift, only as traces of the giver.[23]

It is only in eucharistic celebration that the church is body exactly because there a ritualistic distance obtains that distinguishes the church from itself. Thus, in Milbank's words, the "Church is first and foremost neither a programme, nor a 'real' society, but instead an enacted, serious fiction." So the answer to the question "where is the church?" is to found it "on the site of the eucharist, which is not a site; since it suspends presence in favour of memory and expectation, 'positions' each and every one of us only as fed — gift from God of ourselves and therefore not to ourselves — and bizarrely assimilates us to the food we eat, so that we, in turn, must exhaust ourselves as nourishment for others."[24]

Milbank is, I think, rightly struggling to find a way to remind us that the church is the body of Christ only by the gift of the Holy Spirit — a Spirit clearly not under our control. The problem, then, is how to say that without becoming ecclesiologically docetic or politically domesticated. Put simply, the question is how such an account of the church is consonant with the description provided by Florovsky.

In his "Ecclesial Ethics, the Church's Vocation, and Paraclesis," Reinhard Hütter makes some useful suggestions in this respect. He begins by observing that for all my emphasis on the church, I have a "theologically ambiguous ecclesiology," illustrated by my attempt to mix James Gustafson's *Treasure in Earthen Vessels* and Karl Barth's *Church Dogmatics* IV/2 without explicating the decisive theological differences in their respective ecclesiologies. Though both theologians claim the church as a "natural" reality, Gustafson lacks, in contrast to Barth, any pneumatological emphasis. Without that emphasis, Hütter suggests, the temptation is to approach the church's vocation in the mode of managerial production that seeks to "realize" the church's "ethical nature."[25]

He suggests that the crucial categorical difference is that between a utopian and a pneumatological eschatology. The former envisions the church as a sociopolitical avant-garde for the transformation of a whole society. Human agency on behalf of a progressive eschatology is given salvific or at least redeeming character. In contrast, a pneumatological eschatology understands the church to be the project of God's agency in the Holy Spirit. Therefore, in the church's reality, the eschaton becomes a history, "which becomes again and again transparent to God's eschatological reign by continuously expecting God's present reign in and through the church's activities, procedures, and policies."[26]

Hütter argues that the crucial ethical difference between these two eschatologies is that while the first follows the logic of modern politics, in which the implementation of the end defines the success of the political agents, the second follows the logic of the Spirit, where the ends are embodied in the means in such a way that "success" is defined only by the specific nature of certain ends. Thus, the success of the church's faithful witness can be hidden either through the form of the cross or in the future of God's reign. What is crucial is to acknowledge that the church's "success" can never be made intelligible independent of Jesus Christ's crucifixion and resurrection and God's eschatological reality in the Holy Spirit.[27]

One of the reasons I find Hütter's suggestion useful is because, as he suggests, such an account of the church means that any ecclesiology remains seriously deficient that is not explicated in relation to Israel and the ongoing existence and witness of the Jewish people. This is surely the "sociology" required for any account of what it means for the church to be the body of Christ. As Michael Wyschogrod argues, the being of Israel is embodied being. Jewish theology cannot become pure self-consciousness. Only the Jewish people in their totality can be God's people, and that includes not only those who are saints and mystics but "also the mute and heavy masses who have suffered for the covenant with a minimum of understanding and who have sinned because they responded to the craving of their flesh and the tiredness of their exile, whose significance they understood very little."[28]

He notes that many treat with derision "delicatessen Judaism"—that is the Judaism of gefilte fish, bagels with lox and cheese, the smell of chicken soup. Those who deride such things do not understand that the existence of the Jews is embodied existence. It is fashionable to deny that the people of Israel have characteristic features, but he notes that the typically Jewish face is the result of significant outbreeding over many centuries. There also exists a typical Jewish cuisine that varies in the different cultures in which Jews have adjusted but retains specificity in relation to its gentile counterpart. Such is the Jewish body.

Wyschogrod is well aware that to call attention to the Jewish body is to invite caricature and pathology. But caricature and pathology often point to otherwise unperceived truths.

> The truth we seek is the theology of the Jewish body. We are entitled to speak of such a theology because the divine covenant is with a biological people, the seed of Abraham, Isaac, and Jacob. The biological being of this people comes first. Whatever truth arises out of this people therefore comes first. It is never a truth beyond history, subsisting in any kind of Platonic heaven. Neither is it a universal morality, as so many modern Jews have thought. Judaism can be presented as a system of thought or an ethical philosophy. This is proven by the fact that it has been so presented very frequently. But Judaism is nothing without the Jewish people. Only this people can bring this truth off, almost like a joke that a particular performer can bring to life but when told by others falls flat.[29]

The body that the church becomes, resurrected though it is, cannot be less than the body of Israel, since our Christ is of this body. No doubt the body that is the church is different than the body that is Israel; however, gathered as the latter is from out of the nations, it can be no less physical. That is why, for whatever more the church is called to be, we cannot be less than Sneem.[30]

2

The Church's One Foundation
Is Jesus Christ Her Lord
or In a World without Foundations
All We Have Is the Church

I. Practicing Theology in a World without Foundations

James McClendon has been teaching us how to do theology in a world without foundations before anyone knew what anti-foundationalism was. That he has done so is due partly to his philosophical astuteness as developed in his and James Smith's book *Understanding Religious Convictions*.[1] I suspect, however, his "anti-foundationalism" owes more to his determined stance to do theology in the baptist tradition.[2] The baptist tradition never sought a "worldly" foundation since it knew there is no foundation other than Jesus Christ.

To do theology with no other foundation than Jesus Christ strikes many as dangerous if not irresponsible. Such a theology, it is claimed, surely must be relativistic and fideistic, since it lacks any "rational" basis. Moreover, it has no means to speak to the wider world, thus robbing Christians of any way to serve their non-Christian neighbor. Even worse such a theology invites a triumphalistic attitude incompatible with Christian humility.[3]

I have no intention to try to answer such criticisms on McClendon's behalf. He has already dealt with them time and time again. Instead I am going to offer three exhibits—three sermons—of what Christian practice might look like in a world without foundations. I take such a strategy to be commensurate with what McClendon has taught us. For in a world without foundations all we have is the church. That such is the case is no deficiency since that is all we have ever had or could ever want.

Church, moreover, but names those practices through which the world is known and given a history.[4] Thus, McClendon begins his "systematic theology" not, as recent theology, with doctrine but with ethics. But the ethics he develops is not that of a "theory," since ethics for him is constituted by those practices that make the church the church.[5] Therefore, my use of sermons is an attempt to use a practice central to the church's life in which form and matter are one.

The three sermons I put on display are also meant to exhibit McClendon's account of the strands—the bodily, the social, and the anastatic—that shape his *Ethics*. The first sermon is meant to display the bodily, the second the social, and the third the anastatic. Yet as McClendon emphasizes, the strands cannot stand alone but constitute the rope of Christian existence.[6] Accordingly each of the sermons also have elements of the other two strands.

Though I think each sermon can stand on its own, I will begin each by setting its context and conclude each, not with an explanation, but with further reflection on why and how I think it exemplifies how we can and should go on in a world without foundations.

II. Body Stories

The following sermon was delivered at Aldersgate United Methodist Church in Chapel Hill, North Carolina, July 18, 1993. I followed the lectionary reading appointed for the day. Since I am not ordained but a member of Aldersgate, I used the occasion to challenge the gnosticism so endemic to American Protestantism as well as to direct attention to the importance of the eucharist.[7]

JEWS AND THE EUCHARIST

Genesis 28:10–22
Romans 8:12–25
Matthew 13:24–30, 36–43

We are not a church that often celebrates the eucharist. I regret that and would like us to move toward celebrating every Sunday. There are many reasons why Protestant churches do not regularly celebrate eucharist, but I think the main reason is that most of us no longer believe that our salvation comes through the Jews. I realize that this claim will strike many as fantastic, but by the time I finish I hope it will at least make sense—as well as create in us a hunger to feast with our God.

The text we heard from Romans is, of course, part of the problem. The text itself is not the problem, but how we hear it. We are told not to live according to the flesh, "for if you live according to the flesh, you will die; but if by the Spirit you put to death the deeds of the body, you will live." Our problem is that such a text reinforces our presumption that Christianity is about the "spiritual" and on the whole we like it like that. By spiritual we usually mean it is about stuff that is too deep to understand but nonetheless important.

We also think the spiritual contrasts with all the things that make life good. To be spiritual is to be anti-body, anti-sex, anti-pleasure. So to be spiritual means to be good but dull. This really does not sound like terribly exciting news, but then if Christianity is really about the spiritual then we are pretty much left alone to do what we want with the stuff that really matters—that is the body, sex, and money.

That we associate Christianity with this sense of the spiritual is not surprising, given the world in which we live. If we did not put God in something like the "spiritual realm," we would not know where else God might be. We know that no matter how much our belief in God might matter to us—and I know that it matters a great deal to most of you—most of us live our lives as practical atheists. We think that we need God to give "meaning" to our lives, but if in fact it turns out that God just is not God, most of us, surprisingly, would not have to change how we live. We could go on doing pretty much what we are doing.

For example, Paul tells us that "the creation waits with eager longing for the revealing of the children of God. . . . We know that the whole creation has been groaning in labor pains until now; and not only the creation, but we ourselves, who have the first fruits of the Spirit, groan inwardly while we wait for adoption, the redemption of our bodies." Think about how that set of claims would play in any public school in America. All creation—rocks, plains, mountains, trees, cats, dogs, moles, weeds, and even us—is longing, Paul says, for the revealing of the children of God.

We may think this a colorful way to see the world, but we do not have the slightest idea what difference such a view might make for the way we conduct our science or our everyday life. We need our nature dead, subject to the laws of cause and effect, so we can subject it to our purposes—purposes that are, of course, meant to serve human well-being. We do not believe that what we call nature is best understood as creation. In this sense, the creationists are right to suggest that the way children are taught to view "nature" in the public schools makes irrelevant any claim that we and the world are God's good creation. I know we would like to believe that we and the universe exist as gift, as God's good creation, but it is hard to know what creation means once we have learned to view the world "scientifically."

So Christianity becomes that name for a set of beliefs we cannot "prove"; that is why we call it "faith." Faith is a kind of "knowledge," but it is personal. It means a lot to me, but I cannot presume anyone else ought to share it. Most that come to church probably believe some of the same things I do, but I cannot say that anyone who does not believe what I do is any the worse for it.

The story of Jacob's dream stands in stark contrast with this understanding of "faith." One of the worst sermons that I ever heard was on this passage. The preacher tried to make Jacob meet our understanding of Christianity as spiritual, as a meaningful experience. He noted that Jacob was on the whole a pretty unsavory character—a kid spoiled by his mother, a thief who steals his brother's birthright, a schemer who deserves to have Laban as a father-in-law—but this preacher said Jacob had this wonderful dream that changed his life. Such dreams, he assured us, were the way ancient people described important religious experiences. The way we know Jacob had been changed by this wonderful experience was that the first thing he did on awaking was to pray.

The only problem with this way of viewing this story is it fails to attend to the content of the prayer. Jacob is not in the least changed by his dream. All the dream taught him was that God is present in this place in a peculiar manner, but he is not a bit intimidated by that knowledge. He is the same old Jacob, so he sets out to strike a bargain with God: "If you will give me what I want, take care of my food and clothing, then you will be my God and I will even erect a house for you and give a tenth of what you give me." This is a man who knows how to strike a deal.

As moderns we try to naturalize such passages by giving them a spiritual meaning. By doing so, however, we miss what Jacob, unsavory though he is, recognizes; namely, that God is here at Bethel in a way that God is not everywhere. This place is different because this God is not some generalized spirit which gives meaning to our lives. No, this is the God of Abraham and Isaac. This is the God of this land, the land of Palestine, which is given to Jacob, who is going to need it because he is going to have many descendants.

Moreover, the people of this land, Jacob's descendants, are God's people in a way that no others are God's people. All the families of the earth will be blessed through these people, but they are different from such families. For God says though you, that is the Jews, will spread abroad, you will not escape me. I am going to bring you back to this land because I keep my promises. You may learn to like Babylonia, Spain, or America but as a people you belong in Palestine. Given all they have gone through since the time of Jacob, understandably the Jews sometimes think: "Is this a promise we want?"

Let us confess that the Jacob story bothers us. Is not God everywhere? Yes, but however God is present everywhere does not mean that God is not present in Palestine in a way that is different.[8]

But surely it is an arrogant and elitist claim to suggest that God is peculiarly the God of the Jews (or in a way different from being a God for everyone). It may sound arrogant to those of us who like to think that God is the great democratic politician running the bureaucracies fairly. But I tell you this, if God is not the God of the Jews, then our faith is in vain. Put as starkly as I can put it: if Christian envy of the Jews ever leads to the destruction of the last Jew from the face of the earth, then God will destroy the earth. Our God is not some generalized spirit, but a fleshy God whose body is the Jews.

That God, the God of the Jews, is the God we Christians believe has come in Jesus of Nazareth. We should not be surprised that the God of Abraham, Isaac, and Jacob would so come, since God has no fear of the material—after all it is God's own creation waiting in eager longing. God came in this man, Jesus, to engraft us gentiles into the promise to Israel. God is present in Jesus in a way God is present nowhere else. Through that presence we have been made part of Israel's blessing so that we too might be a blessing to the nations. God does not save us—Jew, Christian, and everyone else—by giving us a better set of philosophical ideas about how to live; God saves us through setting up this rock in Palestine called Jesus. Through Jesus' life, death, and resurrection, we have been made part of God's life with the Jews. All creation rejoices in our creation as God's people, for we are what God has always desired as the end of creation.

That God's salvation is so fleshly, so material, is why we are here to worship God in one another's presence. We know that we cannot hear the word as isolated spirits, but rather we hear God's word as God's body. Through the hearing of the word God creates a unity unknown anywhere else. Of course, that is why nothing could be more scandalous than for Christians to kill one another. When we do so it is not only murder, it is suicide.

That unity God creates by making us the body of Christ is most vividly present in Eucharist. Through this bread and wine, which is the body and blood of Christ, we become God's body. Such presence is made known because our savior is no dead hero, but the resurrected Lord. Resurrection does not mean that Jesus, after laying a few insights and ideals on us, took a flier, leaving us alone to deal with this mess. Resurrection means that when the words are said—this is my body, this is my blood, pour out your Holy Spirit on these gifts—there is nothing we can do to prevent God from being present.

It is frightening, is it not? As Jacob says, "Surely the Lord is in the place—and I did not know it." And then we are told: "And he was afraid." I do not blame him in the slightest. God is frightening. Indeed, I sometimes think the reason that Protestants, and in particular Methodists, are more likely to believe in the "real absence" rather than the "real presence" is that God just scares the hell out of us—and for good reason if God is just this God of Abraham, Isaac, Jacob, and Jesus.

Yet God's unrelenting refusal to be "spiritualized" is particularly threatening in the light of our Gospel for this morning. The parable of the wheat and the tares has been used particularly in recent times to challenge the Christian presumption that we are better than other people or know something others do not. We are, thus, told that in this time between the times we really do not know who has been good and who has been bad, at least until next Christmas. We are comforted by the suggestion that "until the end of the age" we really cannot tell who are the children of the kingdom and who are the children of the evil one. So who are we to judge— particularly ourselves? We are all equally sinners, which is good news because I am freed from thinking how I live matters to God.

But once this parable is read eucharistically we see that it is no accident that the kingdom of heaven is like a good field of wheat. Wheat becomes bread and bread becomes, through the Spirit, the body and blood of Christ. God is present here in this meal in a way that God is present nowhere else. We are that wheat, we are that bread that the families of the world need if they are to know God. We are the people on which the peace of God depends. We are God's eucharist; we are those children for which creation had been longing. In the celebration of this meal God lifts us up, as he lifted Christ on the cross, so that the world might see the beauty of God's creation made real in a people at peace with their world. How can we not hunger to share this meal and share it often? May God continue to make us hungry for it. Amen and Amen!

It is my hope that this sermon displays how the church is storied by God and accordingly stories the world. This, moreover, is a bodily matter that requires Christians to acknowledge that our existence only makes sense as we recognize God's presence in the people of Israel, that is, the Jews. Just to the extent Christians are tempted to tell our story separately from the story of Israel, we become something less than God's body. Thus, McClendon rightly reminds us of the significance of the body in his *Ethics* and also makes the continued existence of the Jews a central issue for his Christology in his *Doctrine*.[9]

III. A Community's Stories

This sermon was preached on August 8, 1993, at Broadway United Methodist Church in South Bend, Indiana. Adam, my son, and I belonged to Broadway during our last years in South Bend.[10] Broadway was celebrating its centennial and the congregation asked some of us back to preach. I again followed the lectionary for the day.

OUR MANY STORIES AND THE UNITY WE SEEK

Genesis 37:1–4, 12–28
Romans 10:5–15
Matthew 14:22–33

It is wonderful to be back. It has been almost ten years since Adam and I were sent out from this place. I use the strange locution "sent out" to remind you that you prayed with us to discern whether we should go. I still remember David saying to me: "I think it all right for you to go if you will put before the seminarians you train what we have taught you here."[11] I have tried to do that, but I cannot tell you that the word I have spread about Broadway has been well received. I know you think I idealize Broadway, and I am sure my memory is selective, but the story of Broadway, even with the most unflattering subplots revealed, remains a challenge for most mainline Protestant denominations.

I do not mean to pour cold water on the celebration of our 100 years, but I would not be faithful to you if I did not speak the truth. The plain truth is that Broadway survives as part of a larger church that is dying. Mainstream Protestantism in America is dying. Actually I prefer to put the matter in more positive terms: God is killing Protestantism and perhaps Christianity in America and we deserve it. By "dying" I do not mean that the institution will not continue to exist. But it is not clear what relation the institution that survives will have to the great tradition we call Catholic Christianity. Paul Ramsey was fond of quoting the Methodist bishop who, during an intense debate at conference, rose to the defense of the church with the claim: "Long after Christianity is dead and gone Methodism will be alive and well." I suspect the Bishop was unfortunately right, if for no other reason than that the ministerial retirement fund will continue to pay dividends whether God exists or not.

In fact, I think this is the reason that the story of Broadway is such a challenge to mainstream Methodism. For if the God we worship does not exist, then this church makes no sense.[12] As David once put it when asked what is the most important thing we do as a church: "Why we come here every Sunday and celebrate the Eucharist." What could be more important than making God present here on Broadway Avenue in this neighborhood at this rather modest church Sunday after Sunday?

I have to tell you, however, that your answer to that question—"that nothing could be more important than the celebration of God's presence in Eucharist"—is not the answer that most Methodists give. Most Methodists think it more important that their churches be friendly than that they manifest the unity that comes only through Eucharist. What matters to us Methodists is that we are an inclusive church: we do not want to believe anything or engage in any practices that might offend and thus exclude anyone.

Our practice of being inclusive is, we think, underwritten by texts like we heard in Romans—"there is no distinction between Jew or Greek; the same Lord is Lord of all and is generous to all who call on him." We think Paul is telling us we should not discriminate on the basis of race, religion, or sex. We read Paul's proclamation of the creation of a new people made possible by Jesus' death and resurrection as the equivalent of democratic egalitarianism.

If you are unsure whether or not Jesus is the second person of the Trinity you can be a Methodist. If you think that God is just as likely to be absent as present in the Eucharist you can be a Methodist. If you think that Christian participation in war raises no moral questions you can be a Methodist. If you see no connection between God's presence in the Eucharist and war you can be a Methodist. But you cannot be a Methodist if you think it proper to exclude anyone else on any of the above grounds.

Such an inclusive church would seem to be one well fitted for success. Yet it is dying. I suspect it is so because people fail to see why they should belong to a church built on being inclusive, since any volunteer service agency will do just as well. Moreover, such agencies are usually better run.

I do not mean for my remarks to sound harsh. In the absence of practices such as the Eucharist that provide compelling examples of unity, it is easy to see how inclusivity could be confused with unity. The unity of which Paul speaks, that between Jews and Greeks, is made possible through the common confession that Jesus is Lord, who has saved us by being raised from the dead. That unity is not based on the acceptance of everyone as they are because we want to be inclusive, but rather comes from the fire of Christ's cross, through which we are transformed by being given distinctive service in God's kingdom.

I remember how John[13] created a hunger in us for this communion by reminding us in sermon after sermon that through word and sacrament God was making us a new people. Then, of course, we would not have the eucharist, but we knew we had missed something we needed. He reminded us that in this feast of the new age we became part of God's life and thus of one another's lives—we became united.

Yet what does that mean? What does it mean for us to be united in Christ? We can say, "The claim of Christian unity is a mystery," by which we mean it is hard to explain. But, of course, that means it is not a mystery since true mysteries are not explanations but realities that can be known only through proclamation—Jesus Christ is Lord.

I think the unity made present in the confession that Jesus is Lord is quite simple, but no less mysterious. It means I will never be able to tell the story of God's formation of my life without the story of Broadway United Methodist Church. This is where Adam was confirmed. This is where John made me go through a year of training before I could join the church since, as he put it, "Your history does not give me much confidence that you understand what it means to be a member of the church." This is where I wandered back into Protestantism, which I am sure made it possible for me to even think about teaching seminarians at Duke and which resulted in my being married to Paula, a Methodist minister.

Of course, I did not come to Broadway as a cipher. I came bringing other stories that in one way or another had claimed me. Certainly the story of being a theologian was important, but that was just a peg on which to hang much more significant engagements. Adam and I, after all, came to Broadway from worshipping God at Sacred Heart. We came, that is, about half-Catholic. Moreover, I had been touched by the witness of non-violence of the Mennonites through John Howard Yoder. In your willingness to include us as part of your stories, those other stories also became part of what it meant to be Broadway. Of course, those stories, Catholic and Mennonite, simply cannot be avoided if you live close to Goshen and a university called Notre Dame.

That Adam and I are no longer here does not mean that our story does not matter. Sarah was quite clear that she did not regard my unwillingness to join a church in Durham as good for my relation with Broadway.[14] So now Aldersgate United Methodist Church in Chapel Hill, North Carolina is part of your story. You want to know who Paula is and what Adam is doing, who he is marrying, not simply because you are curious, though certainly that, but because you know your lives are united with ours. And you know that what God does with our lives makes a difference in how you tell your stories and how we together tell the ongoing story of Broadway.

Our unity is constituted by our inability to tell our stories without one another's stories. It takes time to do that. Indeed, such unity is the way God's patience creates time by providing us the space to have our stories conformed to the story of Christ. Such a conformation does not obliterate our story, but rather it shapes how the story is told, so that it may contribute to the upbuilding of Christ's body—so that finally our stories will be joined in one mighty prayer.

That our unity is so constituted is a great mystery, but here is even a greater mystery: what it means for our lives to confess that Jesus is Lord is that we, finally, are not the best tellers of the story of our lives. When we confess that Jesus is our Lord, our lives are no longer our own, our possession. Although as Christians we inherit a history/tradition which we did not create, yet what we do and how we live does create a history which others will inherit. The very structure of life as church, therefore, is always one of indebtedness, on the one hand, and gift, on the other. This means that those with whom we confess and commune may well know us better than we know ourselves.

That, of course, is why we are such an evangelistic group: we want our lives expanded through telling others of the stories that constitute our lives and, in return, hearing their stories. Paul makes clear that no one can believe who has not heard; no one can hear unless someone proclaims, and proclamation cannot occur unless someone is sent. So we send one another away from Broadway that those whom we do not as yet know might become part of the unity of God's peace.

But what does this have to do with celebrating our one hundredth anniversary in the context of a denomination that is dying? I think something like this: the church lives on memory. In celebrating our anniversary we remember all those who have constituted this congregation. We believe they are celebrating with us today.

I think particularly of Gary.[15] When Gary was ill and unable to be with us, I often felt a kind of dis-ease about whether we should celebrate the Eucharist, unsure if we were whole. I particularly missed him, because it meant that I was left alone to sing off-key. Of course, we no longer need to worry about Gary being present, as we know Gary is in that communion of saints and no illness will ever again prevent his being with us. Our celebration, our continued survival, is a memorial to Gary and all the others who have made us possible by God's grace. We fear the dying of our church because we want the Garys remembered.

It is, therefore, a good thing we have been here a hundred years to be a place of memory. A hundred years is a long time in places like Texas. This church, moreover, has been through some tough times, but it has survived. Current theology is enamored of the image of liberation, but I confess that in the world in which we live survival seems to me to be the greater good. Of course, we do not survive just to survive, but in order that we might be God's speech for those who have not believed.

Yet I am not confident that we will be here in a hundred years. By "we" I do not mean just this particular church, but what we now call "Protestantism" and, perhaps, Christianity. That we Methodist Protestants were called into existence and survived, I am confident, was God's doing. But I am not sure how God will have our story told for the upbuilding of the kingdom. Perhaps God sold us into Egypt that we could prepare the way for the survival of a church that will still have to face, no doubt, a quite different but no less significant Exodus.

Or it may be that we are like Jesus' disciples whom Jesus "made" get into the boat while he went up on the mountain to pray. The disciples found themselves battered by waves and wind, but then they saw Jesus, who seems to have just been out for a stroll, walking, like the Spirit at Creation, on the sea. That he walks so prevents them from "seeing" him, because they have not fathomed that this is the one who alone has the right to command the sea and the stars.

Peter, ever one to test things, says, "Lord, if it is you, command me to come to you on the water." In response to Jesus' command, Peter walks on the water until he notices the wind, becomes frightened, and begins to sink.

I suspect our situation as Protestants is not unlike that of Peter. We were, perhaps, rightly commanded to step out of the ark of Peter to walk on water. We did all right for awhile because we were not that far from the boat, could continue to presume its existence, and we remained focused on the one who had commanded us to leave. But then we noticed the wind. Put quite simply, when we became fearful about our survival, we sank.

For notice that when Jesus and Peter rejoined the others in the boat the wind ceased, and they worshiped Jesus, saying, "Truly you are the Son of God." That, of course, is the heart of the matter: we are not here to call attention to ourselves, to insure our own survival, but quite simply to worship Jesus. Only such a one is capable of constituting us into a unity, of making us a new people, so that the world might know that the God who rules the sun and the stars is also the one found in Jesus Christ. If we try to base our unity on anything other than this one, we will by necessity become fearful and sink. Once Protestantism becomes an end in itself, presumptively believing we can tell our story without the story of our sisters and brothers in the past and present called Catholic, and once we no longer long for the unity only God can give, God will kill us.

But the good news is this: that here in this place we have been made God's own. In a hundred years this building may well not exist, Broadway United Methodist Church may not exist, Methodism may not exist, Protestantism may not exist, but we will be remembered through the unity God has created here through word and sacrament. For never forget that God makes us God's own through faithful worship; and our story together cannot, therefore, be lost. So let us rush to this table, to climb back into this boat, so that we can once again worship our God.

McClendon has reminded us of the importance of the narrative character of Christian convictions. "Jews and the Eucharist" was the attempt to display the cosmic story Christians tell and to celebrate God's creation. In this sermon I have tried to remind us how our "smaller" stories are part of the story of God's creation that longs for the unity of God's kingdom. Just as I tried to suggest in "Jews and the Eucharist" that Christians cannot tell our story without the Jews, in this sermon I wanted to remind Protestants that we cannot tell our story without the Catholics—and, I might add neither can the Catholics tell their story without us. Such tellings will not be easy or without conflict, but Christians do not need to fear conflict since we know our unity is a gift from God.

Some may think this sermon too particular and perhaps too "personal." Few readers of this will know the Johns, Davids, Adams, Sarahs of which I speak. Yet it is in the unavoidability of the telling of such lives that McClendon has taught us that we discover our own lives, our own story. Moreover, just to the extent that such lives exist—and exist for one another—we know God's church, God's society, is real and capable of standing against the powers of darkness.

IV. A Resurrected Life

This last sermon is even more personal than "Our Many Stories and the Unity We Seek." On December 31, 1992, my father died. I was in Egypt. I knew, as I had known for years, I was to preach at his funeral. On January 8, 1993, we celebrated my father's life at Pleasant Mound Methodist Church in Dallas, Texas—the church he had built. I chose the scripture.

CHRIST'S GENTLE MAN

Revelation 7:9–17
Matthew 5:1–12

My father was a good, kind, simple, gentle man. He did not try to be gentle, for there was no meanness in him. He was not tempted to hatred, envy, or resentment. He was kind and gentle, possessing each virtue with a simplicity that comes only to those who are good through and through. It was simply his gift to be gentle, a gift which he gave unreservedly to those of us fortunate enough to be his family and friends.

That his gentleness was so effortless helps us better understand Jesus' beatitudes. Too often those characteristics—the poor in spirit, those that mourn, the meek, those who hunger and thirst for righteousness, the pure in heart, the peacemakers, and the persecuted—are turned into ideals we must strive to attain. As ideals they can become formulas for power rather than descriptions of the kind of people characteristic of the new age inaugurated by Christ. For the beatitudes are not general recommendations for just anyone but, rather, descriptions of those who have been washed by the blood of the Lamb. It is they who will hunger and thirst no more, having had their lives transformed by Christ's cross and resurrection.

Thus, Jesus does not tell us that we should try to be poor in spirit, or meek, or peacemakers. He simply says many that are called into his kingdom will find themselves so constituted. We cannot try to be meek and/or gentle in order to become a disciple of this gentle Jesus; but in learning to be his disciples some of us will discover that we have been made gentle. Jesus' gentleness is nowhere more apparent than in his submission to the cross; and even there he wished no harm to his persecutors. But it is no less apparent in his willingness to be touched by the sick and troubled, to be with the social outcast and the powerless, and in his time of agony to share a meal with his disciples—a meal that has now become the feast of the new age.

Part of our difficulty with the beatitudes is that some of the descriptions seem problematic to us—in particular, we do not honor the meek. To be meek or gentle is, we think, to lack ambition and drive. Gentleness at most is reserved for those aspects of our lives we associate with the personal; but it cannot survive the rough and tumble life of "the world." Yet Jesus is clear that his kingdom is constituted by those who are meek and gentle—those who have learned to live without protection. For gentleness is given to those who have learned that God will not have God's kingdom triumph through the violence of the world. No, that triumph came through the meekness of a cross.

It is surely fitting and right that on the death of my father we celebrate all his gentle presence meant in our lives. It is fitting and right that we mourn the loss of that presence. Yet he would be the first to remind us that his life should be celebrated and mourned just to the extent we remember that his gentleness was a gift made possible by Christ. For the great good news of this day is that my father's life only made sense, that his life was only possible, because our gentle savior could not be defeated by the powers of hate and violence. My father's life is only intelligible insofar as we see in his gentleness the gentleness of our Lord.

For example, in one of the climactic moments of my father's life, when he was honored for supervising the building of Pleasant Mound Methodist Church, the first words he said were: "I would like to say that I am only human; the one we should be thanking is Almighty God. He is the one that gave it to us. Words will not let me express myself." He thanked Don Ragsdale, the construction committee, and Don Wallace, who "did the best electrical job he had ever overseen." He thanked all the Christian business firms, whom he had been doing business with over the years, who gave material at cost. He closed by saying that he had already received all the thanks necessary: "I just thank God and praise God for it."

Plain but eloquent words, they but embody the simple eloquence of his gentle life. His life was like the beauty he taught me to see in a solid brick wall whose bed joints were uniform and whose head joints true. For the simple gentleness of my father was that which comes to those honed by a craft that gives them a sense of the superior good. My father was incapable of laying brick rough, just as he was incapable of being cruel. It literally hurt him to look at badly done brick work just as it hurt him to see cruelty.

Like his gentleness, his sense of craft was also out of step with the spirit of the times. The world wanted work done quickly and cheaply. The world wanted shortcuts. The world wanted him to build houses of brick so soft they would melt from watering the yard. He was incapable of such work, so he was not rewarded as the world knows reward. Yet he lived secure in the knowledge that he never built a house with a "hog in the wall"—that is, with one side of a wall more coarse than the other.

For example, there is a rock building back in the woods outside Mena, Arkansas that my father and mother built. Few people will ever see that building, though it is one of the most stunning rock jobs I have ever seen. My father and mother could not have built it otherwise, for to do so would have offended my father's sensibility. For to lay rock well you must see each rock individually, yet in relation to what may be the next rock to be laid. To see each rock requires a humility founded on the love of the particular that so characterized my father's life.

Perhaps nowhere was that better seen than when one walked with my father through the woods. For my father never saw "nature" in the abstract, but rather he saw this tree or plant, this stream or river, this sky against these particular clouds. As one whose whole life had been in the construction of buildings he seemed to prefer those aspects of our existence that we could not make. Thus he would talk endlessly, and he seldom talked endlessly, about what a wonderful ash tree this was or the wonder that a post oak leaf was—each so different from the others. He, after all, found the holly tree hidden in the woods at our home in Chapel Hill, a tree that I had walked by countless times but had never seen.

I think the wonder he possessed was what made him so fond of children. He did not see children as but potential adults. Rather he enjoyed their wonder at what an extraordinary rock they had found because he too thought the rock, common though it was, extraordinary. If they liked the rock enough to share their discovery with him it was extraordinary. Children loved my father, I think, because they sensed in him the gentle wonder that unfortunately many of us lose in the name of being "grown-up." He loved to teach us to fish or hammer a nail and he could do it with all the patience such teaching requires. Though I have to say I think teaching me to lay brick tested that patience to its limits.

Jesus' gentle life was challenged by the fractious and contentious character of his own people, the power of Rome, and the incomprehension of his followers. My father's gentleness in many ways had a more serious challenge—namely, Texas. Texans have not been a people known for their meekness or gentleness. We are a flinty people formed as we are by a dry wind that blows across a hard land. We are not known for our humility, but for our bluster.

My father was a Texan and he had some bluster to him. Like all Texans he liked to brag—particularly around carpenters. Yet try as he would to be a Texan, his gentleness prevailed. You could feel it in the stories he told of riding his horse to school each day as a young boy. He loved school but even more he tenderly loved that horse. It was that same love I suspect that made Bobby, the bobtail cat that walked out of the Arkansas woods, choose my father as her companion in life. My father accepted that choice as inevitable because he and Bobby seemed to understand one another in a manner that made the rest of us "outsiders."

I suspect that such tenderness also had much to do with one of my father's major failings as a Texan—a failing, I might add, that none of us ever explicitly acknowledged. For if the truth be known, though trained as he was from an early age to be a hunter, he was a terrible shot. My hunch is that his deficiency in this respect did not derive from lack of skill, but rather had more to do with his love of animals. One of my earliest memories was his deferring to a neighbor the shooting of a dog that was suspected of being mad. His gentleness simply would not let him assume the role of hero. Even mother was sometimes frustrated by this, as she could not understand how he could miss the ducks that had landed on their tank in Arkansas. I suspect he just could not bring himself to kill birds, numerous as they are, whose beauty he so admired. Of course armadillos rooting up his azaleas were quite a different matter.

Perhaps a more determinative challenge to my father's gentleness derived from the fact that Texas, at least the Texas in which he was raised, was also "the South." He inherited the habits that separated blacks from whites. Yet those habits could never flourish in his soul. That his gentleness prevailed even here I think had much to do with the unavoidability of the comradeship forged from the crucible of unbelievable hard work. The years he worked with Mr. Henry and George Harper meant that he could never believe their goodness should be ignored on the basis of their color. He, like so many of us, lacked the practices to know how the community formed through hard work could be carried forward in other aspects of our lives, but he also knew the sadness with which we must live in the absence of such practices.

The work that he loved, the work that wreaked havoc on his body, was also a challenge to his gentleness. One side of his hands was worn smooth by the millions of times he held the rough material he laid. The other side of his hands had been made as hard and coarse as the mortar that results when lime and cement are combined. The hardness of the material and the hardness of the work can make bricklayers "hard men." "The job" is no place for the faint of heart or for those of refined speech or taste.

Yet even there my father remained my gentle father. Working as hard as the men he paid, dealing fairly with their weaknesses and strengths, enjoying the "characters"—the Clarence Boduskys, the Jesse Womacks, the Tiptons, Bearhunter, Bobby, and of course, my uncles, George, Rufus, Dick, Tommy, and Bill. He loved and was loved in a world embarrassed to acknowledge that love was even present. Hard men will cry unashamedly when they hear that "Mr. Coffee" is dead because they know they will not see his like again on "the job."

No one knows the gentleness that characterized this man's life more than my mother. She knows that in spite of the tiredness that often gripped his life he never failed to have time for any of us. He never thought that in doing so he was sacrificing his own interest as his love for us was his interest. The tender love my mother and father embodied in their marriage reached out and gave me a brother. That they did so is not surprising, since their love was one in which there was no fear of the stranger.

That my father's life was constituted by such gentleness must surely be the reason that God chose to give him such a gentle death. He lived peacefully and he died peacefully. Of course his dying does not feel gentle for us who loved him. We rightly feel a loss, knowing that such gentle souls are all too rare. How are we to live without him?

But the great good news is that he has joined the other saints of God's kingdom gathered around the throne. He is among those who now worship God, continually sheltered as they are by the one who alone is worthy of worship. He has joined the great communion of saints, that same communion that we enjoy through God's great gift of this meal of gentleness. For in this meal we are made part of God's life and thus share our lives with one another. So we come filled with sadness, yet rejoicing that God, through lives like my father's, continues to make present Christ's gentle kingdom.

Ending with this sermon brings us to where McClendon begins— with lives.[16] For if lives like Dag Hammarskjöld, Martin Luther King, Jr., Clarence Jordan, Charles Ives, Sarah and Jonathan Edwards, Dietrich Bonhoeffer, Dorothy Day,[17] Coffee Martin Hauerwas, and James William McClendon do not exist, then what we Christians practice cannot be true. The attempt to do theology as if such lives did not need to exist is now at an end. God has forced us to see that there is no "foundation" more sure than the existence of such lives. Moreover, just as these lives are witnesses, so McClendon has taught us, our theology is futile unless it too is governed by the witness of such lives.

V. A Concluding Word on Method

Many will find this essay confusing. Will this form or way of doing theology pass muster in the academy? It is so idiosyncratic. Assertions are piled on assertions, but no clear argument or method is apparent. How can one be expected to learn how to do theology in such a mode?

The answer to the last question is simple—through practice. Though I lack the skills of a McClendon—a master craftsman—I have tried to imitate here his "method." For in truth there can be no "method" for theology in a world without foundation. All we can do is follow at a distance.

3

Why *Resident Aliens* Struck a Chord

with *Will Willimon*

I. On Being a "Success"

To ask authors to write an essay about why a book has been successful is an invitation to self-deception. Of course, it is not at all clear that *Resident Aliens* has been all that successful, though we must admit that we have been slightly taken aback by the attention the book has received. Moreover, to ask us to assess why the book has been successful suggests that we might know better than others. We are sure that that is not the case but we are willing to try to say here what we hope the book has done.

In an odd way we feel a little like Paul Ramsey after he wrote an essay called "On a Dignified Death." The essay was picked up and used by people in favor of euthanasia as well as thanatologists who argued that one ought to be more ready to die than Ramsey thought appropriate. So Ramsey wrote a follow-up essay called "On the Indignity of a Dignified Death." Depending on what one means by success, that our book has been in some small measure a success may not be good news.

However, we hope that the book has struck a chord. We regard the book as a rather modest statement of a position that has been articulated by people like John Howard Yoder for years. If the book has struck a chord it is because it did not start a new musical arrangement, but it fits into a growing symphony to which many have contributed, contributors as diverse as Lesslie Newbigen, George Lindbeck, Will Campbell, and others. In other words, we do not want the book to be seen as some new and startling creative challenge but rather as just one voice that is meant to contribute to a community's discussion about what it is and needs to be.

In that respect we think it important that the book is a joint exercise. Hauerwas kids Willimon saying that Willimon has never had a thought that he has not published—and some of them are Hauerwas's. One of the things we hope this book exhibits is how theology is intrinsically a community process. Willimon and Hauerwas have been talking with one another so long that it is unclear whose ideas are whose. If the book has had some success we hope it is because it contributes to that kind of community-building that we think so necessary for the church to be a faithful witness in our world.

The question is often posed, "Whatever happened to the great theologians? Where are the Barths, Brunners, Tillichs, and Niebuhrs today?" (Some who read the opening chapters of *Resident Aliens* were outraged by what they called "Tillich and Niebuhr bashing." We had underestimated how pervasive had been the canonization of these men.) Without denigrating those exceptional and creative minds, we simply must say that we no longer live at a time that the church can and/or should produce such people. Indeed, the very way we try to hold them up as "great minds" is a mistake. To do so makes theology appear as a unique activity that is the product of a creative genius. No doubt we lack their creative genius, but that very image of the lonely genius suggests an understanding of our situation which we think to be mistaken.

Indeed we are very suspicious of the category of "genius," drawing as it does on Enlightenment presuppositions that thought can be free of the material conditions that produce it. For example, the creation of the "history of philosophy" on this model has had a deep, distorting effect on how we understand who "thinkers" are, as well as on what "thinking" is understood to be. By focusing on "thinkers" who seem to think only in reference to other "thinkers," we lose the inherent social and political context that makes philosophy so various. As a result the dependence of thinkers on the tradition that made their work necessary is lost. Theologians then try to model themselves on philosophers, that is, they want to look like thinkers.

That philosophy and theology are dependent on the communities that give rise to them does not deny the creative and critical task, but reminds us that whatever "thinking" is taken to be depends on the substance of a community's practices and convictions. Theologians, like bishops, make sense only when they are understood as secondary to the primary activity of the church. Both bishops and theologians are servants meant to direct the church's attention to the significance of the lives of the faithful. In a very strong sense theology cannot help but be unfaithful if it is "creative."[1]

The "great mind" view of theology is possible only in the waning moments of Christians' hegemony over Western culture. That view of theology is determined by the Enlightenment university, which presumes that theology can be separated from the essential practices of the church. Of course the Barths, the Brunners, and the Niebuhrs would never have thought of characterizing their work in such a way (though Tillich might), but we are suggesting that such Enlightenment presuppositions made possible the way these theologians worked. They presumed an authority which transcended their culture. Therefore, the theologian could write for anyone. This is a byproduct of Western imperialism from which, no doubt, Christianity at once benefited and now suffers. Our culture is quickly losing the generalized Christian "beliefs" that supported the presumption that theology could be written for "anyone," and of course we think that development is a wonderful opportunity for Christians to discover the practices that make theology intelligible as a discipline of the church.

II. On Being "At Home"

We hope the increasing sense among Christians that we are different is one of the reasons *Resident Aliens* may have struck a chord—namely, like Lesslie Newbigin, we believe it is time for the church to recognize that it is in a missionary situation in the very culture it helped create. Of course, we think the church ought to be in a missionary situation at *any* time and in *any* culture. However, it happens that we have lived during a time when Christians thought that they had made themselves a home from which they could become missionaries to others. Because we Western, Northern-European Christians had succeeded in fashioning a "Christian" culture, we could now speak to everyone else's culture. That was a tragic mistake.

The very idea that Christians can be at home, indeed can create a home, in this world is a mistake. As Hugo of St. Victor put it, "The man who finds his homeland sweet is still a tender beginner; he to whom every soil is as his native one is already strong; but he is perfect to whom the entire world is a foreign place."[2] Perfection thus names the form of life Christians call discipleship, which is constituted by their being made part of a journey of a people called church.

Christians' recognition of their status as "resident aliens" was muted when Christianity became a civilizational religion. That project, which in many ways is quite explicable, was the attempt to turn the world into the kingdom. It was the attempt to force God's kingdom into being by making the worship of God unavoidable. It was the attempt to make Christian convictions available without conversion and transformation. There were always forms of resistance to this project outside as well as within the church. Therefore, there is nothing unique about our call for the church to recognize its status as a sojourner except that the material conditions may now exist to force the church to be faithful.

Yet one of the problems of being in a mission situation in a culture you have created is that the very forms the culture takes seem to mimic the reality of the church. For example, consider George Bush's call for a National Day of Prayer in support of the war with Iraq:

At this moment, America, the finest, most loving nation on Earth, is at war. At war against the oldest enemy of the human spirit—evil that threatens world peace.

At this moment, men and women of courage and endurance stand on the harsh desert and sail the seas of the Gulf. By their presence they're bearing witness to the fact that the triumph of the moral order is the vision that compels us.

At this moment, those of us here at home are thinking of them and of the future of our world. I recall Abraham Lincoln and his anguish during the Civil War. He turned to prayer, saying: "I've been driven many times to my knees by the overwhelming conviction that I have nowhere else to go."

So many of us, compelled by a deep need for God's wisdom in all we do, turn to prayer. We pray for God's protection in all we undertake, for God's love to fill all hearts, and for God's peace to be the moral North Star that guides us.

So I have proclaimed Sunday, February 3rd, National Day of Prayer. In this moment of crisis, may Americans of every creed turn to our greatest power and unite together in prayer. . . .

Let us pray for those who make the supreme sacrifice. In our terrible grief, we pray that they leave the fields of battle for finer fields where there is no danger—only tranquility; where there is no fear—only peace; and where there is no evil—only the love of the greatest Father of all. . . .

Let us pray for our nation. We ask God to bless us, to help us, and to guide us through whatever dark nights may still lay ahead. And, above all, let us pray for peace—"Peace, which passeth all understanding."

On this National Day of Prayer and always, may God bless the United States of America.[3]

Such a prayer sounds Christian. But it is idolatrous and pagan, the same sort of prayer Caesar always prays to Mars before battle. So Christians are now in the odd position of trying to destroy, or at least critique, the very culture we created in order that we may be more nearly faithful.

If *Resident Aliens* has struck a chord, we hope it is because our critique seems right to many Christians. C. Wright Mills, the wonderful Harvard radical sociologist, used to say that it was a task of sociology to help people locate their private hurts in profounder social pathologies. We hope that *Resident Aliens* has helped serve that purpose if it has helped people name their pains in a manner that gives them a way to go on. Too often in this culture recognition of our pains invites narcissistic self-absorption rather than locating us in a narrative which puts us in touch with a community that can do something about our pains. So we hope the book has brought to speech pains that people did not even know they had until we named them. Once named, pain can be acknowledged, diagnosed, and rightly ministered to.

In that sense it would be interesting to compare and contrast *Resident Aliens* with that other cultural phenomenon, the book of Robert Bellah and his co-authors, *Habits of the Heart*. No doubt that book also helped name pains under the pathology of individualism. Without denying that much of our difficulty is due to our culture's extraordinary emphasis upon freedom of the individual, we think the pathology runs deeper. Bellah and his colleagues basically want to reconstitute the civil religion of America because America still has the markings of "church." America's civil religion can be preserved provided it is made a bit more civil and a bit less individualistic.[4] In contrast, we do not seek to save *that* church; rather our task is to help

Christians disengage from the Constantinian habits that have so led them to confuse America with God's salvation. America's civil religion is not a cure for individualism but its cause.

That we have taken this path is not surprising. As Hauerwas says, "It is unclear who started looking like whom first, whether Southern Baptist pastors started looking like Texas politicians, or Texas politicians started looking like Southern Baptist pastors." Whatever genetic relations, Christians have been forever tempted to derive our status from those forms of power valued by the wider culture. Thus United Methodist bishops often refer to themselves today as CEOs. The United Methodist *Book of Discipline* is no longer a handbook for church discipline but resembles a handbook for employees of IBM. Pastors are routinely relegated to the ranks of "the health care professions." In the process, the church loses its way. We betray the society to which we were called to witness. No one listens to a church which speaks the same truths that can be heard anywhere other than church.

III. On Being "Characterized"

The desire for social significance has led to quite different reactions from people who read *Resident Aliens*. For example, laity seem to find the book more helpful than people in the ministry. Clergy who are desperate to feel socially significant are offended by the book. Laity, in contrast, are often empowered by the book as they see their membership in the church depicted as having social significance that they had not anticipated. The laity in other words seem to see that the book offers them habits of resistance to the subtle forms of conformity and coercion that our society tempts all of us to accept in the name of being "responsible." Laity seem more ready to accept *Resident Aliens'* ecclesial account that the church first serves the world by being the church.

However, we have also noticed a different reception to the book in terms of age groups of the clergy. Clergy between forty-five and sixty, trained in the theological era which told them that the great virtue is to be open, accepting, and affirming, tend to hate the book. Their ministry, after all, has been built on trying to transform the church into the left wing of the Democratic party. When we suggest that the first social task of the church is to be the church, it sounds triumphalistic and authoritarian. (We do, in fact, think the church should be imperialistic and speak with authority against the state.) In contrast, clergy under forty-five read the book with different eyes. They know that something is deeply wrong and what is wrong is not going to be cured either by breathlessly blessing each new cultural trend or by church growth strategy. Church growth strategy may work, but it is not clear that it will be the church of Jesus Christ that has thereby grown.

We hope one of the reasons the book has struck a chord is because of whom we see as the heroes and heroines in the book. If ethics is the attempt to help us see the significance of the everyday then what we attempted in the book was to help others see theologically the significance of the ordinariness of the church. We tried to show how those ordinary tasks are the most determinative *political* challenge to our culture. Our hero is the Episcopal priest who faithfully serves the eucharist to a parish of 150 souls in South Dakota for many years. That is the most genuine polity this world can know. Through her faithfulness, that minister makes possible the Gladyses who are empowered to speak the unpopular word without which we are lost.[5]

Through the locating of these heroes we hope that we have helped situate the church in America. Good communities are known by their saints. By naming these ordinary but theologically and morally impressive people, we discover resources that we did not know we had.

That is why we are so puzzled by the criticism that the book is "unrealistic," that the church we want does not exist. The whole point of the book is that the church we want *does* exist. We are Methodists, after all, and we will have nothing to do with distinctions between visible and invisible church. The whole point is that we Christians are sitting on a gold mine called the church, but unfortunately the very categories we have been taught as Western Christians make it difficult for us to notice that it is gold.

In this respect one of the virtues of the book is the understanding of theology we hope it exhibits. Theology since the nineteenth century (and prior to that in some forms of Protestant scholasticism) has been under the image of "system." Theology was thought to be like a philosophical system that demonstrated the meaning and truth of religious discourse. So theology became an academic discipline separate from the church.

In contrast, we assume that—no matter how orthodox it may be—theology divorced from the practices of the church cannot help but be ideology. In short, all theology must begin and end with ecclesiology.[6] The very assumption that theology could be an autonomous discipline done for anyone was the result of Constantinian Christianity, which assumed that what Christians believe, anyone would believe on reflection. We decisively reject that presumption, believing as we do that theology cannot escape into "thought" but remains rooted in the practices that constitute the church as a community across time. We are aware that this makes the theological task more complex, but we also think it makes it more interesting and adventuresome.

Indeed one of the chords we hope the book has struck in general is what an exciting and adventurous time we live in as Christians. Put differently, if Christians have a problem today it is not that we are socially conservative; it is that we are just so damned dull. What we tried to do in the book was awaken us to the wonder of being a people who every Sunday gather to worship a crucified God who shares with us the adventure of the kingdom. That worship is the most effective form of resistance to the powers who would determine our lives. What an extraordinary opportunity we have to witness to the world the difference that worship of the true Lord of our existence makes.

Of course, that point only invites a further criticism of the book—namely, we are simply giving a theological justification for a sociological reality. We are trying to make a virtue out of the necessity of the loss of membership in the mainline churches. Small is beautiful. That loss of membership is but one indication of the church's loss of social status and political power. Our critics therefore charge us with "sectarianism" because we are giving up on the church as a public political actor.

We admit that we are making a theological virtue out of a sociological necessity. God knows that the church seldom wills itself faithful, but God, through God's providential care of the church, oftentimes forces us to be faithful. We are simply trying to name what that faithfulness would look like as the church is offered the opportunity rightly to recover its minority status as intrinsic to its mission. It is wonderful to live in a time when Christians have to discover that another person is also a Christian rather than being able to assume it.

However, we reject the claim that thereby we are leading a retreat from social engagement and political significance, or that in fact we are sectarians. We reject the charge that *Resident Aliens* proffers a "new tribalism." Rather, we are reminding the church of how odd it is that we have made that strange entity called the United States of America into a tribe rather than recognizing that the church catholic, spread out across Caesar's artificial boundaries, is our true home. Who taught us that it is a mistake to be tribal? We think that it is Enlightenment presuppositions which presume that before you can be a member of a tribe you first have to recognize that you are an embodiment of something called universal humanity that is enfranchised by the modern nation-state. That is exactly the ideology that justifies genocide against Native Americans. "Tribal" became a dirty word when we realized that it kept some people from submerging themselves and their families into the nation. The church has never cared whether anyone is a member of a tribe or not as long as that membership does not prevent us from sharing the table of the Lord. If that is sectarian or tribal, so be it.

Many respond by noting it is pretty easy for Willimon and Hauerwas to take that position; after all, they are members of the faculty of a mainstream university. Or, as our dean has put it, we continue to draw upon the strengths of residual Christianity to critique that which makes us possible. We bite the hand that feeds us. We do not deny that description. We indeed confess that we are probably more residual Christians than faithful members of the church. But why should we turn the deficiencies of our own lives into justifications for how we think Christians can and should live?

It may be self-deceptive, but we like to think of ourselves as missionaries in the contemporary university. It may well be that our university will decide finally that they have had enough of us and/or Christians in general. But in the meantime we can have one hell of a lot of fun as we remind the university that Christians have some interesting claims to make about this world, not least of which that it is created.

It may be that one of the reasons that *Resident Aliens* has struck a chord is that it at least appears to be non-denominational. Certainly the book does not favor one form of church governance over another and our mail has come from people in an amazing variety of churches. In that respect, the book reflects part of the problem—namely, in the kind of culture in which we live the various denominations are increasingly looking more and more alike organizationally. This is more a reflection that the church finds itself in a buyer's market rather than any authentic catholicity. All the churches are tempted to look as much like one another as possible because a church does not want to stick out in a way that might lose membership. We suspect that is also the reason that in spite of different theologies and ordinations, the various ministries of the church are indistinguishable. You simply cannot tell a strong difference between Methodists, Presbyterians, Baptists, and perhaps even Anglicans and Catholics, when all is said and done. We know that is a generalization that needs much qualifying, but sociologically it still seems to be the case.

IV. On Characterizing Others

Having said that, however, we have noticed a distinct denominational difference in terms of how people respond to *Resident Aliens*. The people who seem to like it the least are United Church of Christ ministers. That may be because the UCC is often characterized as the home of the most liberal clergy in mainstream Protestantism, but it may also be that the UCC still ironically carries the Puritan commitment to America as a city set on a hill. Presbyterians also find the book quite deleterious, perhaps for very similar reasons. They really do not like our critique of Niebuhr's *Christ and Culture*. Presbyterians also talk a lot about the necessity of having a theology of creation that they seem to assume can be abstracted from redemption. By creation they mean that there has to be an independent criteria about nature, separate from christology. They so want to be Niebuhrian transformers of culture that they end up praising "creation" in a way to imply that it does not need redemption.

Our fellow Methodists probably are next in line among those who dislike the book. Methodism, after all, has been the great Protestant religion of America and, having been once established, they certainly do not want to be marginalized people. To a denomination which likes to think that it is still the establishment, still sending more people to Congress every year than any other Protestant denomination, our call for the church to recover its alien status sounds like very bad news indeed. We do not want to call Methodists out of Congress; we just want them to be there as Methodists, for heaven's sake.

Baptists on the whole dislike the book, for the fundamentalists among them note that we are clearly not fundamentalists, just as the liberals among them note that we are clearly not liberal. Among Baptists today it seems that you must be one or the other. We regard this as an indication of the deficiencies of the Baptist tradition insofar as it has almost no catholic sensibilities or ecclesiology. When all you have is the New Testament era and the "now," you are a bit short on resources to stand against the world.

Speaking of the Catholics, however, it seems that they simply have not discovered the book. If they do so they will probably not like it, since part of the project of Catholicism in America over the past century has been to show that Catholics can be good Americans. Constantinianism is a hard habit to break. Interestingly enough, however, among those Catholics who feel strongly about their church's concern for unborn children, they hear what we have to say with quite different ears.

We have a hunch why we have not been read by evangelicals. When we have been read, however, we have often been read poorly, as they want to have the church and the country too. Having once been disestablished, evangelicals are not eager to give up their present establishment. We hope the book, which is quite sympathetic in some ways with some streams of the evangelical tradition, might be an opening for the kind of discussion we need to have between evangelicals and those of us who come from the mainstream. If Christians would really try to evangelize this culture, we will discover how deeply pagan is the USA. In that sense we hope the book is appropriately ecumenical and evangelical.

V. On Being Methodist

However, we have to say, contrary to appearances, the book really is not non-denominational. We admit that we write as deeply committed Wesleyans. We know that to be a deeply committed Methodist may sound like an oxymoron, but nonetheless that is what we avow. By that we mean that at the least we take very seriously the Wesleyan sanctificationist structure of the Christian faith. We Methodists are people committed to being a community capable of sustaining one another in the church's struggle against the world. As such we hope that Methodism is serving its purpose by helping us each find a unity that does justice to the gifts of the distinctiveness of our histories.

Methodism, after all, is a movement that by accident became a church. If we Methodists are not definitively about the unity of the church, we are not about anything. But our unity is not to be discovered in some least common denominator, but rather by drawing on the unity that is part of the church's commitment to Jesus Christ.

Hauerwas, of course, has described himself as a high church Mennonite. While there is no doubt something about that description that lacks seriousness, we believe that is what it means to be a Methodist. For we Methodists are a people with Catholic practices of ministry and eucharist, but at the same time we have a free church ecclesiology. We began as a lay attempt to reform an established church. We have never wanted to let the state establish us. We are established by God, thank you. As free church Catholics we think we stand in a peculiar position to help bind up the wounds of the Reformation.

In many ways *Resident Aliens* stands as a decisive challenge to the Reformation. At least it stands as a decisive challenge to the nineteenth century's understanding of the Reformation. For we believe the association of the Reformation with presumptions of justification by faith through grace as a center of the Gospel was a profound mistake. That emphasis, perhaps unwittingly, underwrote essentially individualistic accounts of salvation that combined with liberal political theory to produce an outrageously accommodated church.[7] Part of our attack on Protestant liberalism is really an attack upon Reformation presumptions insofar as those are based on the idea that the church is somehow incidental to the salvation we have been offered in Christ. Indeed, we believe in the strongest sense that outside the church there is no salvation, for the church offers us participation in light of a people that is an alternative to the world's violence. We know of no way of being saved other than a way which is ecclesial, i.e., political. Therefore, we are really about challenging the assumption that salvation is somehow *extra* political.

For example, it is one of the oddities of mainstream liberal Protestant social theory that because we have an intrinsic social nature, the church must be about social action. But the social theory that informs that social action would create liberal democratic societies that intrinsically privatize religious convictions. Indeed, such a strategy cannot help but reduce Christian practice to religious belief. Thus the widespread assumption that you can be a Christian without going to church. Accordingly, being Christian becomes an intellectual problem (i.e., "Does God really exist?") rather than a practical challenge of discipleship. Put differently, liberal societies make religion more important than the church.[8] If *Resident Aliens* has struck a chord we suspect it is because we challenged those sets of assumptions. *Resident Aliens* is structured on the presumption that our lives are only genuinely social to the extent they have been transformed through baptism into the body of Christ.

That is one of the reasons we find so odd the criticism that we are nostalgic for simpler times such as nineteenth-century America when the church, at least Protestantism, had social status. We look to no golden age which was normative for the church and certainly not the nineteenth century.[9] Rather, we only look forward to the wonderful challenge before us today to be a church that can leave behind past forms of unfaithfulness. If *Resident Aliens* has struck a chord, we hope it has been that one.

4

Whose Church? Which Future?
Whither the Anabaptist Vision?

I. On Picking and Choosing

I am honored to be asked to address you on this important occasion. It is the kind of request you cannot refuse if you respect, as deeply as I do, the people who asked you. So I am not here voluntarily. I am here as an Anabaptist prisoner of war. You just wanted to see someone who has taken the Anabaptists seriously whose name is not Burkholder, Miller, or Friesen. As I often ask my Anabaptist friends—if you guys are a voluntary church why is everyone named Epp or Bender? I realize that is also an inside joke among Anabaptists, which, as I will try to suggest, is a very serious joke indeed.

I do not mind being an Anabaptist POW, not only because of the way you have chosen to conduct the war, but because it lets me say in an appropriate context how much I owe to you and the mothers and fathers of your faith. I am honored to be asked to give this address on the fiftieth anniversary of Bender's *The Anabaptist Vision*. I know enough about Anabaptists to know the importance of Bender and his essay as well as the importance of this event. So I am honored to be honored by you, even though I understand you do not honor honor.

I confess that it did occur to me some time after I accepted your kind invitation to wonder if I had not been set up. Since no one within the Anabaptist world could be asked to do this, for if they were

This essay was written as the keynote address for a 1994 conference at Elizabethan College on the fiftieth anniversary of the publication of Harold Bender's "The Anabaptist Vision." Bender was the president of Goshen College as well as a church historian. "The Anabaptist Vision" served as an identifying document for many Anabaptists.

asked they would display or at least be tempted to display an arrogance or authority incompatible with a servant style of leadership, you asked an outsider to commit that sin. I can tell you, moreover, as long as I am in the business of sinning, I intend to make the most of it.

Anyone should know better than to enter an argument between Jews or the Christian equivalent to Jews—that is, the Anabaptists. Jews love to argue with Jews, just as Anabaptists love to disagree with one another, but as soon as an outsider tries to enter the argument, the former antagonists discover a common interest in keeping the interloper out. At the very least the outsider helps make them friends, as the outsider's lack of sophistication about what "is really at stake," or why X or Y *really* took the position they did, cannot help but remind the antagonists that they have more in common than that about which they disagree. I do not mind serving that function for you. I certainly owe you that much.

However, before I address "whither the Anabaptist vision," I need to be candid with you about my ambiguous ecclesial status. As many of you know, I once described myself as a "high-church Mennonite" and the description stuck. Indeed, in his new book, *The Church as Polis: From Political Theology to Theological Politics as Exemplified by Jürgen Moltmann and Stanley Hauerwas*, Arne Rasmusson describes me as a "Radical Reformation theologian."[1] I confess, it is humbling to be taken so seriously, particularly as I first used that description to confuse my enemies! There was also a serious side to that self-description. In part I was trying to indicate that I am a Methodist or, more accurately, to point out the kind of Methodism that I wish existed but is certainly not readily apparent in most churches that bear the name Methodist.

For I believe Methodism had the potential to be that form of evangelical Catholicism that maintained such continuity with the great confessions of the church because such confessions are integral to sustaining a disciplined community capable of living as a free church. By "free church" I mean a church capable of trusting God to sustain us rather than any arrangement, dependent on state powers, such as the concordat made with liberal societies called "religious freedom." A free church is one with the strength to narrate its life, and in particular the life of the martyrs, on its own terms.

By describing myself as a "high-church Mennonite" I was trying to suggest an image of the sort of church I thought not only should exist, but must exist for faithful witness to the Gospel. Of course, part of my strategy was dictated by my theological training, for I was taught to engage in theology as a tradition-determined activity without my having been determined by any one tradition—other than Yale. I had to find a tradition, or better, hopefully a good tradition would find me. I believe I have been found by such a tradition, mainly through friends, but because it comes through friends it is at once Methodist, Roman Catholic, Lutheran—and even Anabaptist.

We all know some people who are always ready to listen to someone else's troubles. They are often perceived as empathetic and admired for their compassion. In fact, they sometimes turn out to be emotional cannibals who, lacking a rich emotional life themselves, feed off other people's troubles. I hope that I am not an emotional cannibal, but I have to confess I am an ecclesial cannibal. For I am a theologian with a theological position that makes no sense unless a church actually exists that is capable of embodying the practices of perfection. In effect, since my own Methodist church is seldom capable of being such a community, though individual Methodist churches manage to be quite impressive, I live off communities that for varieties of reasons find themselves stuck with strong practices and convictions that they cannot leave behind and remain who they claim to be.

Which at least partly explains why I am at the same time attracted to Catholicism and Anabaptism. To their credit the Catholics are stuck with claims of Christian continuity and unity across the centuries, with questions of what constitutes good order and authority within and between churches in widely different circumstances, and with moral commitments that are embarrassing in liberal cultures. That gives you a lot to work with. In like manner, the Anabaptists are stuck with a history that is so confusing that you cannot even be sure where it is to be begun or who is to be included in it, and with an unbelievable group of "crazies" throughout your history. This means that your story can never be subjected to the normalizing gaze of the "mainstream," and you still have a memory of community discipline along with the oddness of your pacifism. That also gives you a lot to work with.

I am often accused of romanticizing both Catholicism and Anabaptism, and no doubt that is a danger. But the reason I am so attracted to those traditions is that they have managed to keep some practices in place that provide resources for resistance against the loss of Christian presence in modernity. For that is the heart of the matter—namely, practices. Practices make the church the embodiment of Christ for the world. Walter Klaassen argued, rightly I think, in *Anabaptism: Neither Catholic nor Protestant*, that the judgment exemplified by the title of his book can only be made retrospectively and in the light of current developments in church renewal.[2] I am attempting the same kind of retrospective redescriptions in the interest of providing examples of strong Christian practices in a world that increasingly undermines those practices. That should put you on your guard, however, since my primary interest in the "Anabaptist vision," as well as the way I renarrate it, is from the perspective of the pathologies of liberal Methodism.

As a representative of mainstream Protestantism, I can at least warn you against making our mistakes or, even worse, wanting to be like us. I have to confess that I have wondered what a church-growth strategy would look like among the Anabaptists. Could you produce a Lyle Schaller? There are at least some things from which you have been saved because of your ethnic and minority status. Ethnicity and being small are not necessarily signs of faithfulness to the Gospel, but they may not always be a hindrance either.

Yet the critical stance I take in relation to mainstream Protestantism continues to exemplify the practices of the mainstream. Like any good Methodist I get to assume the stance of picking and choosing parts of traditions I like without having to bear the burden of the parts (or, as the English say, "those bits") I do not like. I am like those who hold themselves accountable only to those whom they like and therefore never have to accept the discipline of being corrected by anyone whom they do not like or with whom they are in disagreement.

I have learned, however, not to try to "place" the Anabaptist as an "important minority voice" to which those of us in the mainstream need to listen in order to keep *ourselves* honest. My ambiguous ecclesial stance has at least taught me to drop all pretentions of superiority. I assume, moreover, that is the stance we all must take today as we struggle with questions of "whither the Anabaptist vision." We Christians simply no longer have the space or the time to engage in narcissistic exercises about what makes this group or that group distinctive. Too often claims about ecclesial distinctiveness turn out to be merely reasons for why we must continue to be separate in order to justify the continued existence of the stock portfolio necessary for the ministerial retirement fund.

II. Bender's "Vision"

Harold Bender's great essay "The Anabaptist Vision"[3] not only witnessed the rich results of fifty years of Anabaptist historiography, but
it also has served to set an agenda, both positively and negatively, for
fifty years of historical and theological debate that has now become
part of Anabaptist identity.

Among Bender's many strengths was his refusal to let the enemy
name what makes you Anabaptist—other, of course, than still having
to bear the name given you by the enemy. That, of course, is no easy
task, particularly when your enemy seems more intellectually and
politically powerful than you. Ironically, I first learned the difficulty
of that task watching Catholics resist the Protestants. For example,
during my tenure as Director of Graduate Studies, the Department of
Theology at Notre Dame was going through an external review of our
Ph.D. program. In the final interview one of the external reviewers, a
Protestant theologian with profound Catholic sympathies, registered
surprise that there were no specifically "Catholic courses" on Mary or
the papal office in our curriculum. The chairman of our department,
Father David Burrell, C.S.C., responded by noting that was a very
Protestant observation, since only a Protestant would think what
made Catholics Catholic was their devotion to Mary or their obe-
dience to the Pope.

He observed that Catholics obviously prayed to Mary and thought
the papacy intrinsic to Catholic practice, but to make Mary or the
Pope the center of Catholic life would distort Catholic tradition. No
doubt living in a Protestant culture tempted Catholics and Protestants to emphasize those aspects of Catholic life that seemed to make
Catholics distinctive, but such a process distorts Catholic life and
theology. God, after all, and in particular the God known through
the cross and resurrection of Christ is what makes Catholics Catholic.

Which is but a reminder that the very attempt to locate the
"Anabaptist vision," that is what makes Anabaptists Anabaptist,
may be a mistake. The enemy continues to win just to the extent that
there is a need to find, as Bender puts it, "the true essence of
Anabaptism" (4). I do not wish to make too much of Bender's use of
the notion of "essence," though he uses it several times (13), even
referring at the end of his article to the "essential nature of Christianity" (22). I am certainly not suggesting that Bender was engaged

in a Harnacklike attempt to find the kernel in the husk. Rather, I am suggesting that something may already have gone wrong in Anabaptist life just to the extent that there is a need to discover what makes Anabaptists "distinctive." When you do that you force people to make distinctions that might better be left unmade—e.g., we Catholics are always "just warriors," or we Protestants must always seek to develop a "responsible" social ethic.

It may be objected that I am confusing a historiographical issue with questions of ecclesiology. After all, Bender wrote the essay in 1943 as the annual address required of the outgoing president of the American Society of Church History.[4] Yet, as a good Anabaptist, Bender rightly could not easily distinguish between history and theology. No doubt Bender believed he should write history honestly, but he did not confuse that task with the attempt to write history objectively—that is, from the perspective of anyone. Rather he wrote as a committed Anabaptist trying to reclaim the story of the Anabaptists on Anabaptist terms. He rightly saw that historiography is a necessary theological task and rightly made history serve an ecclesiological purpose. He was so successful that his essay, whether you liked it or not, became the benchmark for the Anabaptist search to discover who they are.[5]

I think it is interesting to note that Bender was not alone in the attempt to use history for a restatement of normative distinctiveness. I do not mean that he was dependent on others working in Anabaptist sources, though that is certainly true and well acknowledged and celebrated by Bender. Rather, I mean "The Anabaptist Vision" was part of a general movement at the middle of this century to use history as a means to come to a self-understanding of what it means to be Lutheran, Calvinist, and even Methodist. Something was and is clearly happening that we probably are not yet in a position to understand nor can we fully appreciate its implications.

III. The "End" of Protestantism

I told you at the beginning, however, that given the no win position I am in, I am going to make the most of it. I am now going to deliver on that promise by making claims well beyond my competence about what I think has happened and is continuing to happen that has fueled this desire for institutional identity. I am a theologian, not a historian, yet like Bender my theological argument involves historical claims. In brief, what I think is happening is that we are coming to the end of what Tillich called "the Protestant era."[6] The differences created by the Reformation, and we must remember that it is only with the Reformation that something called "Roman Catholicism" was created, are now simply no longer interesting, given the challenges before Christians in modernity. But it is exactly because such differences now do so little work that they have become so important. You must maintain distinctiveness when that which created the difference no longer matters.

That the differences that seemed so important at the Reformation no longer matter ironically is the result of practices for which the Anabaptist are given credit. For example, Bender begins "The Anabaptist Vision" with a long quote from Rufus Jones celebrating the contribution of the Anabaptists to the shaping of "modern Christian culture." Bender seconds Jones's suggestion, noting "there can be no question but that the great principles of conscience, separation of church and state, and volunteerism in religion, so basic to American Protestantism, and so essential to democracy, ultimately are derived from the Anabaptists of the Reformation period, who for the first time clearly enunciated them, and challenged the Christian world to follow them in practice. The line of descent through the centuries since that time may not always be clear, and may have passed through other intermediate movements and groups, but the debt to original Anabaptism is unquestioned" (3–4).

It may not be unquestioned, but it is by no means good news. That it may not be good news can be illumined, I think, by noting the tension between discipleship and voluntary church—two of the main characteristics of the Anabaptist vision according to Bender. While there is no inherent conceptual tension between discipleship and voluntary church membership, we at least know that in liberal cultures too often voluntary church membership is translated into the right to make up one's own mind. Accordingly, the church as a disciplined body becomes a community of like-minded individuals who share the conviction that they should respect each other's right to make up his or her own mind. Such a church, moreover, too often reproduces ethnic, class, and national identification in the name of freedom.

Confronted by such challenges, it is not surprising that intellec-
tuals began to scavenge "history" to discover their community's true
"identity." "Identity" becomes the commodification of one's history
to give us something to sell in the religious market. The "selling," of
course, is not primarily directed to those on the "outside," but rather
to convince those who discover they are part of an arbitrary group
called Methodist, Lutheran, Catholic, or Anabaptist that being such
is not altogether a bad thing.

I am not, of course, suggesting that Bender's attempt to articulate
the Anabaptist vision was but a form of marketing strategy. Rather, I
am suggesting that the celebration of his vision may not help us locate
the challenges before those of us who desire to be faithful worshipers
of God. Indeed, it was to Bender's credit that he sought to provide an
account of the "essence of Anabaptism" that was more than the
results celebrated by Rufus Jones. As Bender notes, freedom of
religion is a barren concept saying nothing about the faith or way of
life of those who advocated it. His project was to narrate the Anabaptist historical origins in a manner that resisted the reductionistic
accounts of Kautsky, Niebuhr, Ritschl, and Keller.

Accordingly, he situated the Anabaptist as the "culmination of
the Reformation, the fulfillment of the original vision of Luther and
Zwingli, . . . thus mak[ing] it a consistent evangelical Protestantism
seeking to recreate without compromise the original New Testament
church, the vision of Christ and the Apostles" (9). The Anabaptists
are presented by Bender as consistent Protestant reformers who
insisted that true repentance and regeneration must be a mark of the
church. The Anabaptist "retained the original vision of Luther and
Zwingli, enlarged it, gave it body and form, and set out to achieve it in
actual experience. They proceeded to organize a church composed
solely of earnest Christians, and actually found the people for it. They
did not believe in any case that the size of the response should
determine whether or not the truth of God should be applied, and
they refused to compromise. They preferred to make a radical break
with fifteen hundred years of history and culture if necessary rather
than to break with the New Testament" (13).

But, if we are coming to the end of the Protestant and Catholic era,
Bender's positioning of the Anabaptists as the consistent Protestant
reformers is not a promising narrative. If indeed Anabaptists are
neither Catholic nor Protestant, as Klaassen maintains, then a more

promising mode of narration is required that subordinates past polemics between Protestant and Catholic over "doctrinal matters" to
questions of faithful and unfaithful practices. That is much to ask of
Catholics and Protestants, but, as I shall try to show, it is also much to
ask of Anabaptists who have assumed, under the impact of Bender's
account of the Anabaptist vision, that that is what they have always
been doing.

That challenge is quite simply learning how to exist in a world that
is no longer dominated by something called "Christendom." Ironically, the Anabaptists now live in a world which they said they
wanted—that is, a world in which no one is forced either by the
government or by societal expectations to be Christians—but you, as
well as the churches of Christendom you opposed, are ill prepared for
such a world. You have won the war, largely for reasons beyond your
control, but in winning you have become unintelligible to yourselves
by making a fetish of those aspects of your lives that seemed so
important for the last war.

For example, "voluntary church membership" was a prophetic
challenge against mainstream Christianity, but once Christendom is
gone the call for voluntary commitment cannot help but appear as a
legitimation of the secular commitment to autonomy. In a Christendom world it took conviction to be a pagan or an Anabaptist, but
given the world in which we are now living it is hard to distinguish
pagans from Anabaptists. That is why I emphasize the importance of
practices, which may of course involve "doctrine" as well as "called
membership," since practices provide the material specifications that
help us resist the endemic character of modernity, bent as it is on
turning faith into just another idea.

The habits of Christendom churches may now become a resource
for their members and for Anabaptists to resist letting their church
become just another community in a world desperate for community.[7] For example, Anabaptists are embarrassed about their ethnicity, but it may be that "ethnicity" is one way God provided and
continues to provide for your survival as a people capable of remembering the martyrs that have made you what you are. Bender rightly
understood that historiography is a theological enterprise, but discipleship, the voluntary nature of church membership, and nonresis-
tance must be embedded in a thicker history if they are to continue to
provide us with the skills of Christian faithfulness.

IV. Avoiding Pietism

One of the virtues of putting the matter this way, however, is to reposition current criticism of Bender's account of Anabaptism such as Stephen Dintaman's "The Spiritual Poverty of the Anabaptist Vision."[8] Dintaman contends that even though Bender assumed the evangelical doctrines of the being and work of Christ, as well as the necessity of the Holy Spirit for the living out of the vision, Bender's "vision" resulted in generations of students and church leaders learning some of the behavioral aspects of the Christian faith without learning equally well that discipleship is only meaningful and possible because it is an answer to who God is and what God is doing in the world. Nor did they necessarily experience what it means to have a vital and life-changing personal friendship with the crucified and risen Jesus (2). Whatever the benefits of the Anabaptist Vision, according to Dintaman, it has left Anabaptists with little insight into human behavior and has made peace and justice a substitute for faith.

Dintaman thinks that the emphasis of "The Anabaptist Vision" may account for why the Anabaptist churches have not grown. Anabaptists became quite good at ministry to people who are in control of their lives, but they are no good at all dealing with those troubled souls who seem incapable of change. In short, Anabaptists simply need to recover the Gospel—that is, the faith in Jesus Christ necessary for salvation is not to be confused with peace and social action.

The reasons Dintaman dislikes "The Anabaptist Vision" are precisely the reasons why I like it. I come from a church that has all the insight about human behavior it can use, but it turns out that that insight, separate from practice, does not get you very far. Given Dintaman's agenda, as well as the brief form of his article, one should not expect him to expose his theological presuppositions, but I confess as one long schooled in the discourses of Protestant liberalism "insight into human behavior" makes me uneasy. I am not suggesting that Dintaman is trying to turn theology into anthropology, but "insights about sin and the inner bondage to death and violence" perhaps unintentionally echoes the great enemy of the Anabaptist, Reinhold Niebuhr.

More important for me is that Dintaman's criticism seems to betray an account of salvation closer to pietism than what I have hoped is

Anabaptist practice. I am a Methodist—by the time I was fifteen I had all the experience and self-understanding I can use for a lifetime. I do not want to be "accepted" or "understood." I want to be part of a community with the habits and practices that will make me do what I would otherwise not choose to do and then to learn to like what I have been forced to do. That is why, as I suggested at the beginning, I find the Anabaptists and the Catholics so appealing. Given their history they cannot avoid acknowledging that salvation is about the cosmic transformation of creation in which, by baptism and through God's grace, we have been included. What such an inclusion offers is not acceptance or better understanding, but participation in God's life, God's kingdom, which protects us from the powers raging against that kingdom.

Robert Friedmann in his essay "The Doctrine of the Two Worlds," which appeared in *The Recovery of the Anabaptist Vision*, rightly contrasted the Anabaptist and Pietist understanding of these matters. He noted that little attention has been given to the genuine social ethic of the Gospel message of the kingdom of God, "most likely because it does not fit too well into the ways of the world at large and into the social exigencies of civilization."[9] For the idea of *koinonia* rules out "all individualism and individualistic concern for personal salvation. The old saying that 'there is no salvation outside the church' does not exactly express the underlying idea of this brotherhood ideal; actually that doctrine belongs to a different frame of reference. And yet, it simply is so that the kingdom of God means from its very beginning a togetherness, else it is not kingdom. The mere aggregation of saved souls, as in Pietism, does not constitute the kingdom; it remains just an aggregation, nothing else" (112–13).

"Brotherhood" has now become a problematic way to speak of the communal character of Christian salvation and even more doubtful is that it (or any substitute) should be thought of as an "ideal." Nonetheless, I am sure that Friedmann rightly suggests that salvation for the Anabaptists (and for Catholics) is to be engrafted into a counterhistory made possible by a countercommunity called to be a witness to God's kingdom. Such a history makes the polemics of the Reformation centered around the alternatives of grace and law distinctly a side issue. Just as it has become increasingly clear that what we call Protestantism and Catholicism cannot be mapped by such polemics, it would be irony indeed for Anabaptists to take up those polemics.[10]

I confess that if Bender is to be criticized for what he does not say or for leaving out essentials of the faith, I suspect it is not grace but worship that is missing. Before all else what makes us Christian, whether we be Protestant, Catholic, or Anabaptist, is our worship of God through word and sacrament. It is not unusual for anyone to fail to articulate that which makes them most what they are, but I suspect the failure to notice the significance of worship among Anabaptists may also be why worship does not have the significance it should, not only in Anabaptist theology, but in Anabaptist life. I am aware that I am now drawing on that part of my self-description as "high-church" in a manner that may be unfair, but I confess that I find in Anabaptist worship a lingering Zwinglian rationalism incompatible with your other practices. If non-violence makes no sense without miracle, I fail to see how you can deny the miracle of bread and wine becoming through God's grace the body and blood of Christ?

V. Church "History"

My concern, however, is not what Bender may or may not have left out of "The Anabaptist Vision." Rather I have tried to suggest that Bender's "vision" requires a quite different narration given the loss of Christendom and the peculiar character of modernity. Even if I am close to being right about that, it is not clear where that leaves us. If we must leave the comfort of past categories, we must nonetheless still tell the story of the church. The question, of course, is whose church determines how the history is told in order to confront which future. That future is obviously not one determined by a "new century," since such a designation has no theological intelligibility. The "newness" of the future for the church is that created by our conviction that God continues to create the conditions that the church might be faithful to the kingdom even if that requires the acknowledgement of our past unfaithfulness as Anabaptist, Catholic, or Protestant.

In *Theology and Social Theory: Beyond Secular Reason*, John Milbank observes "we do not relate the story of Christ by schematically applying its categories to the empirical content of whatever we encounter. Instead, we interpret this narrative in a response which inserts us in a narrative relation to the 'original' story. First and foremost, the Church stands in a narrative relationship to Jesus and the gospels, within a story that subsumes both. This must be the case, because no *historical* story is ever 'over and done with.'"[11] The question is how the story is told in order that we know more faithfully how to go on, not as Anabaptist or Methodist, but as those claimed by God to be witnesses to the kingdom of Christ.

Every telling of that story is a covenant with the past. If the way of characterizing your history as exemplified by Bender no longer serves to help us confront the challenges before us, does that mean that those that have made you what you are will be lost?[12] It may or at least it may mean that how they are remembered will be different. All remembering is equally a forgetting. Which is a reminder that we Christians can take the risk of remembering, and forgetting, that task we currently call history, because we know that God rightly remembers all those who constitute the communion of the saints.

I do have one suggestion. I think that if Anabaptists are to help God's church (as it appears even among mainstream Protestant and Roman Catholics) to remember our story for faithful living, you will do so by following the example of *Martyrs Mirror*. I take this suggestion from Nicholas Lash's wonderful article "What Might Martydom Mean?" in his *Theology on the Way of Emmaus*. Lash observes that only an incorrigible idealist (in Marx's sense) could suppose that the cross is a symbol to help us deal with or make sense of suffering. Such a view would simply "leave everything as it is." That is not the witness Jesus bore of himself, it is not that to which those who first interpreted him as God's self-interpretation witnessed, nor was it how God "interpreted himself."

The "martyrdom of God" is not the condition for a more or less satisfactory account of the human condition, but rather

> the transformation of that condition: divine utterance is "performative". Similarly, the transformative power of Christian "martyrdom", of "sharing the testimony of Jesus" is a condition of its truthfulness. What might "witness" or "martyrdom" mean today? The form of the question, derived from models of interpretation the inadequacy of which I have tried to indicate, is unsatisfactory. It should rather be: What form might contemporary fidelity to "the testimony of Jesus" appropriately take? And this is a practical and not merely a theoretical question. It is a question that will continue, often in darkness, strenuously to engage all those resources of

integrity and discernment without which patterns of human action are not responsibly undertaken or pursued. And it will also continue to engage all those resources of textual, historical and literary criticism without which the New Testament scholar (and church historian) cannot competently perform his indispensable function. That function is an aspect, but only an aspect, of the broader task of Christian interpretative practice, of the attempt to bear witness faithfully and effectively of God's transformative purpose and meaning for mankind.[13]

That seems to me to get the issue right for all of us: namely, we will not know how to tell our story well unless we are able to know what martyrdom even today might look like. I should like to think that Bender would be happy to be reminded by Nicholas Lash, a Roman Catholic, that the story the church tells, the story in which God has embedded the church, is a story of sacrifice that is meant to challenge the stories of a world bent on sacrificing to false gods.[14] That, I take it, is the challenge before us.

PART II

In Catholic Company

5

A Homage to Mary and to the University Called Notre Dame

"Just seven." With that answer I knew this was going to be different. I had just been hired to teach in the theology department at the University of Notre Dame. It was one of the obligatory occasions to meet "the faculty." I assumed that they were, like me, academics before they were anything else. I confess that I thought it curious that the economist who sought me out actually thought *Rerum Novarum* might have something to do with economics, but what caught me completely off guard was his answer to the ritualistic question asked on such occasions when you are desperate to find something in common: "How many kids do you have?" — "Just seven."

With that "just" I knew I had entered a strange new world. Nothing in my old world had prepared me for that "just." Even being from the South was insufficient to prepare me for all that that "just" involved. My father was one of six bricklaying brothers, but that was "back then." One of the brothers, Rufus, had five children, but Aunt Christeen was from an East Texas farm and was used to it. Even then all their cousins thought five was a lot. No one in the family would have thought "just five." Not even Uncle Rufus. Catholics were going to be different.

Of course, from my growing up I was not entirely without knowledge of Catholics. After all, I played "war" and tried to figure out what "sex" was with Charlie Jurek. Charlie said he was Catholic, but that did not seem to make that much difference in Pleasant Grove, Texas. There did not seem to be enough of them to make any difference. I knew there were more Catholics than just Charlie, since he told us that he went to a church weirdly called Saint August-stein, or so we

pronounced it. I assumed that what it meant to be Catholic was going
to a church that did not have a real name—like Pleasant Mound
Methodist. Of course, as I got older I learned that Charlie was Czech,
or something foreign, and he could do anything he wanted during the
week and get forgiven for it with no sweat.

By the time I got to Notre Dame I thought I was more knowledge-
able if not sophisticated. I had been to Yale Divinity School and had
gotten a Ph.D. in theological ethics. I knew a lot about Catholics or
at least something called church history. I was even an "expert" on
Aquinas's *Summa*. I had actually read the whole damn thing, which is
more than most Roman Catholic theologians can claim. I had stud-
ied *Rerum Novarum* as well as the other social encyclicals. Hell, I was
ready to go!

But that "just" threw me. What kind of people would produce that
"just." Of course, I would learn over the next fourteen years that many
Catholics would have nothing but disdain for that "just." The kids I
had in class, who were the "just," now explained that the "just" was an
"ethnic thing" which they had no intention of repeating. After all,
that was why they were at Notre Dame—to become good Americans
who had small families, who could get ahead. Yet for good or ill,
whether they had learned to hate it or love it, that "just" was part of
their history.

By God's grace it is now part of mine. Though I did not realize it at
the time, coming to Notre Dame was going to change my life. I
thought I was simply making, a "vertical move," from Augustana
College (Rock Island, Illinois) to a "real" university. I did not anticipate that I was going to have to think about as well as even begin (to
be sure in a hesitant and awkward way) to become "religious." My
theological training had not prepared me for this development.

At Yale you are trained to be a theologian by writing books about
other people's books. There is nothing wrong with such training, but
it always has the danger of becoming an end in itself. For example you
can easily forget that the subject of theology is God. There are good
reasons to forget that, moreover, given the character of the modern
university. God, to put it mildly, just does not sound like a university
subject. How do you study that?

Of course that is a good theological question. Most of Christian
theology has insisted we know God more by what God is not, than
what God is. All positive predication of God's attributes is qualified

by the negative apophatic reminder. I learned, however, that this means something quite different when said by a priest who begins each day in prayer than when I say it. There is no substitute for being around significant practitioners. Notre Dame was filled with such practitioners.

No doubt such practitioners were at Yale, and even Texas, but I did not notice them and if I had I would have probably ignored or dismissed them as "pious." What made Notre Dame different is you could not miss them. They were simply there in the way the "just" was simply there. Mary requires that they exist. Without them you would not know what it means to pray to Mary and how such prayer produced such a strange people called "Catholics." For what I was learning is that "Catholic" names not a set of "beliefs about God," but a world of practices called "church." It simply had not occurred to me that church, that is, practices as basic as prayer or having children, are intrinsic to what we mean by God. Suddenly Wittgenstein had implications I had not anticipated.

For good or ill, what it means to be a "Catholic" is to be a member of the church. I can illustrate the difference by calling attention to what it means to be an atheist in Judaism, Protestantism, and Catholicism. When Jews say that they do not believe in God, they mean that God is an unjust son-of-a-bitch and they will be Goddamned if they will worship him. When Protestants say that they do not believe in God they mean this is all there is. You might as well eat, drink, screw, and die. When Catholics say that they do not believe in God, they mean they are mad at the church.

Thus, I soon learned that ex-Catholics disbelieved with an intensity I could only admire. They could get angry at the Pope about the teaching on contraception, or at the priests for being such pricks, or at the nuns for the way they had taken out their frustration on the kids in the second grade, and so on. What was remarkable, however, is that they had been part of a people who had actually marked them for life. The deepest marking for most was, of course, having been a "just." What a wonderful gift, even if it took the rest of your life to get over it.

Such was the world I entered as one of the first Protestants to teach theology at Notre Dame. Of course, there were many non-Catholics at Notre Dame, but not many in theology. I was so new to the Catholic world that I did not even understand that I was an "experiment." I just thought any "good department" would want someone as smart as me. What a shit I was. Of course, in some ways my blissful arrogance worked out well for everyone, since it never occurred to me I ought to hedge my bets. Even if it had, I probably would not have known how to do it.

It is important to note, for those unfamiliar with the Catholic world, that the very presence of a theology department in Catholic colleges and universities, and in particular at Notre Dame, is a relatively new development. Theology was what you taught priests in seminary. Why would good Catholic kids, most of whom knew better than to think about becoming priests, need to know anything about theology? That is what priests, or at least some theologian priests, and the church are for. All you need to do is know when to show up for Mass. The Jesuits, of course, thought that was not enough. They thought smart Catholics ought to know something about philosophy. So Catholic laity got taught Plato to make them Catholic. What a world!

Theology as an undergraduate subject became necessary for Catholics to answer Protestant questions. After all, America is one of the first countries where Catholics have had to live among a majority whose intellectual and cultural habits, for good or ill, had been established by Protestants. So when graduates of Notre Dame went to live in the South, they encountered Southern Baptists who asked them if it was really true that they obeyed a little Italian guy in Rome or worshiped Mary. No graduate of Notre Dame would know how to answer questions like that. Praying to Mary is as natural as being a Notre Dame football fan. It simply comes with the territory.

So the very existence of theology at Notre Dame was a response to the Catholic break out from the ethnic "ghetto." The department had originally been founded to provide a more or less advanced catechism. After Vatican II they thought it ought to be more scholarly, which meant you ought to hire some smart guys from Europe. That is not a bad idea, except most Notre Dame undergraduates were not overly impressed with theology done with an accent. So I got hired.

What a strange department it was. For example, I discovered that we were offering a Ph.D. in liturgy. Moreover, those involved in teaching those courses were damned smart. It just did not sound like an academic subject to me, but then I thought, "What do I know?" After all, in the general run of things my field of Christian ethics is probably no less weird. Just ask the faculty at Duke.

I even discovered that one department member's specialty was ecclesiology. Besides he was expert in a field called "Mariology." He was personally stiff, theologically conservative, but also one of the leaders of the Catholic charismatic movement. The Spirit sure could play tricks on folks. Over the years I learned to love him and I hope he even learned to care for me a bit.

Our relationship had not started well, I later discovered. During my initial interview at Notre Dame I had introduced myself to him by saying, "Hi there. My name is Stanley Hauerwas. I am from Texas. You know that is where it takes six syllables to say "Gawddamn." I was not aware at the time that this could be offensive. Indeed, it meant so little to me that it was only some time later when others told me the story that I knew I had done it. Of course, it was not long after that incident when the same man refused to serve me the eucharist in a university-wide Mass. I just went to a different line.

Yet this same man was always unfailingly courteous to me. He could be vicious with his more liberal Catholic colleagues, but he was always pastorally sensitive in his dealings with me. I always thought he had no use for the Catholic liberals, since they should have known better, but since I had the disadvantage of being brought up in a false religion, one could be more patient in the hope of winning me to the true church. As I have reflected on my time at Notre Dame, I take great comfort that he thought I might some day make a Catholic.

My hiring had been one of the last official acts of my chairman, Rev. James Burtchaell, C.S.C., prior to his becoming Provost of the university. He was and is an extraordinarily impressive person, having done his Ph.D. in New Testament at Cambridge. I learned by watching him that those who have been humbled by Mary do not have to be afraid of exercising authority. I thought that, being urbane and cultured, he would be for "openness," but instead he used his bully pulpit to insist that Notre Dame must work to remain Catholic.

At the time I could not conceive how Notre Dame could be more Catholic than it already was. The student body was ninety-eight percent Catholic. There were priests all over the place saying Mass. Catholics made up the majority of the faculty. However, as things worked out he was right.

I only began to know what Catholicism was, however, by learning to know the acting chairman of the department—Charlie Sheedy, C.S.C. Charlie was professor of moral theology, but had spent years as the dean of the college. Charlie had become a moral theologian because he was the last to speak up when his friend who was then chairman of the new theology department, Rev. Theodore Hesburgh, C.S.C., had been passing out the jobs. They probably thought Charlie was a good candidate for moral theology, since he also had a law degree from Catholic University. Of course, Charlie was too fascinated in all things human to be tied down to reading in a field—there were all those French novels to read and baseball season was always just around the corner.

I always thought the order was wise to keep Charlie around in the novitiate and seminary after his retirement from University teaching. The young priests were too tempted to be the mirror image of the old-time priests—rather than giving conservative answers they thought they had to give liberal answers. Charlie, who had always fought alcoholism, knew he had few answers but he knew he was a priest.

They said that Charlie was that piece of humanity that they threw into the gears of Catholic and university bureaucracy to bring them to a halt. He was surely that, but for me, he was my friend and priest. I vividly remember our last conversation. I was now teaching at Duke. Charlie was by this time long retired and was suffering from emphysema. I had not seen him for over a year. We agreed to meet on a bench in front of the Dome. Never one for small talk, the first thing he said was, "What do you think heaven is going to be like, Stanley?" He is now in the process of learning.

David Burrell, C.S.C., a philosopher, became the chair of the department for the next nine years. They were exciting and intellectually stimulating years. David already was a friend, as our offices in the basement of the library were close to one another. Through David I had become an active member of the philosopher's seminar at Notre Dame. I had never before been around people who took argument so seriously. We spent a whole year reading Witgenstein's *Philosophical Investigations* line by line. I thought Notre Dame was intellectual heaven.

It took me several years to discover that Notre Dame had its fair share of intellectually dull faculty. On the whole, however, I kept meeting interesting people who thought being Catholic ought to make a difference for how they thought and taught. Even in the law school and business school could be found people who thought being Catholic mattered for what they did as scholars and as teachers.

Burrell was the kind of chairman who actually thought ideas mattered for what we did. Convinced that Judaism could not be just the "background" to Christianity or just another "religion," we became committed to hiring in Judaica. I found myself so engaged in the building of a department that was neither denominationally confessional nor "religious studies," that I forgot I was not Catholic.

I became a theological anthropologist. My Catholic colleagues complained about the lack of diversity, by that they meant non-Catholics, in the student body. In contrast, I felt I was part of a people zoo with no cages. I never knew this many different people existed. I discovered Eastern Europe, the Philippines, Mexico, Central America, South America, and, in an odd way, a Texas I never really knew, through colleagues and students at Notre Dame. Notre Dame, it turns out, does not serve a state, nation, or ethnic group. It serves Mary wherever she appears.

At the time I did not realize I was becoming Catholic. It was certainly not anything I was trying to do. It just seemed more important after a while to read *Commonweal* than *Theology Today*. Even though I was developing a C.S.C. prejudice against the Jesuits, I even read *America*. Catholicism constituted a world into which I was inextricably drawn. The intelligence and charm of Irish priests like Ernan McMullin and Enda McDonagh are hard to resist. In fact, I was beginning to wonder if my liver would survive the goodbye parties for those who from time to time returned to Ireland.

What makes this world possible, of course, is the Mass. I had actually begun to go to church again when I taught at Augustana. The Lutherans, at least Swedish Lutherans, had a wonderful liturgy. When I moved to Notre Dame the only people I could find who worshiped like the Lutherans were the Catholics. I had gotten used to having the eucharist every Sunday and I was damned if I was going to give it up. I am not sure why I thought eucharist so important, but I was sure if Christianity made any sense it surely had something to do with eating that meal. Or, to quote Flannery O'Conner, "If it is just a symbol, then to hell with it."

I also had a son, Adam, to raise. He was at that rambunctious age that makes it difficult if not impossible to stay still. Much to his and my delight I discovered that I could take him to Mass each Sunday in the pit of Grace Hall. Burrell said Mass there for sleepily hung over undergraduates, so the noise my kid made, along with the many other

families who had discovered this system, made a positive contribution. Adam simply assumed you were supposed to stand alongside the
priest during the great thanksgiving.

As an anthropologist utilizing the participant-observation method,
I noticed that Catholics worshiped quite differently than Protestants:
Catholics are noisy and not particularly "worshipful." Though I was
at first bothered by this, I began to realize that Catholics do not have
to be "holy" at worship, because they think God is going to show up
anyway. If the priest gets it right there is not a thing they can do to
prevent God from being present in Eucharist.

In contrast, most Protestants believe in the "real absence" rather
than any presence. Accordingly, we have to be especially "holy"
because otherwise we are afraid "God" will go away. I suspect that one
of the reasons Protestants are so serious in worship is our un-
acknowledged presumption that there is no difference between what
is happening in our own subjectivities and in God. Though I would
have difficulty spelling it out, I think this has to do with the Protestant inability to party the way Catholics can really put it on.

As Adam got older, we discovered that we liked going to Mass at
Sacred Heart. As a kid growing up I seldom liked going to church. It
was just so boringly wordy. In contrast, I do not remember Adam ever
suggesting, even on the coldest snowy mornings, that he did not want
to go. It was, after all, a feast for the senses. Processions with flags and
horns, smells and bells, thrilling music, and a meal to eat. What a way
to find out what Christianity is about. I was learning right along with
my kid.

Of course, there were things that bothered me. The maleness of it all
was often a bit overwhelming. Yet I kept meeting all these strong
women who, I thought, should not be there given the maleness of
Catholicism. For example, my summer school classes were filled with
sisters from all over the country—Sisters of St. Joseph, Franciscan
Sisters of the Perpetual Adoration, Sacred Heart, and on and on. I
have often wondered if anyone in Catholicism has any idea how many
orders there are. What I discovered in these women was the strength
that comes from doing hard but good work well. There is no question
that the future of the orders is grim. The reasons are no doubt complex,
but I suspect it most has to do with the loss of the work to do.

In truth, I was at Notre Dame when civil rights and the Vietnam
War, not feminism, were the social agenda. I do not know how it

would "feel" to be there now. At least at that time, a time when undergraduate women were first admitted, I did not notice that docility was rampant in the women students. What I noticed instead was that the intellectual quality of my classes went up.

In truth, more troubling for me during this time than questions having to do with the role of women was the dramatic gestures we were expected to make in worship. I was beginning to get used to prayers addressed to Mary, but on "Good Friday" I found I was not only supposed to adore the cross but kiss it. Moreover, it was a crucifix. I did it, but I did not like it. I kept thinking that the Italians must have done this to make the Germans feel uncomfortable.

It took ten years, but I did finally discover I was a Protestant. I do not know what it means for me to be a Protestant, but some folks at Notre Dame finally got nervous about the theology department having so many strange people in it. They appointed a Catholic liberal, a non-C.S.C. priest, to be our chairman. It was his job to make the department more Catholic. That is how I found out that I was a Protestant. He told me I was and I guess he was right. He said that what we had been doing under Burrell was trying to be a non-denominational department of theology, but from now on we were going to be denominationally Catholic.

Of course, given my experience in universities formed by Protestants, I think that our attempt to form a theology department that took God seriously was possible only because we were sustained by the Catholic church—not exactly just another Protestant denomination. Now I was being told that Catholics were going to try to be like Protestants. I suppose that is the way you have to go if you are going to make it in America, but I found it very sad. After all, what can you expect when your new chairman proclaims, in print no less, that if he had not become a theologian, what he would most liked to have been was a United States Senator.

Of course that message had been there all along. The subtext of Notre Dame had always been that Catholics can now make it in America. After all, the Protestant establishment is running out of energy, or at least kids. They sure as hell do not know what makes them Protestant any more unless it is class. So the Catholics might as well seize the opportunity. Notre Dame says that you can become as rich and powerful as the Protestants—only your Catholicism means you want to use that wealth and power to do "some good."

So I left Notre Dame. It was a sad leaving, but I am glad that the years there left their mark on me. For even though I am not a Catholic, I feel what it means to be one in the contemporary university. I suspect that the last legitimate prejudice on campus is against the Catholics. After all, they continue to remain members of a hierarchical institution that maintains some extraordinarily conservative moral practices. As hard as they try to be good Americans, Mary just keeps following them around.

6

The Importance of Being Catholic:
Unsolicited Advice from a
Protestant Bystander

I. On "Being" Catholic

"I was a Communist for the FBI" was the way the fifties television show began. In a similar manner, for fourteen years, "I was a moral theologian, if not for the Roman Catholic Church, at least for some Catholics around the University of Notre Dame." Of course, there is a great deal of hubris in that claim, since many Catholics, both at Notre Dame and elsewhere, would be quick to point out that few ever counted me among those who held the high office of moral theologian for the Church of Rome. No doubt they are right. At best, I was a Christian ethicist who was graciously given the opportunity to live, work, discuss, argue, and most importantly, worship with Roman Catholics. Moreover, my stay with Roman Catholics left its mark on me, for which I shall ever be grateful. I have been given more than I ever gave. I am, therefore, grateful that through the Wattson Lecture* I have been given the opportunity to make some contribution to the ongoing discussion of Roman Catholics about moral theology and/or how to think and live as Catholics in the American context.[1]

You really left yourselves open when you invited me to address questions of ecumenical ethics. I did not spend fourteen years laboring in Roman Catholic vineyards for nothing! I learned a great deal while I was with you, and I have been dying to have an opportunity to unload on someone what I think that I learned. It just so happens this is the first opportunity I have had since I left Notre Dame, so you are

This essay was given as the Tenth Paul Wattson Lecture at the University of San Francisco on February 27, 1989.

going to bear the brunt of it. You will probably get exactly what you do not need—unsolicited advice from a Protestant bystander. For example, my Roman Catholic friends often pointed out to me that I could afford to be enthusiastic that Catholics had the resources to make authority an issue, but only because I did not have to obey those who would exercise that authority.

That, of course, is a fair criticism. Yet, most of the time that I was at Notre Dame, I did not think of myself as a Protestant ethicist. I thought, no doubt with a great deal of naiveté, that I was Catholic. This delusion derived partly from the fact that I was and am still a Methodist. This is an ecclesial commitment I never got most of my Roman Catholic friends to appreciate, since they assumed all Protestants were Baptists, especially if they were from the South. I could not convince them that, at least on some readings, Methodism is not a Protestant tradition but stands centrally in the Catholic tradition. Methodists are even more Catholic than the Anglicans who gave us birth, since Wesley, of blessed memory, held to the Eastern fathers in a more determined way than did any of the Western churches—Protestant or Catholic. Of course, this account of Methodism has very little to do with the reality of the contemporary Methodist church, but it means a great deal to some of us who became Christians through the rediscovery of the Catholic substance of John and Charles Wesley. We were committed to a rediscovery of the disciplined nature of the church and thought Wesley provided some important theological and institutional expression of that; or, as someone put it, "If Wesley had not been Wesley, he would have been Ignatius."[2]

Of course, the other reason I thought I was a Catholic was because I was trained at Yale. I remember being asked during my interview at Notre Dame what problems or differences I thought being a Protestant ethicist would create for my teaching. I replied that I hadn't the slightest idea because I did not consider myself a Protestant theological ethicist—after all, I had gone to Yale! Aquinas was as much my theologian as he was the Catholics'. After all, Aquinas could not have known he was a Roman Catholic because you do not become Roman Catholic until you have Protestants. Moreover, I had been taught to regard the encyclical tradition as essential to any Christian theologian's work. Father Bernard Häring and Vatican II were part and parcel of my education.

To be sure, I did not know enough then to know what I did not know, but I soon found myself thoroughly pulled into the Catholic world and Catholic moral theology in particular. What I discovered is that Catholicism was a world rich with textures and colors that I had not known existed. As a relatively homeless WASP, I felt I had discovered a community where moral discourse still mattered. What more could someone trained in ethics ask? Couple this with the extraordinary generosity of Catholics to welcome and put up with me—even be willing to take me seriously—naturally I thought I was a Catholic.

However, as one of my colleagues put it as I was leaving Notre Dame, I was mistaken to think I was ever really a Catholic. I had taken theology too seriously as defining what makes Catholics Catholic. Catholicism is more than "doctrine" and theological reflection on doctrine. It is also habits and practices that take a lifetime to understand. I appreciate that point. Indeed, it is one on which I want to draw, since what I have to say here is basically a pep talk to keep Catholics Catholic, even in America. I have begun with this personal word, however, in the hope that what I have to say will not be received as coming from one who is completely an outsider, but at least from one who was, and hopefully still is, a little Catholic. I am a bystander because I want you to be better Catholics than I can be or perhaps am prepared to be.

In that respect, I suspect Catholics should be a bit suspicious of Protestants who are enthusiastic about the current possibilities of the Church of Rome. For example, Richard Neuhaus, in his wonderfully intriguing book *The Catholic Moment: The Paradox of the Church in the Post-Modern World*, cannot say enough in support of John Paul II and Cardinal Ratzinger. I am very sympathetic with Neuhaus's castigation of Catholic liberal theologians who imitate Protestant theologians' tendency to make theology but a form of anthropology.[3] Despairing of the incoherence of theological discourse in mainstream Protestantism, some of us cannot help but think that Catholicism still possesses enough substance to mount a good argument. As Neuhaus says, prior to Vatican II "The problems of Roman Catholicism were 'their' problems; now they are our problems."

And, conversely, many of our problems have become theirs. The nature and mission of the Church, the relationship between Church and world, the role of Scripture and tradition, the question of teaching authority (the "magisterium") within the Christian community, the connection between teaching authority and theological exploration, the meaning of doctrine and dogma—the Roman Catholic Church is working through these questions on behalf of the entire Christian community. Of course, there are other Christian communities addressing these questions. Some communities, however, are not capable of that. Much of liberal Protestantism has lost the points of reference, even the vocabulary, required for deliberation and debate on such questions. Most of conservative Protestantism, especially fundamentalist Protestantism, is not aware of the questions.[4]

Catholics are suspicious of the Protestant enthusiasm for Catholicism that Neuhaus and I represent because many Catholics have spent their lives reacting against an authoritarian church. I am often sympathetic with such concerns, but the problem with that perspective is that it creates a false sense of security. The church could be criticized, because it was assumed that the structure would simply remain in place—bishops would continue to be bishops, Rome would still be Rome. In like manner, the "old Catholic moral theology" could be criticized without fundamentally challenging the assumption that the distinction between moral theology and fundamental theology made sense—Catholic moral theology should no longer be "legalistic," but yet the structure of moral theology was assumed to be sound. As a result, criticism of the church has too often been a distraction from the real business at hand: namely, helping the church face the challenge of modernity. Catholics, in the name of reform, work to make the church look like American democracy, failing to see that that cannot help but result in a church that is no longer capable of challenging the status quo. If I seem too uncritical of Roman Catholicism therefore, it is only because I have to live out the presuppositions of the alternative. However, let me try to make these remarks more concrete by attending to the question of ecumenical ethics.

II. On the Very Idea of Ecumenical Ethics:
Or, Why Natural Law Is a Misleading Idea for Catholics

I have been asked to address the issue of ethics and ecumenism because Catholics find themselves in a quandary raised by the issue of abortion. For example, I was told that Catholics, particularly in California, face a challenge in this respect because they would like to participate in the California Ecumenical Council but the latter has already taken a position that is pro-abortion, at least in terms of the public policy alternatives. The question seems to be how Catholics can continue to be good ecumenical citizens while at the same time maintaining the integrity of Catholic moral insights.

My simple answer is that I do not want you to be good ecumenical citizens—I want you to be Catholics. I also want to say that there is nothing more important for the future unity of the church than for you to be Catholic. For unless you draw on the integrity of your hard-won wisdom about matters such as abortion, you will have failed in your calling to be the church that holds itself in judgment for the church's disunity. For I take it that inherent in the Roman Catholic commitment to the magisterial office is the willingness to see the divided nature of the church as a sign of Catholic unfaithfulness: you have failed to help us see why we Christians who find ourselves separated from Rome should be what you think we should be.[5] In short, you have been so anxious to be like us you have failed in your ecumenical task to help us see what it means for any of us to be faithful to the Gospel on which our unity depends.

Of course, there is every reason for you to be confused about these matters. After all, it was the strategy of most ecumenical movements in this century to concentrate on deeds rather than creeds. We assumed that there was little chance of reaching agreement in matters of belief, but at least we could join hands as people of goodwill to fight for justice, to protest on behalf of the oppressed, to stand for basic moral values. Moreover, such a stance seemed peculiarly well-suited to Catholicism, since your ethics was putatively based on natural law and thus did not require any peculiar theological justification or ecclesiological practices to be rendered intelligible.[6]

Therefore, unlike Protestant accounts of the moral life that, at least in theory, maintained a much tighter connection between our theological conviction and moral behavior, Catholics seemed to have a moral tradition particularly well-suited for ecumenical endeavors. In other words, it matters not whether Protestants believe in the authority of the magisterial office or have a correct understanding of nature-grace. All that matters is that Catholics and Protestants can agree that certain forms of behavior are encumbent on Christians and all other people of goodwill. We may not be able to agree about the status or nature of the sacraments, but at least we can agree that all Christians, Protestant and Catholic, ought to be for justice. If natural law means anything, it ought to mean that.

At a theoretical level this seems straightforward and clear. The problem, however, is that this kind of account of natural law ethics failed to acknowledge or notice that it was intelligible only so long as Catholicism presupposed a social order whose practices had been formed by Catholic habits. I remember a story that nicely illustrates this. A Protestant observer at Vatican II told me about a bishop who inquired of his theological advisor, "Now explain to me again why only Catholics seem to believe contraception is wrong even though our position is based on natural law reasoning common to all people." It is tempting for me, at this point, to launch into a critique of certain kinds of natural law accounts that seem to make theological claims secondary. These, I think, hardly do justice to Aquinas's account of the meaning, or role, of natural law. I look forward to the yet to be written history that demonstrates how Aquinas's position was distorted by being read through the eyes of German idealistic philosophy. For Aquinas, natural law serves neither as a principle that justifies a "universal ethic" abstracted from a community's practices nor as a substitute for agents' character and virtues. Rather, natural law is an exegetical principle necessary for the reading of the Old Testament as well as for helping us understand that when confronted by God's law we always discover that we are sinners. I say that I am tempted to provide a theological account of natural law, but I am going to refrain, because my interests here are more properly described as a theological and social commentary.

For in an odd way, when Catholics came to America you learned (but it is not yet a lesson you have taken to heart) that your "natural law" ethic was community- and tradition-specific. You came to America with a moral theology shaped by the presuppositions of Catholic Constantinianism. Natural law was the name you gave to the moral practices and principles you had discovered as essential to Christian living, if not survival, in that barbarian wilderness we now call Western civilization. You could continue to believe in the theoretical validity of a natural law ethic even, or perhaps especially, interpreted through Kantian eyes as long as you saw the sociological and historical center of your life in Europe. After all, Protestantism, whether in its Lutheran, Calvinist, or Anglican form, still had to make do with societies that had been formed as Catholic. This is but a reminder that Protestantism remains both theologically and sociologically a parasitical form of the Christian faith. Without Catholicism, Protestants make no sense—a hard truth for Catholics and Protestants alike to acknowledge.

Yet that changed when you came to America. By "came" I mean when Catholics took up the project of being Americans rather than Catholics who happen to live in America. For when you came to America, for the first time you had to live in a society which was putatively Christian and yet in which you were not "at home." The church knew how to live in cultures that were completely foreign—in India and Japan—but how do you learn to live in America, a culture which at once looks Christian but may in fact be more foreign than China?

It was a confusing challenge for Catholics. You came here with the habits and practices of a Constantinian ethic allegedly based on natural law presumptions, and you discovered that to sustain those habits you had to be a "sect." Protestant Constantinianism forced Catholic Constantinians to withdraw into your own enclaves—into your own ghettos—in order to maintain the presumption that you possessed an ethic based on natural law grounds. What a wonderful thing God did to you. Contemplating it can only confirm what an extraordinary sense of humor God must have. For example, you came to America thinking that societies had the obligation to educate children about the true and good. Yet, confronted by a putatively neutral public education which presumed that everyone agreed that church and state ought to be separated, you were forced to build your own school system. Where else would Catholics learn that the life of the mind could not and should not be separated from the life of prayer?

I do not wish to be misunderstood. I am aware that there were many reasons for Catholics to live in ghettoes, not the least of which was Protestant anti-Catholicism, which is still more virulent than Catholics generally are willing to acknowledge. Nor do I wish to invite you to wallow in romantic nostalgia for the often wonderful and terrible forms of life that those ghettoes produced. I simply want to call your attention to the sociological form that it seems was necessary to sustain the Catholic project of a natural law moral theology.

III. Catholics in the Hands of Tolerant Protestants: Or, Being Killed by Kindness

Of course, the problem for Catholics is no longer how to survive in a hostile environment dominated by Protestant and Enlightenment presuppositions. Now the great problem is how to survive liberal tolerance. Until recently you could depend on Protestant prejudice to keep Catholics Catholic—i.e., it may not be clear what it means to be Catholic, but at least Catholics could depend on Protestants to tell them why they were peculiar. However, as Protestants have become increasingly unclear about what it means for them to be Protestant, it has become equally difficult to know—at least in matters moral—what difference it means to be Catholic. From a Protestant perspective, as long as we are characterized by a general uncertainty about what we are about, it just seems to be a matter of courtesy to invite Catholics to become part of our amorphous search for identity.

This is a particularly dangerous situation for everyone. Catholics desiring to show that they have a positive attitude toward Protestants end up telling Protestants what we already know—e.g., that moral matters such as abortion and divorce are extremely complex, so it is very hard to have predetermined moral stances about such issues. But if Catholics, thus, end up telling Protestants what they already know, consider the plight of Protestants! We end up telling secularists what they already know! Strange results for traditions that are called into the world on the presumption they have something to say that the world needs to hear!

In short, one of my worries is not that Catholics will fail to be ecumenical but that when they come to cooperate with Protestants they will have become what we already are—that is, a denomination. In his book *The Restructuring of American Religion*, Robert Wuthnow documents the decline of mainstream Protestantism in America.[7] He confirms what I think many have sensed: that members of Protestant churches now depend less on belief in the particular theological and ecclesial heritage of that denomination than on how that religious organization provides a means for individuals to express their particular interests. Therefore, American Protestants are no longer determined by whether they are Presbyterians or Methodists but by whether they are "conservatives" or "liberals" within their denominations. Moreover, the meaning of "conservative" and "liberal" is determined primarily in terms of options within the context of the American political system rather than by theological and moral questions.

This has not happened to American Protestantism by accident; rather it is the result of our success. Conservative and liberal Protestants could disagree about the divinity of Christ, but they were in agreement that there was a pivotal connection between personal faith and the larger society. Wuthnow has characterized their reasoning as follows:

> The good society depends on individuals acting responsibly to uphold moral and democratic values; but a sense of personal responsibility is best supported by conceptions of individual accountability to the sacred; and this sense of accountability requires acknowledging the higher authority of the divine, guilt and punishment whenever responsibility to the divine is not maintained, and the possibility of divine forgiveness, redemption, and even ennoblement.[8]

In our current context this sounds remarkably conservative, so it is easy to overlook the underlying assumption that the primary social task of mainstream Protestantism was to create and sustain a society that provided freedom for something called the individual—that is, our task was to make democracy work. Wuthnow suggests, therefore, that the supermarket with its myriad consumer products more than the traditional flag-waving Fourth of July parade has become a symbol of freedom. "Freedom means the opportunity to choose from a variety of products, to select a full complement of goods that meet our individual needs and desires. It means having the financial resources with which to purchase any gadget of seeming use in our quest for personal development and self-expression[9]—and of course, it means freedom to choose our "faith."

In short, Protestantism helped to create, but even more, to legitimate, a form of social life that undermined its ability to maintain the kind of disciplined communities necessary to sustain the church's social witness. In an essay written over twenty years ago but still unsurpassed in its keen appraisal of our situation, James Gustafson noted in "The Voluntary Church: A Moral Appraisal" that the movement from the "gathered church" to the voluntary church almost irresistibly involves a compromised form. The decisive criteria for the latter is no longer holiness of life but, in Gustafson's words, "the will to belong."

The theological and experiential marks of authority on which the in-group was defined from the outgroup have lost their power. The zest for purity in the churches has given way to an acceptance of the impossibility of its achievement, and consequently to a more or less open membership. Now, instead of being gathered out of the body of strangers into the family of saints, the strangers volunteer to join the community of those like themselves, who find something meaningful in religious life for themselves, their children, or their neighborhood. Men admire the saints among them, and perhaps wish to join their small number. If they fail, however, there is no serious disruption of church life.[10]

What I find so interesting about this process is that it is also happening to Roman Catholics. You are becoming like Protestants, one denomination among others. No true church here, but rather one more association of people who, at best, share a common search for meaning. No doubt there is little you can do about this, as you are subject to economic and social forces that make this process almost inevitable. What I find odd, however, is that the kind of moral theology you are generating in the name of freedom underwrites this process as a good.

IV. Catholic Moral Theology and the Ecumenical Task

So let me at last turn to issues that I suspect you invited me to address in the first place—namely, how should Catholic moral theology be done if Catholics are to be full participants in ecumenical dialogue and action? I have not begun with that question because I think it makes little sense to try to answer it in the abstract. The question makes sense only in the context of the forces that have produced it. Moreover, it is exactly those forces that make the question of how Catholics relate to Protestants of relatively little moment compared to the issue of how Catholics and Protestants alike can maintain communities, in this American context, capable of disciplined moral discourse as Christians.

Yet, it is exactly that challenge that most Catholic moral theo-logians, whether they be of the left or the right, fail to make central for their work. Catholics on the left want the church to be a morally disciplined community in order to speak in a determinative fashion about war and economic justice but to speak less decisively about

redescribe

abortion, contraception, and divorce. Catholics on the right want the church to speak decisively about abortion, sexual ethics, and divorce but less decisively about war and economic justice. One would think that this difference would be the result of some fundamental disagreements about methodology of moral theology, but I think that is not the case. Rather, I fear this kind of dispute already reflects a church that has lost its theological moorings for ethical reflection.

Indeed, I want to put the issue in an even starker fashion, for I want to maintain that the natural law basis, particularly as it was shaped by neo-Thomism, of Catholic moral theology was insufficient to prepare Catholics for the challenge of negotiating a society like America's. As a result, disputes between conservative Catholic moral theologians and liberal Catholic moral theologians do little to help Catholics locate the challenge they continue to face in America. For natural law underwrote the assumption that Catholic moral theology could be written for anyone, irrespective of his/her relation to faith in Jesus of Nazareth. But "anyone" in America turned out to be the "individual" of the Enlightenment, whose very being depended on the refusal to acknowledge or spell out his/her particular history.

Thus, Catholic moral theologians have embraced the American project as part and parcel of what it means to do faithful moral theology. For example, consider some of the titles of recent works by Catholic moralists—Charles Curran, *American Catholic Social Ethics: Twentieth-Century Approaches*;[11] John Coleman, *An American Strategic Theology*;[12] David Hollenbach, *Justice, Peace, and Human Rights: American Catholic Social Ethics in a Pluralist Context*;[13] Dennis McCann, *New Experiments in Democracy: The Challenge of American Catholicism*;[14] the anthology *American and Catholic: The New Debate*;[15] and George Weigel, *Catholicism and the Renewal of American Democracy*.[16] It would be a mistake, of course, to read too much into titles, but it is at least interesting that Catholic thinkers seem to think that Catholics can and should be modified by the designation "American."

This emphasis on "America" might be interpreted in a purely descriptive manner meant to denote the unavoidability of the American reality. No doubt at times it does mean no more than that. Yet, it also means more, since there is the suggestion, not only in these authors but generally in American Catholic moral theology, that

"American" is a normative recommendation that should change how moral theology is done. Moreover, it is a recommendation that is in continuity with the deepest wellspring of past Roman Catholic moral theology—namely, that grace completes nature. So, moral theology can first be based on the assumption that there is no fundamental tension between general societal ethos and specifically Catholic moral conviction.

For example, Dennis McCann in his *New Experiment in Democracy* argues that the Americanist heresy condemned by *Testem Benevolentiae* is not a heresy at all. Rather Americanism:

> is not shameful "indulgence" but, as Max Stackhouse has recently pointed out, "a liberation to new duty given by the grace of God, which leads to voluntary community, disciplined personal life, lay intellectuality, and social outreach." Indeed, as Leo XIII feared, this liberation is a liberation from the church; but he failed to grasp the Americanists' hope that such a liberation also occurs for the sake of the church. At stake in the "certain liberty" for which Americanists stand condemned is, in Stackhouse's terms, the revolutionary American principle of "self-governing association" and its extension to all the institutional sectors of society. America thus is an experiment in which the basic, primordial freedom of the church to order its own life is taken as the basis for the organization of political, economic, educational, familial, and other aspects of life.[17]

The difficulty, according to McCann, is the "certain liberty" valued by Isaac Hecker and later by John Courtney Murray, has not been fully realized by the church's "search for self-identity" after Vatican II.[18] Yet, he is convinced that the future is with the Americanist as it is the:

> consistent tendency of Catholics to define their own integrity in terms of this nation's ongoing experiment in "self-governing association." In this sense, the Americanist heresy is rooted in the very foundations of Christianity in this country, a heritage common to the whole spectrum of American Protestant and Catholic communities of faith. It has become, and inevitably must become, the agenda for American Catholicism whenever Catholic people consider fully the logic of their circumstances here—how it is that their habitual patterns of organizing themselves for participation in our common life are religiously significant.[19]

McCann, thus, argues that it is the task of the future not only to make America more American by fuller institutionalization of that "certain liberty," but the church itself must be made American by becoming the same kind of voluntary self-governing institution that already characterizes most of American life.

According to McCann, the primary virtue for a church so constituted, internally and externally, is civility. Appealing to John Courtney Murray, McCann suggests that civility should be understood as "a disposition to conduct politics not as open warfare among conflicting interest groups, but as skilled and self-disciplined public 'conversations.' "[20] As such, civility is not just a political necessity, but a religious virtue:

> Its faithful exercise makes each of the communities participating in the American "public church," as well as their respective members, more disposed to regard each other in public as mutually interdependent, as bound to each other, in Martin Marty's terms, "by explicit or tacit agreement, to mutual communication, of whatever is useful and necessary for the harmonious exercise of social life."
>
> "Civility" thus is the ecumenical virtue par excellence; for in our pluralistic context, it is an indispensable precondition for building the Kingdom of God in America. Pluralism may exist without "civility," but a pluralistic society cannot, if it lacks the sense of social interdependence which this virtue fosters among diverse communities who, both because of and in spite of their differences, remain pledged to one another for the sake of the common good.[21]

I must admit that I thought, after John Murray Cuddihy's *The Ordeal of Civility: Freud, Marx, Levi-Strauss, and the Jewish Struggle with Modernity*,[22] that no one would be able to recommend civility without apology again. For as Cuddihy points out, civility is that part of the modernization process that requires the bureaucratization of private affect and public demeanor. It is the great bourgeois project to adapt the individual's inner life to the socially appropriate.

> "Niceness" is as good a name as any for the informally yet pervasively institutionalized civility expected—indeed required—of members (and of aspirant members) of that societal community called the civic culture. Intensity, fanaticism, inwardness—too much of anything, in fact—is unseemly and bids fair to destroy the fragile solidarity of the surface we

call civility. Civility, as the very medium of Western social interaction, presupposes the differentiated structures of a modernizing "civil society." Civility is not merely regulative of social behavior; it is an order of "appearance" constitutive of that behavior. This medium is itself the message and the message it beamed to the frontrunners of a socially emancipating Jewry came through loud and clear: "Be nice." "The Jews," writes Maurice Samuel looking back on the epoch of Emancipation, "are probably the only people in the world to whom it has ever proposed that their historic destiny is—to be nice."[23]

It may well be unfair to juxtapose Cuddihy's account of civility to that of McCann's. McCann would certainly protest that he is concerned to save particularity in the name of healthy pluralism. But it is not enough to affirm pluralism. One must be able to show, given the context of the Enlightenment ideology and institutions indicated by Cuddihy, that the forces of modernity that grind all genuine disputes into calm "conversations" can be resisted.

Nor is it enough, as McCann and Hollenbach do, to appeal to "justice as participation," as if the very evocation of that phrase represents a coherent social theory or policy. Hollenbach, for example, notes that the disagreements between John Rawls, Robert Nozick, Michael Sandel, and Michael Walzer concerning justice could be seen as a vindication of MacIntyre's and Hauerwas's analysis of the moral anarchy of our society and our allegedly "sectarian" social strategy. Rather than a confusion about justice, according to Hollenbach, what we have is the beginning of a genuine argument about justice. We do so, that is, if we realize:

> that there is not one meaning to justice in some univocal sense. All of the interlocutors in the current disputation have got their hands on some part of the reality we are in search of. Socrates knew this phenomenon well: dialectic, that is argument, is a process of sorting through a host of opinions to discern what is true in each, in search of that which is most true, most good. The argument about what justice means is as old as Western civilization. The quality of the argument today may well determine whether this civilization has a future, or whether its future will be in any sense civilized. In the face of these high stakes, I think the sectarian retreat of MacIntyre and Hauerwas is ultimately, if unwittingly, a failure of nerve. It fails to appreciate new possibilities present today for expressing love of one's neighbor by engaging in the march of cultural transformation.[24]

"Justice as participation" turns out to be another way to say Catholics should be good Americans.

Of course, I do not mean to imply everyone who calls for an "American Catholic moral theology" agrees with McCann's and Hollenbach's understanding of that project. Indeed, I assume that there are significant differences between the two of them. In particular, I find John Coleman to be especially sensitive to the challenge facing American Catholicism. As he notes:

> What seems abundantly clear is that the American Catholic Church cannot have its cake and eat it too. It cannot hunger after unitary prophetic strategies which presuppose authoritarian patterns within a largely hierarchical church or a restricted lay autonomy and, simultaneously, foster a human relation and voluntary model premised on pluralism and personal freedom. . . . It [the church] cannot accept the game of pluralism and still expect to impose its unique agenda on the societal outcomes.[25]

He thus urges the church to explore all the creative possibilities of the human relations and voluntary model of the church in spite of the liability of that church's penchant to become captured by class-based moral consensus. As he puts it, "with the collapse of the immigrant church and the increasing education of American Catholics, the church is fated to that model in America."[26] A sobering prediction indeed.

At stake in these ecclesial observations is not only the question of the church's accommodation to this society but questions of how moral rationality is understood and practiced, for in the interest of joining the arguments about such matters as abortion in our culture, the church is tempted to underwrite those forms of Enlightenment rationalism that deny their traditioned character. Catholics, more than any other people, must resist the presumption of modernity that those from other traditions are "really just like us," since we can make their behavior intelligible because we speak a putatively universal language. What must be admitted is that Catholics and non-Catholics live in different worlds. That is why Christians finally do not seek to convince the other, we seek to convert. These are complex matters involving questions of relativism and truth that cannot be explored here. Suffice it to say, however, that at least one of the ways we know the truth of the

Catholic faith and its capacity for knowing and worshiping God rightly is its unwillingness to let the reality of the church devolve into an amorphous voluntary society grounded in an equally ambiguous notion of natural law.

V. Abortion and Ecumenical Relations

I am aware that I have said little about how abortion fits into this account. Indeed, it may seem I have said little about moral theology but have only been talking generally about the historical and sociological situation of Catholicism in America. Moral theology is more properly about concrete issues such as how to reason about abortion, suicide, contraception, etc. Instead of talking about such issues, I have used this occasion to criticize the Americanism of Catholic social ethics in order to defend my "sectarianism"; or, to put the issue summarily, I have suggested that there is nothing wrong with Catholics that could not be made better if they would just quit being nice and let the nasty side come out.

Yet, I do think what I have said is important for how Catholics think about abortion and how they articulate their concern about abortion to the wider society. Michael Schwartz, in "The Restorationist Perspective: Catholic Challenge to Modern Secular America," an article I wish I had written, notes that abortion has become the test case for the honeymoon between "Americanist Catholics—who are usually well-educated and upwardly mobile—and the secular culture to which they have surrendered."[27] These Catholics, Schwartz notes, are subject to the paradoxical attitude that secular culture adopted toward postconciliar Catholicism. That is:

> Catholicism is still despised to the extent that it claims to teach with authority, but that contempt is no longer mixed with fear, only with condescension. The pope is unable to assert his authority effectively over even the clergy, much less the laity. And so we have the new strain of anti-Catholic sentiment expressing itself by praising those Catholics who separate themselves from the beliefs and practices of their church. To the extent that the reality of the church is despised, so individual Catholics who subordinate their Catholicism to some secular ideology are held up as models of intellectual honesty, courage, and all-around decency. The only good Catholic, it would seem, is a bad Catholic.[28]

Schwartz observes, however, that for such Catholics a crisis was occasioned exactly when your "new-found ecumenical friends decided that the next great step in the advance of civilization was to authorize the killing of babies. We were tolerant, and we desperately wanted to be accepted. But we were still Catholics, not barbarians. We drew the line at murdering the young."[29] In opposition to those in power, Catholics knew this was not another question to be resolved by interest-group politics. Catholics knew they had a duty to stand for life, to choose, as Schwartz puts it, Christ over Caesar.[30]

This seems to me to put the issue just right. For if the strategy I have followed in this essay is close to being right, it is to remind you that opposition to abortion involves much more than just opposition to abortion. In fact, it does nothing less than put Catholics at odds with the primary ethos and institution of the liberal culture which has just accepted you. To be against abortion as meaning politics as usual—to be for or against Bush (or Clinton)—is no longer possible. As Schwartz says:

> The unfortunate truth is that most Catholics in America look to something other than the church for their basic direction in life. There are among us today people who call themselves Catholics but who are, above all, something else: feminists, Marxists, Republicans, evolutionists, pacifists, or whatever. Not everything in these ideologies is in conflict with Catholicism, and not everything in them is in harmony with Catholicism. But where these secular ideologies are in conflict with Catholicism, those who have placed their faith elsewhere insist that the church must change to conform itself to the higher truth proclaimed by the ideology of their choice. No secular ideology can save. None of them, ultimately, is the truth. Only the Catholic faith answers the hunger of the human heart. Only the Catholic faith is true. Only the Catholic faith can bring us to the wholeness which consists in seeing God as God really is. It is not, I am saying, the church which must change to accommodate to the things of the world, but the world must be transformed, folded under the mantle of the Bride of Christ.[31]

I have resisted using this occasion to critique the methodology of past Roman Catholic moral theology except for a few generalizations about natural law as the presumed starting point for Catholic reflection. But if Schwartz is right, as I think he is, it means that moral theology cannot be divorced from those practices and virtues that derive their intelligibility from theological convictions. After all, the Catholic convictions about abortion have never been derived from abstract principles about the "right to life," but rather have been rational just to the extent that Catholic people were formed by practices that made them a community capable of welcoming children. What is "natural" about that is that is the way we were created— a claim about "nature" that unavoidably requires acknowledgment that there is a Creator.

As a way to make these issues concrete, let me suggest a different way to test the issue of ecumenical ethics. Rather than thinking about how Catholics can participate in the California Council of Churches, ask whether the bishops ought not to commend to all Catholic's participation in Operation Rescue. There is a test for you. You would have to associate with the most despised of our society— Bible-believing fundamentalists—in non-violent action. Indeed, as was reported in the December 8, 1988 *Wall Street Journal* article "Anti-Abortion Movement's Anti-Establishment Face," there are tensions between Catholics and Protestants in the movement. Charlotte Tow Allen, the writer of the article, reports:

> Evangelicals rely exclusively on the Bible for moral authority. "I don't see how someone could believe abortion is murder without believing in the Bible," says Michael Hersh, director of Operation Rescue in Atlanta. This can be disconcerting for those who believe abortion violates natural law as well. Catholics have a long tradition of incorporating natural law principles into their theology, which makes it easier for them to discourse on moral issues with Jews, atheists, and other non-Catholics.

Yes, far too easy, but what a wonderful opportunity God has given you to discover the richness of being Catholic and, therefore, to call us all to the unity of God's good kingdom.

7

Work as Co-Creation:
A Critique of a Remarkably Bad Idea

I. A Broadside

A great chorus of praise greeted Pope John Paul II's encyclical *Laborem Exercens*, but I cannot join it. *Laborem Exercens* is a disaster both in the general perspective it takes toward work as well as its specific arguments. I wish I could find a way to interpret the encyclical in a positive manner, but I find that I cannot. My dis-ease with this encyclical goes deeper, however, since the problems with *Laborem Exercens* may well signal the end of the social encyclical tradition that began with Leo XIII's *Rerum Novarum*. For *Laborem Exercens* glaringly reveals the methodological shortcomings inherent in the encyclicals from their beginning.

Obviously this kind of broadside attack demands careful and detailed argument and that is exactly what I will try to provide. My concern with *Laborem Exercens* involves two interdependent arguments: (1) the theological analysis of work is deficient, and (2) this results in a social and economic theory that systematically distorts the nature and significance of work in most people's lives. I will, therefore, try to show that John Paul II's understanding of work is theologically arbitrary, romantic, elitist, and certainly an insufficient basis for an adequate social theory or critique.

This document typifies Vatican encyclicals in the generality of its analysis. Concrete implications remain unclear or uncertain; when the encyclical tries to become concrete, it simply errs, or supports or condemns positions no one holds. That such stylistic deficiencies characterize the encyclicals no longer seems surprising, since they remain paradigmatic documents of a Constantinian church always wanting to mount social criticism while continuing to seem supportive of the powers that be.

To begin on a positive note it is interesting that *Laborem Exercens* does not appeal explicitly to natural law as the basis for its analysis of work or to determine the moral principles relevant for the evaluation of economic systems. Rather, more than in any past social encyclical, John Paul II attempts to ground his perspective directly in scripture. At least his intent is to avoid using scripture to buttress positions determined on other grounds. He employs an extensive discussion of scripture, in particular the creation account in the first three chapters of Genesis, to establish a theological perspective on work. He explicitly says that "the Church's social teaching finds its source in sacred scripture, beginning with the Book of Genesis and especially in the Gospel and the writings of the apostles" (3).[1]

Yet I fear that John Paul II's use of scripture is highly selective and comes close to being dishonest. For example, why does he use Genesis when other texts of scripture might be equally relevant or even more appropriate? To be sure, the Gospel and apostolic writings are footnoted, but that never goes beyond very general observations. Certainly scripture provides little support for the claim that work, no matter how interpreted, is the "key," even the "essential key," to the "whole social question" (3). Surely deserving at least an equal claim is the Pauline emphasis on the powers and/or the Johannine theme of church and world. Therefore, one cannot help but feel that, in spite of claims to the contrary, John Paul II is only using scripture to buttress a theory arrived at on other grounds. Indeed, his excerpting a narrow segment of Genesis reflects an implicit but continuing reliance upon the natural law presumption that creation itself furnishes sufficient grounds for universally relevant moral assessment. Such selective subordination of scripture and the Gospel to a fundamentally anthropological perspective can only undermine the theological significance of Jesus' life for our discernment of God's creative activity and purpose.[2]

Some may feel that this kind of criticism is unfairly directed at a document like *Laborem Exercens*. After all, John Paul II is not writing a treatise that tries to do justice to every theological nuance. Rather, he is trying to give moral and pastoral direction to people of goodwill as they are confronted by the complex and troubling economic realities of our day. Concern for theological fine points constitutes intellectual carping by those who lack the courage to take a position on anything—much less one concerning economic matters and based on scripture.

Such a response fails to recognize that how the encyclical argues is as important as what it says. For if the encyclical lacks the theological integrity which John Paul II wants to claim by his very use of scripture, then it compromises even some of the reasonable positive strategies he recommends. Therefore, while it is not necessary for John Paul II to touch all the theological bases to justify his position, he at least owes us an explanation why he has touched the ones he has.

II. In the Beginning

Yet, even if we concede his choice of Genesis as the key text, his interpretation remains doubtful at best. In essence, John Paul II argues that Genesis 1:27–28 entails the view that "work is a fundamental dimension of human existence on earth" (9). Even more, work is that activity provided through which man, created in God's image, is invited to share "by his work the activity of the Creator" (25). God means for man to continue to perfect or extend his creation through the advancement of "science and technology, and, above all, to elevat[e] unceasingly the cultural and moral level of the society within which he lives in community with those who belong to the same family" (1). Thus, it seems, we are invited to think of ourselves as nothing less than co-creators with God.

The images John Paul II uses to discuss how we became co-creators through our work are interesting. Drawing on the Genesis account, the Pope tells us our task is to subdue the earth (4), but our subduing is accomplished only as we "dominate" and each becomes "more and more the master of the earth" (4). We rightly "dominate" the earth through the domestication of animals, the cultivation of the earth, the extension of our powers through technology, but perhaps most of all through our creation of culture itself (5). Indeed, the very meaning of rationality involves our power to dominate the earth (6) and that is why work is the characteristic unique to humanity, as we alone have the power necessary to dominate. Only man can imitate God, because only man has the unique characteristic of likeness to God—i.e., to create through his work (25). Therefore, work is not simply an opportunity for us, but a duty (16).

John Paul II's use of Genesis appears shockingly naive at best, as he seems to assume that these texts are clear, if not self-interpreting. No attempt is made to substantiate his reading in relation to the whole of scripture and/or, more importantly, how these readings should be Christologically shaped. John Paul II works much like the preachers who write their sermons and then look for texts to support them.

There is, I think, little support for the way John Paul II construes these texts. This is particularly the case insofar as he legitimates the idea that work is the way mankind is invited to be a co-creator with God. For that is exactly opposite to how these texts have been read in Christian tradition. The good news of the creation account is that God completed his creation and that mankind needs do nothing more to see to its perfection. That is exactly why God could call it good and rest—and, more importantly, invite us to rest within his completed good creation. Indeed, John Paul II's interpretation of the invitation to become co-creators is uncomfortably close to the view Eve accepted by allowing herself to be tempted by that subtle serpent.

Of course, John Paul II is quite right that the terms "subdue" and "dominion" are in the text, but I think it is a theological mistake to read them as inviting us to be co-creators with God because we are made in God's image. Indeed, the force of those words in relation to our being God's image is meant to have a quite different effect. As Gerhard Von Rad argues:

> the distribution of weight in the Priestly account of man's creation speaks less of the nature of God's image than of its purpose. There is less said about the gift itself than about the task. This then is sketched most explicitly: domination in the world, especially over the animals. The commission to rule is not considered as belonging to the definition of God's image, but it is its consequence, i.e., that for which man is capable because of it. The close relation of the term for God's image with that for the commission to exercise dominion emerges quite clearly when we have understood *selem* as a plastic image. Just as powerful earthly kings, to indicate their claim to dominion, erect an image of themselves in the provinces of their empire where they do not personally appear, so man is placed upon earth in God's image as God's sovereign emblem. He is really

only God's representative, summoned to maintain and enforce God's claim to dominion over the earth.[3]

A representative is not a co-creator. A representative does not "share by his work in the activity of the creator," but instead reflects what that activity has already accomplished. Therefore, "subdue" and "dominion" should not be interpreted, as John Paul II does, in terms of "dominate." To be sure the Hebrew *rada* is a strong expression meaning tread as in a wine press.[4] But even so we see from the text that man does not exercise this dominion by dominating, but rather by maintaining God's good order.

Particularly significant in this respect are verses 29 and 30 in chapter 1 of Genesis. For they clearly indicate that man's dominion did not extend to the domestication of animals to obtain his food. Rather, for nourishment man was graciously given "every plant yielding seed which is upon the face of all the earth, and every tree with seed in its fruit." And to the animals God has given "every green plant for food." Therefore, perhaps the original paradigm of "domination"— i.e., the human pretension that it is our right because of "special" rational nature to kill and eat animals—is clearly seen in Genesis to be antithetical to God's design and command.[5] John Paul II's underwriting the language of domination by man of the animals is but another example of the long history of human inability to accept that God's eschatological kingdom is genuinely one of peace.

John Paul II's stress on "domination" seems particularly insensitive in that we live at a time when many Christians and non-Christians alike are recovering a sense of our commonality with nature and the animal world. We are learning that our task is not so much to dominate as it is to learn to live in a covenant with God's good creation. As James Gustafson has recently suggested, our task is not to control but to consent to God's good order.[6] While I am certainly not suggesting that the Vatican should underwrite the ecological romanticism so prevalent today, at the very least the Pope should have felt some discomfort with any theological legitimation of the arrogance of our species' superiority and correlative assumption that we have the right to rape, or as John Paul II puts it, to "master" the world (4).

Equally troubling in this respect is the blessing of technology in *Laborem Exercens*. Of course, he is certainly right to suggest that technology can be our ally as it "facilitates, perfects, accelerates, and augments" our work (5). Yet our increasing mastery of technology can, ironically, just as easily master us. Just to the extent we seek to control through technology, we become controlled by it. For technology too often becomes a substitute for human cooperation and community; and if technology itself fails, then we cannot easily reclaim those forms of cooperation and community which have been replaced. I am certainly not suggesting that John Paul II should have taken a "small is beautiful" attitude, but at the very least he could have tried to help us understand more profoundly the ambiguity of technologically enhanced work.

III. Work and Idolatry

It may be objected that I have read far too much into John Paul's language of "share in the work of the creator," "dominate," and "master." After all, he is careful to limit man's mastery and dominion to the "visible world" (4, 21). Yet this qualification is hardly sufficient, since the "invisible world" seems to stand simply as an external limit to man's using this earth as the playground for the exercise of power. Such a limit does little to help us understand better the kind of dominion we ought to exercise in this world.

Or again it may be objected that I have overlooked John Paul II's clear understanding that sin has disordered work. As a result of sin, toil too often is an ever-present aspect of work. Though John Paul II does not elaborate exactly what he means by toil, he seems to have in mind those aspects of work that are laborious in the sense they are physically tiring, dangerous, or unfulfilling (9). In short, toil is when work is no longer "for man," but man is defined as "for work" (6).

Yet this understanding of work and the effect of sin seems neither theologically or empirically warranted. John Paul II suggests that while sin may have affected work it has not changed its essential nature. Work still provides the means for us to participate in God's creative purposes. As he suggests, perhaps even because of the toilsome aspect of work it remains a good thing for us. Work is good because it is "something worthy, that is to say, something that corresponds to man's dignity, that expresses this dignity and increases it" (9). For it is through work that man "achieves fulfillment as a human being" and indeed in a sense becomes "more a human being" (9).

But in fact we know most of the work in which we engage does not promise that kind of fulfillment, and more importantly it is by no means clear that it should. Indeed, one must ask if scripture does not contain a much more realistic account of work and its status for human community than John Paul II's account. For by attributing such an extraordinarily high theological status to work he is led to describe work basically as a self-fulfilling activity. While it may be true that any kind of work may have periods of intrinsic pleasure and interest—i.e., bricklaying, running a punch press, writing, painting—nonetheless most work is not intrinsically fulfilling, but a necessity for survival as well as contributing to our interdependence as social beings.

One of the interesting features of scripture's treatment of work is that work need not be regarded as ultimately significant. Work is simply common as it is the way most of us earn our living. Indeed, if there is a grace to work it is that we do not need to attribute or find in our work any great significance or salvation. Our work does not need to have or contribute to some grand plan; its blessings are of a more mundane sort. Work gives us the means to survive, be of service to others, and, perhaps most of all, work gives us a way to stay busy. For while work may not be ultimately fulfilling, it is at least a great gift—a hedge against boredom. Attributing greater significance to work risks making it demonic, as work then becomes an idolatrous activity through which we try to secure and guarantee our significance, to make "our mark" on history.

Therefore, sin or its consequence is not to be found in the lack of fulfillment that John Paul II seems to associate with toil. Rather, sin is found in the corruption of work resulting from our rebellion against our status as creatures. John Paul II is quite right to remind us that work itself is not the result of sin—it was man's task to till and keep the garden prior to sin (Genesis 2:15)—but such tilling and keeping was still common work. Our sin was and is exactly to try to make it more than that.

No doubt John Paul II's account is motivated by an attempt to call attention to the dignity of common labor. But in doing so he underwrites what can only be described as a romantic and elitist view of work. Thus he says, in perhaps the worst paragraph in *Laborem Exercens:*

The ancient world introduced its own typical differentiation of people into classes according to the type of work done. Work which demanded from the worker the exercise of physical strength, work of muscles and hands, was considered unworthy of free men and was therefore given to slaves. By broadening certain aspects that already belonged to the Old Testament, Christianity brought about a fundamental change of ideas in this field, taking the whole content of the gospel message or its point of departure, especially the fact that the one who, while being God, became most like us in all things devoted most of the years of his life on earth to manual work at the carpenter's bench. This circumstance constitutes in itself the most eloquent gospel of work, showing that the basis for determining the value of human work is not primarily the kind of work being done, but the fact that the one who is doing it is a person. The sources of the dignity of work are to be sought primarily in the subjective dimension, not in the objective one. (6)

This may be the implication of a philosophy of personalism based on the work of Scheler, but it has precious little to do with the Gospel. It is ludicrous to assume that Jesus' occupation as a carpen-ter—an assumption for which there is no scriptural evidence—should suffice to raise work to a new status. I find such reasoning nothing less than embarrassing, coming from a source who should know better. But even worse are the ethical assumptions supported by such reason-ing, for they in fact can legitimate some of the most inhumane forms of work as long as the person participating subjectively feels his "personhood" is being enhanced. Put more strongly, such a position virtually entails the view that we should be able to find work fulfilling no matter what its objective character. I am aware that John Paul II does not wish for such implications to follow, but I do not see how they can be avoided.

Of course, it is possible to interpret his suggestion in a very radical manner so that any just economic system would require the elimina-tion of all forms of unfulfilling work. Yet such a suggestion is a fantasy that unfortunately would destroy human community. The issue is not that certain forms of work are not fulfilling but that they are improp-erly compensated by a society which fails to appreciate the need for someone to pick up the trash. Some of the passages in *Laborem Exercens* seem to suggest that John Paul II would prefer a society of happy peasants and self-initiating artists, but such a society is not only impossible, even more we should not desire it. The unpleasant and necessary character of work forces us to discover and enhance communal aspects of our lives which we might otherwise ignore.[7]

Yet the story grows worse. For John Paul II is not content to use Jesus' life to underwrite romantic versions of the "dignity of labor." He goes further and suggests that through the toilsome aspect of work we are able to share in Christ's very work. "By enduring the toil of work in union with Christ crucified for us, man in a way collaborates with the son of God for the redemption of humanity. He shows himself a true disciple of Christ by carrying the cross in his turn every day in the activity he is called upon to perform" (27). Such a claim comes very close to trivializing the cross of Christ by identifying every kind of suffering or onerous task with Jesus' cross.

John Howard Yoder has argued that the cross is not some general symbol of life's difficulties. Jesus' suffering on the cross is the kind of suffering to be expected when the power of non-resistant love challenges the powers that would rule this world by violence.[8] That it was such does not mean that other forms of our suffering are unimportant or humanly insignificant. Indeed, the church must be the kind of community in which we can care for one another in our sufferings. But we are able to be that kind of community only because Jesus in his cross has in fact redeemed humanity in a manner that does not require our "collaboration." Rather it requires our willingness to live trusting that the power of his cross is more profound than the powers of this world.

Thus exactly what we do not find in our work is "a small part of the cross of Christ" (27). On the contrary, what we find in our work is opportunity of service to one another, reminding us of our need as a people for being a community in which our work, while often not fulfilling in itself, is a service to one another. John Paul II's attempt to give work an intrinsic status by underwriting the dignity of common work only underwrites our already overwhelming temptation to attribute too much significance to our individual efforts.

It is useful to ask ourselves why John Paul II considers it necessary to renew our sense of the dignity of common work. For his account has all the marks of the kind of things that those who no longer have to work feel they need to say about those who do. Perhaps then, the best definition of work is "that from which the rich are exempt." The rich thus must attribute meaning to work in an effort to morally legitimate their own parasitical status.

But there are also ecclesiological presuppositions at work here. His account of work lacks any sense of how work contributes to the growth of actual communities such as the church. To be sure, he notes that work "first and foremost unites people" (20), but he neglects to mention that uniting occurs because we see how often our very mundane tasks contribute to the lives of others. That I have a plumber I can trust means more to me than some of the things we classify as "really important." Exactly because we know we can count on one another as people, we do not need to attribute overriding significance to plumbing itself.

The church is crucial for sustaining work not because it can provide a philosophy of work, but because it is a group of actual people who have learned to rely on one another, to depend on one another. We do not need to attribute ultimate significance to our work because we see how our work helps sustain the lives of other people. Moreover, we know that work can estrange as easily as it can unify—we therefore require a community whose unity can see us through the conflicts that our interaction in work can so easily entail.

John Paul II's theological analysis of work does not describe the character of work as we actually experience it. In effect his account develops a systematically distorting analysis which fails to encounter the economic challenges of our day and in particular the contribution the church can and should make.

IV. The Problem with *Laborem Exercens*'s Economics of Work

On a more positive note it is extremely important that *Laborem Exercens* represents a welcome return to the economic issues that inspired and generated *Rerum Novarum*, *Quadragesimo Anno*, and *Mater et Magistra*. Moreover, John Paul II has rightly reemphasized some of the profound insights of those encyclicals. Particularly strong is his return to the theory of just wage and the common good as crucial indicators of the justice of an economic system. Thus he says:

> the justice of a socioeconomic system and, in each case, its just function-
> ing, deserves in the final analysis to be evaluated by the way in which
> man's work is properly remunerated in the system. Here we return once
> more to the first principle of the whole ethical and social order, namely
> the principle of the common use of goods. In every system, regardless of

the fundamental relationships within it between capital and labor, wages, that is to say remuneration for work, are still a practical means whereby the vast majority of people can have access to those goods which are intended for common use: both the goods of nature and manufactured goods. Hence in every case a just wage is the concrete means of verifying the justice of the whole socioeconomic system and, in any case, of checking that it is functioning justly. (19)

This strikes me as a sober and realistic position that is in many ways at odds with John Paul II's more romantic theology of work. For here work is rightly seen not as providing fulfillment or playing a role in God's continuing creation, but rather as the way we earn our living. Moreover, the just wage has the virtue of being concrete and empirical. For a just wage precisely is that "remuneration which will suffice for establishing and properly maintaining a family and for providing security for its future" (19). Of course, there will be arguments about what will constitute such a wage and how best to accomplish it, but at least such a standard puts the argument where it should be.

The attractiveness of the just wage is that it does not pretend that in order to bring a moral perspective to economics we are required to provide an alternative theory to either capitalism or socialism. Rather, it simply directs our attention to the important moral and social purposes our economic systems are meant to serve—namely, to support and sustain our ability to have and raise children. Moreover, this criterion reminds us that all economic questions are also fundamentally moral questions insofar as they draw on our assumptions about what we are or should be as a society capable of welcoming and sustaining future generations.

Of course, the standard of the just wage leaves many questions unanswered. For example, what kind of family must an economy be capable of supporting? Do the number of children make any difference for our consideration of what kind of remuneration the society must provide? Does it make any difference if the family is understood in intergenerational terms? What kind of child-rearing practices and educational opportunity must the economy make possible? Why, for example, does John Paul II assume mothers, rather than both parents, should be made free to nurture and educate children? Why should men be excluded by economic necessity from accountability for that most important role?

Such questions are left unanswered in *Laborem Exercens*, and rightly so. For they are exactly the questions that the appeal to the just wage is meant to occasion as central for any society's setting of economic priorities. The just wage, so to speak, is not an economic theory but, rather, a moral challenge to any theory or system in that it reminds us what we should be about. While it involves no utopian ideal of a harmonious or egalitarian economic system, it stands as a simple reminder that any system must at least deal with these matters.

Alas, John Paul II could not leave it at that but assumed that a theory beyond the just wage was needed. He thus attempts nothing less than to supply us with a new "meaning of human work" (2) that can provide a perspective for all economic questions from production to distribution. The church, in its lofty position as universal teacher, must by extension supply mankind with an alternative global economic theory through which our problems will be ameliorated. We are told that "work is the key to the whole social question" (3), not merely in the sense of the just wage, and that from an analysis of work rightly understood, a theory which avoids the weaknesses of both capitalism and socialism can be developed and implemented.

The basic premise of this theory is the "principle of the priority of labor over capital" (12). This is assumed by John Paul II but never analyzed or demonstrated as foundational. Rather, we are told that the theory entails that "labor is always a primary efficient cause, while capital, the whole collection of means of production, remains a mere instrument of instrumental cause" (12). This principle is the economic restatement of the primacy of man over things — i.e., work is to serve human purposes, not vice versa.

On the basis of this theory John Paul II supports positions that are generally recognized as commendable. Thus, in line with past social encyclicals, he supports private property, yet he reminds us that ownership can be subordinated to the right of common use (14); he supports the right to employment and to unionize, as well as the rights of farmers, the disabled, and the particular responsibility states have in the process of immigration. The problem, however, is that John Paul II did not need his elaborate theology and theory of work to arrive at and support these particular positions.

Even more problematically his theory distorts a realistic account of our economic alternatives. Because he utilizes a "personalistic" account of work he neglects exactly the primary issue at stake in any labor dispute—i.e., power. He fails to point out that the issue is not work itself, but why the holders of capital should be able to have power over others simply because they possess the resources to define the value of work.[9] What John Paul II either does not recognize or does not confront is that the very definition of terms of modern economic theory already entails and underwrites power relations that may well be unjust in terms of his own criteria of just wages. It is, of course, a good thing to condemn "rigid capitalism" (14), but that is not very interesting, since that species exists now for the most part only in the ideology of the Republican party. The problem with John Paul II's analysis is that he simply fails to direct our attention to where the real conflicts are occurring within and between advanced capitalist economies and the developing nations.

It is, for example, simply misleading and distorting to tell us on the basis of a "correct understanding of work" that in principle capital cannot be opposed to labor (13). Nor is it the case that an economy, almost by a will of its own, is or can be coordinated to achieve the common good (10). And it is naive in the extreme to assume that the "mutual dependence of societies and states" is sufficient to sustain a call for them to collaborate to secure international full employment (18). The assumption of an organic and harmonious theory of society as in social encyclicals of the past fails to acknowledge the inherent power-relations of economic systems. Some possess power over others; they are not about to relinquish that power because it fails to sustain a system of fulfilling work for everyone.

As Christians, however, we need no alternative social and economic theory to capitalism or socialism to recognize that injustice exists. We need only the presence of the poor, the uncared-for widows and orphans, the disabled, the unemployed. All we need to know is that a worker cannot support his or her family. Based on that knowledge, we can challenge the greatest pretensions of all economic and social theories—whether capitalist, socialist, supply-side, Keynesian, or even papal. For the pretext of all such theories is the claim that they really know what is going on and as a result ask some to suffer for the good of the whole on the basis of theory. Such is the ideology that the Pope must challenge; unfortunately it is missing from his *Laborem Exercens*. Instead of a prophetic challenge to the pretension of those who claim to be in control, who claim to know what is going on economically, we get only another theory.[10] Thus,

the church abdicates its most important role, which is simply to point
out: "The Emperor has no clothes."

IV. Are Social Encyclicals Still a Good Idea?

The problem with *Laborem Exercens*, however, is not in many ways
unique but, rather, exhibits characteristics of the more recent encyclicals. In those the church, as represented by the magisterial office,
is seen as a universal teacher of basic truths for all people. As a result,
most of what they say is of such a general nature that it cannot be
rescued from the charge of being platitudinous. The encyclicals seem
to be written in a purposively ambiguous manner so that all sides are
left to interpret them in a manner that does not challenge our
essential self-interests.

For example, John Paul II, echoing recent encyclicals, tells us that
"Commitment to justice must be closely linked with commitment to
peace in the modern world" (2). The problem with such claims is that
they in no way indicate the price that is required for anyone to hold
them. For example, nowhere does John Paul II indicate that in the
interest of peace we must seek to achieve justice in a manner that
may be less effective than violence for eradicating immediate forms
of injustice.[11]

Laborem Exercens is no exception in this respect; nowhere does
John Paul II indicate what kind of costs might be required for the
achievement of the just wage. The encyclical gives the impression
that universal employment and just wage are compatible demands
requiring only the cooperation of people of goodwill. In fact, goodwill
is not enough, not only because we cannot assume its universal
existence; even if goodwill existed on everyone's part it by no means
follows that we know how to form an economy sufficiently productive
to create the resources for just wages for everyone.

As a result the social encyclicals, and *Laborem Exercens* in particular, appear to many to be less than morally serious documents.[12] They
have next to no effect on people who are having to make the
economic decisions that affect thousands of lives. Rather, they primarily reinforce the notion that the church, through the papal office,
has some ideas about economics but these ideas are not very clear or
useful. Although some are pleased with the impression that the

church has taken a courageous stand, in fact that stance has required little of the Pope or members of the church. Moreover, exactly because the church must try to address all people and situations, John Paul II must base his position on a general theological and economic theory that simply cannot stand up to analysis. As a result, the church reiterates to the world little more than what has been known for some time.

Perhaps, then, the papacy should cease celebrating the anniversary of *Rerum Novarum* by writing new encyclicals. For the encyclicals betray the church's very most important social fact—namely, its presence throughout the world in diverse social settings and economic contexts. The great moral strength of the church is that it is of a people scattered amid the nations in a manner defying all geographical and political boundaries. Yet instead of drawing on that rich resource the papacy articulates universal political and economic theories that cannot help but be lifeless abstractions. In contrast, what the papal office should be doing is providing the means for Christians in diverse lands to show that the unity formed through sharing a common eucharistic meal requires them to defy the economic injustices created by clan and nation.

For example, at the very least the church should remind its rich members that our souls are in danger because of our possessions. If the church, not the Church of Rome but the Church of the Holy Redeemer of Peru, Indiana, raised that question seriously, we might well find that the church would have something interesting to say about work and the economic order. For then the membership would have paid the price that is required by genuine challenge to our assumptions about the naturalness of the economic inequities that surround us. What is required is not better economic theory or a more profound account of work, but a church more ready to be a people caring for each other rather than economic systems.

It may be objected that calls to be concerned about people rather than economic systems are romantic at best but, more importantly, a false alternative that comes close to being immoral. After all, economic systems are people. Of course, that is right, but it is a point that fails to take seriously my challenge. Attention to actual economic relations might help us see that the church must draw on its best resource when dealing with such matters—namely, the actual experience of Christian men and women who must find ways to negotiate the extraordinarily complex economic systems in which we find ourselves caught.

For example, it might be extremely wise for the church to raise once more the issue of usury as a significant moral issue for discussion in the church. No doubt the prohibition of usury was defended by some remarkably bad arguments, but the principles informing it are still relevant. Namely, is it appropriate for Christians who are pledged to care for one another to take advantage of others who are in economic distress?[13] Of course, it is true that money is often lent for reasons other than economic distress, but that is exactly the kind of distinction that the required discussion might make in trying to deal morally with questions of the legitimacy of usury. Such an issue does not ask us to choose between capitalism, socialism, or some "middle way;" it reminds us that if we are to make any headway on the morality of certain transactions, we must begin by asking how Christians should conduct their economic relations with one another—e.g., how does the Vatican pay those who clean and repair St. Peter's? Only by so beginning can we know whether, if, and how Christians might have something to say in general about what modern economies are doing to our lives as Christians, in particular, and to "all people of goodwill."

8

In Praise of *Centesimus Annus*

I. On Not Burying the Encyclical Tradition

I wrote an essay in response to John Paul II's *Laborem Exercens* called, "Work as Co-Creation: A Critique of a Remarkably Bad Idea." In the first paragraph of that essay I said,

> A great chorus of praise has greeted Pope John Paul II's encyclical *Laborem Exercens*, but I cannot join it. *Laborem Exercens* is a disaster both in the general perspective it takes toward work as well as its specific arguments. I wish I could find a way to interpret the encyclical in a positive manner, but I find that I cannot. My dis-ease with this encyclical goes deeper, however, since the problems with *Laborem Exercens* may well signal the end of the social encyclical tradition that began with Leo III's *Rerum Novarum*. For *Laborem Exercens* glaringly reveals the methodological shortcomings inherent in the encyclicals from their beginning.[1]

By "methodological shortcomings" I meant the abstract nature of encyclical pronouncements. The encyclical by necessity must be written at such a generalized level that their pronouncements seem platitudinous and irrelevant for policy decision. Moreover, the encyclicals of the past have often been based on "natural law" presuppositions that underwrite the abstract character of their discourse. As a result, I contended, the encyclicals were giving the impression that the church, at least through the magisterial office, could speak in an ahistorical fashion for all times and places.

I write as one who has to eat his words. For even though I do not think I was wrong about *Laborem Exercens* (though I might have interpreted it in a more charitable light), I have to say that I think *Centesimus Annus* is a worthy successor to *Rerum Novarum*. Coming from me this is high praise in that I believe that *Rerum Novarum* marks the high point of the social encyclical tradition; for *Rerum Novarum* was written before Catholics, and in particular the popes, felt obliged to make their peace with modernity and in particular with liberalism.

What I like about *Rerum Novarum*, in other words, is its anachronistic character. Leo XIII still pictured himself as a priest of a large parish called "Christendom." He unapologetically set about showing where things had gone wrong by appealing to principles such as the just wage in a way that was remarkably premodern, as if Europe needed and wanted, and would readily receive, the pastoral care of the church. Many years ago, in a response to a paper by Charles Curran which praised the later encyclicals in opposition to *Rerum Novarum*, I pointed out that Leo XIII and Karl Marx were friends.[2] Both were fundamentally conservative radicals challenging the kind of society being produced by the development of industrial capitalism. They rightly saw such developments as destroying any form of community that can sustain a sense of human solidarity. In Leo's case, of course, any account of human solidarity depended on the acknowledgement that what we share in common is our worship of God. Thus in *Rerum Novarum* Leo reminds state authorities and owners of their duty to provide for Sabbath observance as well as feast days so workers can go to Mass. He writes as a concerned pastor.

What I like about *Centesimus* is that it assumes a similar posture. I cannot deny that *Centesimus* accepts more from the later encyclicals than I would like, but in many ways I think it could signal a return to the radical ecclesial vision of *Rerum Novarum*. Therefore, I will focus my remarks on this new encyclical with some reference to *Rerum Novarum*. I had originally intended to concentrate on *Rerum Novarum*, but this new encyclical is so interesting that by concentrating on it we may be able to grasp once again Leo XIII's insistence that the foremost social witness of the church for the world is our worship of God. The assumption at work here is unmistakable and profound: it is the church, and the church alone, which provides the world with the means to know the substance of the good society.[3]

II. On Historical Modesty and Ethical Judgment

One of the attractive features of *Centesimus* is the modesty of its claims. Much has been made of John Paul II's praise of market economies, but more important, I think, is his statement in *Centesimus* that

> The church has no models to present; models that are real and truly effective can only arise within the framework of different historical situations through the efforts of all those who responsibly confront concrete problems in all their social, economic, political and cultural aspects as these interact with one another. For such a task the church offers her social teaching as an indispensable and ideal orientation, a teaching which, as already mentioned, recognizes the positive value of the market and of enterprise, but which at the same time points out that these need to be oriented toward the common good. (43)[4]

The Pope does not invite us to speculate about a "third way" between capitalism and socialism. The issues before us are far more important than that choice suggested, since what is at stake is not an alternative "model" of economics the church can put forward, but rather how the church stands as an alternative to *all* such models. In effect, the Pope's modesty about economics is based on his rightful immodesty about the significance of the church.

It is exactly this "immodesty" in *Centesimus*, in contrast to more recent encyclicals, that seems to free John Paul II to argue in a historical and concrete manner. Not only do we get a remarkably specific account of the 1989 revolution, but the encyclical explicitly acknowledges the more general point that history and truth are not incompatible categories. Thus, the Pope contends that the church does not close

> her eyes to danger of fanaticism or fundamentalism among those who, in the name of an ideology which purports to be scientific or religious, claim the right to impose on others their own concept of what is true and good. Christian truth is not of this kind. Since it is not an ideology, the Christian faith does not presume to imprison changing sociopolitical realities in a rigid schema, and it recognizes that human life is realized in history in conditions that are diverse and imperfect. (43)

The crucial thing to note here is that these reflections are the product of a church that is confronting the contingencies of history.

Of course, the trick is to work in a historicist perspective without translating "what is" into "what ought to be," without, in other words, underwriting the prevailing economic order by declaring its particular patterns of production and consumption as normative; something that both Leo XIII and John Paul II went to great lengths to avoid.

On this score, there is some slippage in the encyclical. It is one thing to say that the church has no economic theory, but the very way the Pope describes current economic options may betray such a theory. For example, in the context of developing a quite powerful critique of how modern economic developments destroy our ability to welcome children into our midst, we are told that these criticisms are directed not so much against an economic system as against an ethical and cultural system.

> The economy in fact is only one aspect and one dimension of the whole of human activity. If economic life is absolutized, if the production and consumption of goods become the center of social life and society's only value, not subject to any other value, the reason is to be found not so much in the economic system itself as in the fact that the entire sociocultural system, by ignoring the ethical and religious dimension, has been weakened and ends by limiting itself to the production of goods and services alone. (39)

The problem here is that the Pope's attempt to distinguish the economic from the political and cultural system may reflect the very liberal ideology that in other contexts the encyclical means to challenge. For it is liberalism that tries to make the economic realm an independent realm determined by its own laws and processes. Indeed, such a presumption is the basis for the idea that economics is a science that is separable from politics and ethics. This presumption, it seems to me, is exactly what *Rerum Novarum* rightly challenged by making central just wage as *the* criterion for good economic relations. For the "just wage" is determined by calculating what is required for the sustaining of families and children, not by the exigencies of the autonomous market.

Of course, the case can be made that the distinction between "the economic" and "the cultural" may simply be a way for the Pope to remind us that those activities we name as economic are in service to more determinative goods. But by so humbling the "economic," it is important that such humility does not become an ideology for capitalism. For example, if economics are to be judged by the service they provide for the flowering of the family, then it might well mean that we must challenge the tendency of the modern corporation to make efficiency the criterion of good business.

One of the ways that John Paul II avoids abstractions such as capitalism and socialism is by focusing on the nature of work. Work becomes the hermeneutical key to reveal the character of any regime. In other words, John Paul II rightly sees that the way to avoid overly formal and ultimately false alternatives is by forcing us to look concretely at what is actually happening to people. In this respect the encyclical stands in the tradition of *Rerum Novarum* and *Laborem Exercens*. Here, however, John Paul II gives an account of the communal dimension of work that puts the emphasis on the "creative" aspect of work in *Laborem Exercens* in a new perspective; thus he notes, "It is becoming clearer how a person's work is naturally interrelated with the work of others. More than ever, work is work with others and work for others: It is a matter of doing something for someone else" (31). Later we are reminded that "By means of his work man commits himself not only for his own sake, but also for others and with others. Each person collaborates in the work of others and for their good" (43). Thus John Paul II reminds us that what is crucial is not that our work in and of itself is "creative," but rather that it is of service to others—i.e., let us praise those who pick up our trash and clean our offices.

The power of this perspective is illustrated by another East European leader who also compels us to look at labor not in the abstract but in the concrete, Václav Havel. In an essay on *Living in Truth* entitled "The Power of the Powerless," Havel tells the following story:

In 1974, when I was employed in a brewery, my immediate superior was a certain Š, a person well versed in the art of making beer. He was proud of his profession and he wanted our brewery to brew good beer. He spent almost all his time at work, continually thinking up improvements and he frequently made the rest of us feel uncomfortable because he assumed that we loved brewing as much as he did. In the midst of the slovenly indifference to work that socialism encourages, a more constructive worker would be difficult to imagine.

The brewery itself was managed by people who understood their work less and were less fond of it, but who were politically more influential. They were bringing the brewery to ruin and not only did they fail to react to any of Š's suggestions, but they actually became increasingly hostile towards him and tried in every way to thwart his efforts to do a good job. Eventually the situation became so bad that Š felt compelled to write a lengthy letter to the manager's superior, in which he attempted to analyse the brewery's difficulties. He explained why it was the worst in the district and pointed to those responsible.

His voice might have been heard. The manager, who was politically powerful but otherwise ignorant of beer, a man who loathed workers and was given to intrigue, might have been replaced and conditions in the brewery might have been improved on the basis of Š's suggestions. Had this happened, it would have been a perfect example of small-scale work in action. Unfortunately the precise opposite occurred: the manager of the brewery, who was a member of the Communist Party's district committee, had friends in higher places and he saw to it that the situation was resolved in his favour. Š's analysis was described as a 'defamatory document' and Š himself was labelled a 'political saboteur'. He was thrown out of the brewery and shifted to another one where he was given a job requiring no skill. Here the notion of small-scale work had come up against the wall of the post-totalitarian system. By speaking the truth, Š had stepped out of line, broken the rules, cast himself out, and he ended up as a sub-citizen, stigmatized as an enemy. He could now say anything he wanted, but he could never, as a matter of principle, expect to be heard. He had become the 'dissident' of the Eastern Bohemian Brewery.[5]

John Paul II and Havel are reminding us that good societies are ones that encourage good brewers to brew good beer. Before neo-conservatives rejoice in the Pope's acceptance of market economies, I think they might well ask whether in fact most capitalist societies are able to meet *Centesimus's* understanding of the moral character of work. For economic transactions cannot be "spiritually empty" if we are to serve one another and the goods thereby embodied.[6]

The fact that work has a moral purpose is something that "liberals" and "conservatives" forget. They become too enamored with issues of distribution. This is why John Paul II reminds us that "economics" is not just a matter of which economic systems can produce the most units to be more widely distributed, but what kind of people we become through those economic systems. How our work engenders trust in ourselves and others is surely more important than the assumption that good economics are those subject to constant growth.

III. Why Truth and Love Are More Important than "Rights"

The great strength of this encyclical is that it directs us to the question, "What kind of moral habits and institutions are necessary to encourage good brewers to brew good beer?" It is on this score that *Centesimus* stands in such prominent continuity with *Rerum Novarum* and its critique of liberalism. Specifically, in contrast to more recent encyclicals the liberal language of "rights" in *Centesimus* is distinctly muted. Certainly "rights" are still used to mark important goods, but the notion that rights are primary moral notions is clearly rejected.

Rights are subordinate to prior obligation.[7] But the specification of such obligation requires an understanding of goods that are more than simply an appeal to the right of the individual to make up his or her own mind.[8] Put in terms of *Rerum Novarum*, this encyclical assumes that truth is prior to any account of rights. As John Paul II says,

> Finally, development must not be understood solely in economic terms, but in a way that is fully human. It is not only a question of raising all peoples to the level currently enjoyed by the richest countries, but rather of building up a more decent life through united labor, of concretely enhancing every individual's dignity and creativity, as well as his capacity to respond to his personal vocation, and thus to God's call. The apex of development is the exercise of the right and duty to seek God, to know him and to live in accordance with that knowledge. In the totalitarian and authoritarian regimes, the principle that force predominates over reason was carried to the extreme. Man was compelled to submit to a conception of reality imposed on him by coercion, and not reached by virtue of his own reason and the exercise of his own freedom. This principle must be overturned and total recognition must be given to the rights of the human conscience, which is bound only to the truth, both natural and revealed. The recognition of these rights represents the primary foundation of every authentically free political order. (29)

Here we see the traditional claim that freedom is not and cannot be an end in itself. Rather freedom is subordinate to the discernment and articulation of truth. Thus the Pope assumes that so-called "free speech" is "free" only insofar as it is in service to a more profound good. Christians are not about the creation of "free" societies, but rather of societies in which people can worship the true God truth-fully. All that we do depends on our wills being rightly directed to the One who alone is worthy of worship.

Of course, this creates a problem about the status of the church in liberal societies, but it is far better to recognize this as a continuing problem than to assume that it can be easily solved by some false notion such as "freedom of religion." The Pope rightly knows that Catholicism is not "a religion" in an abstract sense, but rather a people committed to the evangelization of the social orders in which it finds itself. There is no question, therefore, of the church being pushed aside into a private personal realm in the name of "freedom of conscience." The church cannot, in the name of becoming "free," underwrite a social policy that makes it a matter of indifference whether one worships or does not worship God.

By emphasizing the organic relationship between the church and society, John Paul II stands in deep continuity with Leo XIII. In this regard, one of my favorite passages in *Rerum Novarum* (22) is the following:

> Of these things there cannot be the shadow of doubt; for instance, that civil society was renovated in every part by the teachings of Christianity; that in the strength of that renewal the human race was lifted up to better things—nay, that it was brought back from death to life, and to so excellent a life that nothing more perfect had been known before or will come to pass in the ages that are yet to be. Of this beneficent transforma-tion, Jesus Christ was at once the first cause and the final purpose; as from Him all came, so to Him all was to be referred. For when, by the light of the Gospel message, the human race came to know the grand mystery of the Incarnation of the Word and the redemption of man, the life of Jesus Christ, God and Man, penetrated every race and nation, and impreg-nated them with His faith, His precepts, and His laws. And, if Society is to be cured now, in no other way can it be cured but by a return to the Christian life and Christian institutions. When a Society is perishing, the true advice to give to those who would restore it is, to recall it to the principles from which it sprung; for the purpose and perfection of an association is to aim at and to attain that for which it was formed; and its operation should be put in motion and inspired by the end and object which originally gave it its being. So that to fall away from its primal constitution is disease; to go back to it is recovery. And this may be

asserted with the utmost truth both of the State in general and of that body of its citizens—by far the greatest number—who sustain life by labor.

Thus, in response to the ills of modern industrial society, Leo XIII prescribed the only true cure, "a return to Christian life and Christian institutions." I am aware that such claims tend to make Catholics in America squeamish, but there is no way around them if we are to honestly hold, with Leo XIII, that truth derives from truthful worship.[9]

Think, for example, of what this means for how Christians might conceive of social policies concerning divorce. In *Costi Connubii* Pius XI maintained that "it is clear that marriage even in the state of nature, and certainly long before it was raised to the dignity of a sacrament, was divinely instituted in such a way that it should carry with it a perpetual and indissoluble bond which cannot therefore be dissolved by any civil law."[10] I am not suggesting that such a position would necessarily commit the church to one social policy concerning basic issues like marriage and divorce, but at the very least it means that any policy must be based on more than what is socially expedient or "good" for individuals.

It is in regard to such concrete matters as these that the encyclical tradition stands in continuing tension with the presuppositions of liberal democracy. Liberal democracies are both justified and formed on the presumption that no one knows the truth or, to put it perhaps more charitably, that whatever we mean by "truth" can only be discovered through the "marketplace of ideas." Yet neither Leo XIII nor John Paul II can make their peace with any such presumptions nor with any societies so constituted. Indeed, John Paul II reminds us that at the heart of the church's vision of the social good is the principle of solidarity. "This principle is frequently stated by Pope Leo XIII, who uses the term *friendship*, a concept already found in Greek philosophy. Pope Pius XI refers to it with the equally meaningful term *social charity*. Pope Paul VI, expanding the concept to cover the many modern aspects of the social question, speaks of a civilization of love" (10).

Such language may appear foolish or naive in the face of our so-called political realities, but I think there can be no greater realism. For example, the analysis of Havel is not dissimilar. He notes the crisis facing the societies of the West in that our technologies are out of control. Hoping to use technique as a substitute for genuine community, the "freedom" acquired through technique has enslaved us and compelled us to participate in the preparation of our own destruction. Moreover, there is, according to Havel, no evidence that democracies of the West (of traditional parliamentary type) offer any solution. Indeed, Havel suggests

> that the more room there is in the Western democracies (compared to our world) for the genuine aims of life, the better the crisis is hidden from people and the more deeply do they become immersed in it.
>
> It would appear that the traditional parliamentary democracies can offer no fundamental opposition to the automatism of technological civilization and the industrial-consumer society, for they, too, are being dragged helplessly along by it. People are manipulated in ways that are infinitely more subtle and refined than the brutal methods used in the post-totalitarian societies. But this static complex of rigid, conceptually sloppy and politically pragmatic mass political parties run by professional apparatuses and releasing the citizen from all forms of concrete and personal responsibility; and those complex focuses of capital accumulation engaged in secret manipulations and expansion; the omnipresent dictatorship of consumption, production, advertising, commerce, consumer culture, and all that flood of information: all of it, so often analysed and described, can only with great difficulty be imagined as the source of humanity's rediscovery of itself. In his June 1978 Harvard lecture, Solzhenitsyn describes the illusory nature of freedoms not based on personal responsibility and the chronic inability of the traditional democracies, as a result, to oppose violence and totalitarianism. In a democracy, human beings may enjoy many personal freedoms and securities that are unknown to us, but in the end they do them no good, for they too are ultimately victims of the same automatism, and are incapable of defending their concerns about their own identity or preventing their superficialization or transcending concerns about their own personal survival to become proud and responsible members of the *polis*, making a genuine contribution to the creation of its destiny.[11]

Thus Havel asks the question, What then are we to do? And in a language not far from John Paul II, he answers by suggesting that all of us, East and West, have one fundamental task from which all else follows:

> That task is one of resisting vigilantly, thoughtfully and attentively, but at the same time with total dedication, at every step and everywhere, the

irrational momentum of anonymous, impersonal and inhuman power—the power of ideologies, systems, *apparat*, bureaucracy, artificial languages and political slogans. We must resist their complex and wholly alienating pressure, whether it takes the form of consumption, advertising, repression, technology, or cliché—all of which are the blood brothers of fanaticism and the wellspring of totalitarian thought. We must draw our standards from our natural world, heedless of ridicule, and reaffirm its denied validity. We must honour with the humility of the wise the bounds of that natural world and the mystery which lies beyond them, admitting that there is something in the order of being which evidently exceeds all our competence; relating ever again to the absolute horizon of our existence which, if we but will, we shall constantly rediscover and experience; making values and imperatives into the starting point of all our acts, of all our personally attested, openly contemplated and ideologically uncensored lived experience. We must trust the voice of our conscience more than that of all abstract speculations and not invent other responsibilities than the one to which the voice calls us. We must not be ashamed that we are capable of love, friendship, solidarity, sympathy and tolerance, but just the opposite: we must set these fundamental dimensions of our humanity free from their 'private' exile and accept them as the only genuine starting point of meaningful human community. We must be guided by our own reason and serve the truth under all circumstances as our own essential experience.[12]

Because John Paul II and Havel share the presumption that good societies are finally about truth, they refuse to accept liberal nostrums for social problems. For example, John Paul II rightly resists formalistic appeals to economic justice as a solution to poverty (57). The poor will not be served by empowering them to become consumers. Indeed, the Pope insightfully suggests that liberalism is an attempt to defeat Marxism by its own form of materialism, that is, through the creation of needs without any concept of our true good.

A given culture reveals its overall understanding of life through the choices it makes in production and consumption. It is here that the phenomenon of consumerism arises. In singling out new needs and new means to meet them, one must be guided by a comprehensive picture of man which respects all the dimensions of his being and which subordinates his material and instinctive dimensions to his interior and spiritual ones. If, on the contrary, a direct appeal is made to his instincts—while

ignoring in various ways the reality of the person as intelligent and free —
then consumer attitudes and lifestyles can be created which are objectively improper and often damaging to his physical and spiritual health.
Of itself, an economic system does not possess criteria for correctly
distinguishing new and higher forms of satisfying human needs from
artificial new needs which hinder the formation of a mature personality.
Thus a great deal of education and cultural work is urgently needed,
including the education of consumers in the responsible use of their
power of choice, the formation of a strong sense of responsibility among
producers and among people in the mass media in particular, as well as
the necessary intervention by public authorities. (36)

The question, of course, is how we can be so educated in the midst
of market economies, since they generate exactly the kind of consumer demand that he sees is at the heart of the problem. Thus, John
Paul II reminds us that the economy cannot do this alone but depends
on educational and cultural forces. Yet such strategies seem undermined by the capacity of market economics to subordinate everything to issues of economic rationality. So we need to know more
about what should be left outside market forces. For example, should
we allow blood to be bought and sold?[13] Or to put it in the most
offensive possible way, there is no question that the *Centesimus*, like
Rerum Novarum, is about the subordination of the economic and
political orders to love.

The question, particularly in liberal societies, is how that is to be
done. Liberal societies train us to believe that our own self-interest is
legitimate, that our greed through market mechanisms serves the
common good. But that "good" turns out to be little more than an
aggregate of our self-interests. For those of us produced by such
societies to speak about love and economics surely sounds like madness. Yet John Paul II has profoundly challenged such societies. And
for that we are in his debt. The question remains, however, what
alternative do we have?

IV. The Violence of Economics

It is exactly in relation to this kind of question that the history of the
revolution of 1989 provided in chapter 3 of the encyclical is so important. This is a new development in the encyclical tradition that bodes

well for the future, for it is nothing less than a theological commentary on the developments in Eastern Europe from World War II to the present. It is at once the source that shapes the moral vision of the encyclical and the central example that gives power to that vision.

Through that history John Paul II criticizes socialism for its assumption that the individual person is simply "an element, a molecule within the social organism so that the good of the individual is completely subordinated to the functioning of the socio-economic mechanism" (13). This is an old and rather tired argument. But the Pope deepens the point by arguing that lurking behind this reduction of the human person is, quite bluntly, atheism. Moreover, it is not just any atheism, but the atheism born of the rationalism of the Enlightenment "which views human and social reality in a mechanistic way" (13).

Such atheism, according to John Paul II, is the source of the socialist presumption that societies are caught in unavoidable class conflicts. Moreover, such a presumption is also the source of the militarism of modern societies.

> In a word, it is a question of transferring to the sphere of internal conflict between social groups the doctrine of "total war," which the militarism and imperialism of that time brought to bear on international relations. As a result of this doctrine, the search for a proper balance between the interests of the various nations was replaced by attempts to impose the absolute domination of one's own side through the destruction of the other side's capacity to resist, using every possible means, not excluding the use of lies, terror tactics against citizens and weapons of utter destruction (which precisely in those years were beginning to be designed). Therefore class struggle in the Marxist sense and militarism have the same root, namely, atheism and contempt for the human person, which place the principle of force above that of reason and law. (14)

Given the Pope's own experience of Poland, it is not surprising that his analysis in this regard is primarily directed at socialism. Yet capitalism is based on the same atheistic presupposition he finds in socialism. Moreover, capitalist societies have been at least as militaristic as socialist societies, if not more. Both capitalist and socialist societies are predicated in violence. And both are legitimated by modernist social theories which, as John Milbank has argued in his stunning book *Theology and Social Theory*, are grounded in the assumption that violence and not peace (which the Pope calls "love") is the basic characteristic of the human condition.[14] Milbank argues, I think rightly, that the social world that secular economics and sociology "describes," thereby making such social arrangements appear inevitable, is the very condition that produced the social sciences as legitimating forms of thought for the liberal project. Thus, social sciences can pretend to possess predictive power exactly because they train us to act as individuals in competition with other individuals for survival.

In this respect, we might have wished that the Pope would have been more critical of the so-called "free" or "market" societies. As Herbert McCabe, O.P., has pointed out to me, the Pope goes to great lengths to suggest that there are many different kinds of market societies, e.g., distinguishing between market and capitalist societies, but he does not in similar fashion make it clear that socialism is equally diverse. Even more helpful would have been the Pope developing his criticism of the rationalism of the Enlightenment to suggest how we are all now caught in alternatives that presume the necessity of violence.

That is why I think the Pope's account of the history of Eastern Europe so important. For he tells that story as the story of the triumph of truth and love over violence. "It seemed," the Pope writes,

> that the European order resulting from World War II and sanctioned by the Yalta agreements could only be overturned by another war. Instead, it has been overcome by the non-violent commitment of people who, while always refusing to yield to the force of power, succeeded time after time in finding effective ways of bearing witness to the truth. This disarmed the adversary, since violence always needs to justify itself through deceit, and to appear, however falsely, to be defending a right or responding to a threat posed by others. Once again I thank God for having sustained people's hearts amid difficult trials, and I pray that this example will prevail in other places and other circumstances. May people learn to fight for justice without violence, renouncing class struggle in their internal disputes and war in international ones. (23)

By no means has the Pope become a pacifist, but this testimony is unmistakable in its significance. For the Pope is suggesting that we Christians best serve the societies in which we find ourselves by developing habits of truth and non-violence.

For Havel too, truth and non-violence are the power of the power-less, for only through truth can we resist the lies that are the source of violence. Such truth may be as simple as that of a greengrocer in a socialist society who refuses to display in his or her shop window the sign "Workers of the world unite." As Havel points out, to display such a sign seems harmless in and of itself, but the greengrocer knows it to be a lie that confirms the surrounding presumption that social-ism is a worker's paradise. Exactly because so little seems to be at stake in such a display, those who put the sign in their window lose their hold on the truth and submit to the order of violence.[15] Similarly, John Paul II, through his narrative of Eastern Europe, invites us to become part of God's people by refusing to submit to violent narra-tives that capture our souls by asking us to submit to false economic and political orders through seemingly meaningless and insignificant acts—acts like putting yellow ribbons on Church doors.

V. On Theological History

The striking account of the revolution in Eastern Europe of 1989 reflects the theological method employed in the encyclical. I have said little about these matters to this point because I think *Centesimus* is distinguished exactly in that it does not concentrate on "method." There are simply no extended discussions of natural law. Instead, the Pope unapologetically works with explicit theological categories.

Thus the Pope makes clear, in contradistinction to liberal Chris-tian theologians such as Reinhold Niebuhr, that sin is first and foremost a theological claim. We only know we are sinners because we have been revealed so by Christ. The Pope writes that

> man, who was created for freedom, bears within himself the wound of original sin, which constantly draws him toward evil and puts him in need of redemption. Not only is this doctrine an integral part of Chris-tian revelation, it also has great hermeneutical value insofar as it helps one to understand human reality. Man tends toward good, but he is also capable of evil. He can transcend his immediate interest and still remain bound to it. The social order will be all the more stable, the more it takes this fact into account and does not place in opposition personal interest and the interests of society as a whole, but rather seeks ways to bring them into fruitful harmony. In fact, where self-interest is violently suppressed,

it is replaced by a burdensome system of bureaucratic control which dries up the wellsprings of initiative and creativity. When people think they possess the secret of a perfect social organization which makes evil impossible, they also think that they can use any means, including violence and deceit, in order to bring that organization into being. Politics then becomes a "secular religion" which operates under the illusion of creating paradise in this world. (25)

That is why the Pope describes the encyclical *Rerum Novarum* as part of the church's evangelizing mission (54). For what we have here is no independent anthropology that can be known by anyone apart from christological claims. In the encyclicals the church

> proclaims God and his mystery or salvation in Christ to every human being and for that very reason reveals man to himself. In this light, and only in this light, does it concern itself with everything else: the human rights of the individual and in particular of the "working class," the family and education, the duties of the state, the ordering of national and international society, economic life, culture, war and peace and respect for life from the moment of conception until death. (54)

There is no "natural law" minimalism in this encyclical. There is no false humility about the place of the church in society or the correlative theological task. Rather, the Pope boldly and rightly calls our attention to those whose lives only make sense in light of the God who is disclosed in the life, death, and resurrection of Jesus of Nazareth. It is as the basis of that Christian witness that the Pope can write the history of 1989 as the triumph of truth and love over violence.

Of course, that triumph came only through the willingness of many to suffer. The Pope does not avoid the question of suffering. On the contrary, he writes,

> The newness which is experienced in following Christ demands to be communicated to other people in their concrete difficulties, struggles, problems and challenges, so that these can then be illuminated and made more human in the light of faith. Faith not only helps people to find solutions; it makes even situations of suffering humanly bearable, so that in these situations people will not become lost or forget their dignity and vocation. (59)[16]

Yet finally, one might have hoped that the Pope would have developed this theme of suffering with the depth of Leo XIII in an encyclical promulgated one year after *Rerum Novarum*. The encyclical was entitled *Rosary and Social Question*.[17] In it Leo XIII noted that one of the greatest evils gripping modern social order is a repugnance to any kind of suffering. He lamented that as a result most people

> are thus robbed of that peace and freedom of mind which remains the reward of those who do what is right, undismayed by the perils or troubles to be met with in doing so. Rather do they dream of a chimeric civilization in which all that is unpleasant shall be removed, and all that is pleasant shall be supplied. By this passionate and unbridled desire of living a life of pleasure, the minds of men are weakened, and if they do not entirely succumb, they become demoralized and miserably cower and sink under the hardships of the battle of life. (4)

I know of no more prophetic words for our times and no more effective analysis of the ills that afflict societies like the United States of America. As a remedy Leo XIII directed our attention to Christ.

> We see Him bound like a malefactor, subjected to the judgement of the unrighteous, laden with insults, covered with shame, assailed with false accusations, torn with scourges, crowned with thorns, nailed to the cross, accounted unworthy to live, and condemned by the voice of the multitude as deserving of death. Here, too, we contemplate the grief of the Most Holy Mother, whose soul was not only wounded but "pierced" (John xix, 37) by the sword of sorrow, so that she might be named and become in truth "the Mother of Sorrows." Witnessing these examples of fortitude, not with sight but by faith, who is there who will not feel his heart grow warm with the desire of imitating them?
>
> Then, be it that the "earth is accursed" and brings forth "thistles and thorns" (Gen. iii, 14), be it that the soul is saddened with grief and the body with sickness; even so, there will be no evil which the envy of man or the rage of the devils can invent, nor calamity which can fall upon the individual or the community, over which we shall not triumph by the patience of suffering. For this reason it has been truly said that "it belongs to the Christian to do and to endure great things," for he who deserves to be called a Christian must not shrink from following in the footsteps of Christ. But by this patience, We do not mean the empty stoicism in the enduring of pain which was the ideal of some of the philosophers of old, but rather do We mean that patience which is learned from the example of Him, who "having joy set before him, endured the cross, despising the

shame" (Hebr. xii, 2). It is the patience which is obtained by the help of His grace; which shirks not a trial because it is painful, but which accepts it and esteems it as a gain, however hard it may be to undergo. The Catholic Church has always had, and happily still has, multitudes of men and women, in every rank and condition of life, who are glorious disciples of this teaching, and who, following faithfully in the path of Christ, suffer injury and hardship for the cause of virtue and religion. They re-echo, not with their lips, but with their life, the words of St. Thomas: "Let us also go, that we may die with him" (John xi, 16). May such types of admirable constancy be more and more splendidly multiplied in our midst to the weal of society and to the glory and edification of the Church of God! (4)

No celebration of *Rerum Novarum* is complete without these words of Leo XIII, for they remind us that the virtue most necessary for the life of non-violence is that of patience and that patience is formed by the life of prayer.[18]

9

Living in Truth:
Moral Theology as Pilgrimage

with *David Burrell, C.S.C.*

Writing on the media coverage of the Pope's visit to Denver in August of 1993, Peter Steinfels (in his capacity as religion writer for the *New York Times*) noted that reporters are adept at writing about events in an old way, but seem stymied by the genuinely new. The language they have been provided in their briefings by the experts sets them up to look for certain things, which they proceed to find and to comment on; but what happens when those very experts are outflanked by something fresh in the event itself? And that, after all, is what events have the capacity to unleash.

In this case, an accomplished media person—Steinfels—sensed something happening in Denver, especially to and among younger people, which outstripped the tired clichés about polarizations within the Catholic Church that the experts had prepared the journalistic Pope-watchers to look for. Others of us who heard about the event in Denver from certain eyewitnesses were able to catch something of their inspiration occasioned by the person of the Pope and the way he had incarnated what they believed and what had come to animate their lives of faith. All of the observations of cultural anthropologists about pilgrimage—the need to see and to touch and to do so in the company of others—seem fulfilled in this dual pilgrimage scenario: the Pope journeying to meet young people while they journeyed to meet him. And what has always fascinated cultural anthropologists about pilgrimage—from Chaucer on—is the way unexpected things happen.

Something analogous took place with the publication at last of the long-touted encyclical *Veritatis Splendor*. Its reputation had preceded it, for the experts had generated an ominous foreshadowing of papal excoriation of unacceptable positions and even rumored that John Paul II might "up the ante" in matters involving morality by a declaration of infallibility. With those fears in the foreground, however, commentators had a difficult time finding items to focus on, since the encyclical's argumentation is dense and its scolding muted. That did not, however, keep the BBC from remarking that the Pope had reasserted "rigid Catholic morality," either because such was already their image of Catholic morality, or of the Pope, or both.

The text, however, outflanks all the commentators, sounding a genuinely inspirational call to link ethical reasoning with faith by offering a clear object lesson in doing so. But most outflanked of all are the experts, especially Catholic ones, who have long been attempting an elaborate accommodation with the spirit of the age. Their mode of argumentation, dubbed "proportionalism," is presented and countered in the text, so that, by taking issue with the form in which it has been presented, they can continue the discussion. It is entirely fair to argue that one has been unfairly represented; the crucial point to note, however, is that this encyclical makes the effort to present before it criticizes and others should return the favor, even though to do so demands close reading.

The outflanking, however, is the more noteworthy event, for the Pope's manner of argument promises to shift the character of the discussion for those more interested in extending it than in defending themselves. And it does so by being—despite its length—an inspiring text. (When that can be said of moral theology we are indeed on the threshold of something new.) What makes it new is the method employed: begin with scripture, show how rational argument contributes to faith seeking understanding, and return to a church life and practice informed by scripture. Jesus, not "natural law," is the paradigm throughout, while the argument focuses on human dignity and the way in which the figure of Jesus insures that dignity.

And the proper context for reading this document is not the tired and uninformative intrachurch polarity of "liberal/conservative," but the fresh perspective on politics offered in Václav Havel's *Living in Truth*. What impressed us about Havel's analyses when they first appeared was the way in which living in a totalitarian society demanded that he rethink the political, and in the wake of his rethinking, readers in the West could begin to see just how tired our debates had become. And irrelevant to boot, as the social fabric crumbled in our national capital as well as in the urban areas surrounding the very universities in which the discussions were being carried on. Are those debates significantly different from the views on freedom, conscience, and ethics that this encyclical presents in order to criticize? Asking ourselves this question will help us to locate the Pope's constructive efforts, and will also prepare us to understand his appeal to younger people, by catching something of the inspiration of this document ourselves.

Beginning with an extended commentary on the encounter of Jesus with the rich young man and its consequences for Jesus' own disciples (Matt. 19:16–26) allows the Pope to forge an "intrinsic and unbreakable bond between faith and morality." So "the moral life presents itself as the response due to the many gratuitous initiatives taken by God out of love for man," and "the commandments are linked to a promise." Thus keeping them "must not be understood as a minimum limit not to be gone beyond, but rather as a path involving a moral and spiritual journey towards perfection, at the heart of which is love." Yet respecting "all the moral demands of the commandments represents the absolutely essential ground in which the desire for perfection can take root and mature," precisely because this next step "requires mature human freedom."

John Paul's later claims concerning the universal character of the negative commands of natural law must be understood in this context. Such precepts are not a minimum but are meant to put us on the way to perfection. John Paul knows that any decision to follow Jesus, once made, requires reaffirmation. For Jesus asks us to begin a journey, a following of him, that will make all our actions glorify God. In short, we usually only notice that we have become disciples of Christ retrospectively.

Thus freedom grows toward maturity only by being directed to the truth, and that direction comes from the Scriptures as they orient us to the same one to whom the young man was drawn, Jesus. It is this rich affirmation of the "inseparable connection between the Lord's grace and human freedom, between gift and task," which sets up the middle and longest section of the encyclical, offering "discernment and teaching, in order to help [us] in [our] journey towards truth and freedom." Its four sections—freedom and law, conscience and truth, fundamental choice and specific kinds of behavior, and the moral act—keep in the foreground the inherent orientation of human intentionality to what is true and what is good.

Citing Aquinas on the "eternal law," the Pope counters the familiar charge of heteronomy ("who's going to tell me what I can or cannot do?") with the reminder that this "law must therefore be considered an expression of divine wisdom: by submitting to the law, freedom submits to the truth of creation." We never find this "eternal law" codified anywhere, of course; "Saint Thomas identifies it with 'the type of the divine wisdom as moving all things to their due end.' " Yet by recalling our status as creatures, we are invited into a domain in which we find our ends or goals given to us, along with the rational means that help us discern them. In Aquinas's words, "this participation of the eternal law in the rational creature is called natural law." Yet as the very structure of the encyclical displays, these rational means are never sufficient to complete our discernment; one must always return to the figure of Jesus.

While he does not rest any argument on "natural law," the Pope will defend moral arguments that have rested their case on it from the charge of "biologism" by reminding us of the role the body plays in presenting to us "the anticipatory signs, the expression, and the promise of the gift of self, in conformity with the wise plan of the Creator." This is contrasted with those who would view us primarily "as rational being[s, who] not only can but actually must freely determine the meaning of [our] behavior." In short, he opposes the "autonomous individual" to an embodied creature whose nature evinces certain "permanent structural elements," variously expressed in diverse cultures yet paradigmatically displayed in "Christ . . . who, having taken on human nature, definitively illumines it in its constitutive elements and in its dynamism of charity towards God and neighbor." These "permanent structural elements" will find moral expression in the negative commandments which, by setting a lower limit to that "dynamism of charity" which has no higher limit, directly challenge those who would violate human dignity in the name of ideologies of any sort.

The primacy of conscience in Catholic moral thought demands that the Pope treat extensively this interior call to faithfulness to what is right. He takes issue with those who "no longer call its actions 'judgments' but 'decisions': who say that only by making these decisions 'autonomously' would [we] be able to attain moral maturity."

And he does so by recalling that "the judgment of conscience is a *practical judgment*": it "does not establish the law; rather it bears witness to the authority of natural law and of the practical reason with reference to the supreme good," thereby making manifest "the link between freedom and truth."

With regard to the formation of a sensitive conscience, however, he cites Aquinas: "What is essential is a sort of '*connaturality between man and the true good*.' Such a connaturality is rooted in and develops through the virtuous attitudes of the individual . . . : prudence and the other cardinal virtues, and even before these the theological virtues of faith, hope, and charity."[1] So conscience is not some inaccessible and utterly mysterious interiority by which individuals express their autonomy (and isolation), but rather that capacity of discernment that deals, in Aristotle's sense, with "matters that can be other," the capacity that attends anyone who has developed those habits of action that both faith and reason conspire to nurture in the minds and hearts of those who would follow Jesus.

This perspective allows the Pope to question a position that pretends to offer a "deeper" way, in which "the properly moral assessment of the person is reserved to his fundamental option, prescinding in whole or in part from his choice of particular actions, of concrete kinds of behavior." He counters this ideology with a panoply of texts from scripture showing how the admittedly radical "decision of faith" is "actually exercised in the particular choices of specific actions," thus confirming sound philosophy and the good sense of any partner who rightly objects to professions of love in the face of infidelities. Accordingly, he reminds us that we must be wary of thinking that we are different from what we do, since what each of us often insists is not the real "me" turns out to be who, in fact, I am. That such is the case is but a reminder that the Christian moral life cannot be an individual achievement but requires a community of friends we call the church to challenge our endemic drift toward self-deception. John Paul in this encyclical is reminding us what friends owe one another, particularly when faced with the ethos of freedom.

This is the reason for his critique of any moral theory that attempts to detach the moral specificity of human acts from anything other than "the faithfulness of the person to the highest values of charity and prudence" in such a way that moral "precepts should be considered as operative norms which are always relative and open to exceptions." The reasoning here mimics the murkiness of "proportionalism," as this theory has been dubbed by its promoters, and we can leave it to them to challenge the accuracy of the Pope's resumé of their thought. What such a focus on "the highest values" can easily overlook, however, is the intrinsic connection of actions with their object—a connection unavoidable if we are to be people of virtue. Thus John Paul II's reminder that it is not enough to do good works if they are not done well, that is, as people whose life is directed to pleasing God. For as Aquinas insisted, even the precepts of the New Law will kill if they are not formed by the work of the Holy Spirit.

For those who may find this way of putting the matter less than helpful, we can find it echoed in Gandhi's reminder that moral matters are fairly defined by the need to regard means as intrinsic to the ends they propose to attain. Keeping the two insulated from each other not only promotes self-deception but in turn fosters institutional arrangements which keep that deception from coming to our attention. So however it may be articulated, "by acknowledging and teaching the existence of intrinsic evil in given human acts, the Church remains faithful to the integral truth about man; she thus respects and promotes man in his dignity and vocation." Such a summary statement recalls us to the context of Václav Havel: there are certain actions that no human being is entitled to perpetrate, whatever ideological justifications may be forthcoming. This is not only because of the harm such acts do to others but, equally important, the harm such acts do to the perpetrator.

Such an account of the moral life (1 Cor. 1:17) recalls that "the relationship of [human] freedom to God's law . . . is ultimately the question of the *relationship between freedom and truth*": the freedom we possess is that of creatures, revealed in Jesus by his life and words as a "freedom acquired in *love*, that is, in the *gift of self*." So we are exhorted to discover the reaches of that freedom in faith rather than by a pretended "autonomy," and reminded—startlingly—that its test is the willingness to die for what is true and right. It is "the personal dignity of every [person that] demands [to be] protected by those moral norms which prohibit without exception actions which are intrinsically evil." And while accommodation is the name of the game we play, it is "martyrdom [which] rejects as false and illusory whatever 'human meaning' one might claim to attribute, even in 'exceptional' conditions, to an act morally evil in itself," and so stands as "the high point of the witness to moral truth."

This clarion call gives existential bite to the assertion that such "norms represent the unshakable foundation and solid guarantee of a just and peaceful human coexistence" and a stark reminder of how "they help to preserve the human social fabric and its proper and fruitful development . . . by protecting the inviolable personal dignity of every human being." One thinks of those who gave their lives that political institutions accountable to the people might take root or be restored in one country after another. And a comparably radical note is sounded for us when this encyclical cites an earlier one (*Centesimus Annus*) to remind us: "If there is no ultimate truth to guide and direct political activity, then ideas and convictions can easily be manipulated for reasons of power. As history demonstrates, a democracy without values easily turns into open or thinly disguised totalitarianism."

Our response to this encyclical probably depends in large measure on how we respond to that assertion, which returns us to Václav Havel. Those who are satisfied with current political and social arrangements in the West, or who contend that some tinkering will set them right, will be inclined to find the Pope's perspective classical and quaint, perhaps even rigid and unyielding. Those of a more radical bent, on the other hand, may well recognize here a voice clearly and unequivocally on the side of human dignity and one which offers the figure of Jesus as a compelling ideal and a compassionate guide along the way. Is it any wonder that a generation whose moral guides focused on accommodation find an inspiring leader in this voice? It is this context of "evangelization, aimed at generating and nourishing 'the faith which works through love,' . . . [that sets] the proper place which *continuing theological reflection* about the moral life holds in the Church, the community of believers."

PART III

Ecclesial Ethics

10

The Liturgical Shape of the Christian Life: Teaching Christian Ethics as Worship

I. Beginning at the Beginning

In Texas we love to tell an apocryphal (maybe) story about the head coach of a not very good high school football team. As is well known, Friday night high school football is the most significant liturgical event in Texas.[1] This coach's team unfortunately found itself behind 75 to 0 at halftime. Rather than begin with the pep talk or the "chewing out" that is usually expected at halftime, this coach, holding a football in front of him, said: "Boys, I think we need to begin at the beginning—this is a football."

There is nothing like being completely trounced to force teams, communities, or traditions to get back to the basics, to rediscover those elementary habits and practices that make them intelligible to themselves. I am not suggesting that Christians and in particular, theologians, are rediscovering the centrality of worship for Christian life and thought because we are currently being trounced, but I do think it is no accident that, as a people who are beginning to realize they are in a conflict, what Dan Hardy and David Ford in their *Jubilate: Theology in Praise* describe as "praise of God"[2] turns out to be a battle cry. Hardy and Ford advance the extraordinary claim that praise is the very character of Jesus' relationship with the Father, so they are making not "just" an empirical generalization but a full-bodied metaphysical claim.

Yet the theological metaphysics they develop, I believe, is crucial for a church that finds it is in a fight and already behind 75 to 0 at halftime. For a church so situated nothing could be more salutary than being reminded that what makes Christians Christian is our worship of God.[3] Of course, the praise of God cannot be limited to "liturgy," but it is nonetheless the case that Christians learn how to be praiseworthy people through worship.[4] The account of praise Hardy and Ford provide, if it does nothing else, reminds us where Christians necessarily begin.

In order to suggest what I take to be the fruitfulness of Hardy's and Ford's reflections, I want to report on how I have tried to teach the basic course in Christian ethics at the Divinity School at Duke for the last ten years. I realize that such a report is not the normal way to do "theology." But abstracted from those activities integral to the life of Christians too often turns out to be systematically elegant but empty.[5] By focusing on a course, I hope to exhibit why we Christians insist it is hard to distinguish between what we think and what we do—particularly as both what we think and what we do is constituted by God's praise.

I had taught seminarians at the University of Notre Dame, but since I was not Catholic I thought it inappropriate for me to teach their basic course in moral theology. So I had not really been challenged to ask myself how a basic course in Christian ethics should be structured until I came to the Divinity School at Duke.[6] I was sure that it did little good to teach seminarians Christian ethics as a series of alternative positions—e.g., Reinhold Niebuhr stresses the importance of sin and/or Calvinists concentrate on the importance of covenantal relationships. While no doubt such teaching gives students some quite valuable information, it seldom initiates students into the activity of moral reflection by which they acquire skills necessary for their ministry.

It occurred to me that whatever else the ministry may be said to be about the one thing ministers clearly do in an embattled church is lead their congregations in worship. So my colleague Professor Harmon Smith and I designed a course in Christian ethics shaped around worship.[7] Our task, after all, is to train seminarians for ordination to the church's ministry. It is no doubt true that many churches are currently unclear about what power ordination confers, which results in the ennui and cynicism that currently grips the lives of so many in the ministry. We thought a course constructed around worship might counter some of the unclarity surrounding the ministry just to the extent that the course embodied the presumption that there is literally nothing more important for the Christian people to do than praise God.

We also hoped that by patterning the course on the liturgy we could defeat the dreaded "and" as in "theology and worship." That "and," of course, reflects the current irrationalities of the theological disciplines enshrined in seminary curriculums. As a result, students who suffer the disadvantages of seminary education are left with questions such as "what is the relation between systematic theology and preaching?" This is particularly a problem for those of us who "do ethics," since "ethics" too often is understood by theologians and ethicists alike as what you do *after* you have the theoretical issues straight in theology. This results in a convenient peace treaty that defines turf—i.e., the theologian does not have to be concerned with "ethics" and the ethicist does not need to do any "theology." Through the liturgical shape of the course, we hoped that students might learn that part of the problem is found in those practices that make the distinction between theology and ethics appear to be intelligible.[8]

The course begins with lectures that are meant to help the student understand why the course is shaped by the liturgy. These lectures contain everything that will be said over the whole course, but I have learned that you cannot repeat yourself too often. Indeed, I try to help the students understand why repetition is intrinsic to worship, since the God we worship requires repetition exactly because our God is a God of surprises. As Hardy and Ford observe, "God is free and one cannot make rules for how he may speak and act. Yet the complementary point is that God is faithful and consistent, the sort of God who takes part in liturgies as well. The further perspective that embraces both these is that God is above all to be praised, and that he is well able to guide individuals and communities to do so."[9]

Through the introductory lectures I challenge many of the presuppositions of political liberalism that are the basics for the assumption that "ethics" and "politics" can be distinguished. That distinction, moreover, reinforces the widespread idea that ethics is primarily about "quandaries" and/or decisions rather than the formation of virtuous people. Yet the formation of Christians through the liturgy makes clear that Christians are not simply called to do the "right thing," but rather we are expected to be holy. Such holiness is not an individual achievement but comes from being made part of a community in which we discover the truth about our lives. And "truth" cannot be separated from how the community worships, since the truth is that we are creatures made for worship.

Fergus Kerr rightly contends that "it is because people exult and lament, sing for joy, bewail their sins and so on, that they are able, eventually, to have thoughts about God. Worship is not the result but the precondition for believing in God. Theological concepts are rooted in certain habitual ways of acting, responding, relating, to our natural-historical setting. It does not follow that the idea of God has a place in the conversation simply because we enjoy singing hymns: but if we cannot imagine what it is to observe rites, enjoy singing hymns and the like, the nature of religion is bound to remain opaque."[10] The focus on worship is a constant reminder that knowledge of God and knowledge of ourselves is interdependent and that interdependence is what "ethics" is about.

Accordingly, any account of truthfulness as well as the rationality of theological convictions cannot be considered apart from worship. Through worship we not only come to know God, but we are changed by our knowledge of God, morally and also rationally.[11] Once theology is liturgically shaped we may hope to recover theology as a tradition-determined craft in contradiction to the ahistorical accounts of truth and rationality so characteristic of modernity.

Students might then begin to get a hint that worship is not something Christians do to make them "moral" and that worship and the holiness of life intrinsic to worship cannot be related as cause to effect. Rather, the activities of worship are not intended to effect a direct consequence exactly because they are purposefully directed to God. Because worship puts all that we do before God, we are made part of God's praise and joy. That is why the first task of the church is not to make the world more just, but to make the world the world. For the world can only know that it is the world through its contrast with the church that rightly knows the joy of worshiping the true God.[12] Insofar as ethics has a task peculiar to itself, that task is to assemble reminders from the training we receive in worship that enable us to rightly see the world and to perceive how we continue to be possessed by the world.[13]

II. From Gathering to Sending Forth

The course is organized around the basic movements of the liturgy. To so structure the course challenges the presumption that ethics is about how general principles or concepts, such as love or justice, should be "applied." If our lives are shaped through the worship of God, any abstraction that requires application indicates something has gone wrong.

That Christians must be gathered to worship, for example, in itself is a "morality." Gathering indicates that Christians are called from the world, from their homes, from their families, to be constituted into a community capable of praising God. The basis for such a gathering derives from the great commission given in Matthew 28:16–20. The church is constituted as a new people who have been gathered from the nations to remind the world that we are in fact one people. Gathering, therefore, is an eschatological act as it is the foretaste of the unity of the communion of saints. Such a unity is possible only for a people who worship the true God.

The focus on gathering makes it impossible to divorce Christian ethics from ecclesiology. MacIntyre rightly argues that every moral philosophy characteristically presupposes a sociology, but from the perspective of the gathered church the church determines what counts as the "sociological."[14] That eleven o'clock on Sunday morning remains the most segregated hour in North Carolina has a different significance once the necessity of gathering is acknowledged. For the segregated character of the church is not problematic because it offends democratic egalitarian presumptions, but because a church so constituted is not gathered and therefore not able to properly worship God.

Our account of the gathered church, I argue, renders problematic Troeltsch's well-known characterization of church, sect, and mystical types, as well as H. Richard Niebuhr's famous "five types" of the relation of Christ and culture. Such typologies not only derive their intelligibility from quite doubtful epistemological assumptions, but, more troubling, their very heuristic power tempts us to forget that even the "church type" is gathered. Such typologies are arguments disguised as sociological analysis that presuppose the practices of liberal Protestantism. Schooled by such intellectual habits, Christians lose the skills derived from our worship to see well the world in which we live.

Under the influence of Troeltsch and Niebuhr, Christians can lose any sense that the way they think about the world is different than how others may think about the world. In particular, Troeltsch and Niebuhr underwrote the assumption that Christian ethics should be an ethics for anyone, since such an ethic was a necessary correlative to the presumption that Christianity is a civilizational religion. In contrast, I argue that the very fact that Christians must be gathered to worship suggests that the audience for Christian ethics must be those who have been shaped by the worship of God.

Obviously, Christians think what we have learned from our worship about living well is true for anyone. That is why we have the obligation and joy of witnessing to what God has done for us. But the very notion of witness means we cannot presume that those to whom we witness already have learned what we have learned by the necessity of our being gathered.

I have some students, usually quite conservative evangelical students, or ones who have had in their undergraduate training a bad introductory course in philosophy, who begin to be worried about the "relativism" they think is implied in this approach. I try to help them see that the very description "relativism" depends on epistemological presuppositions that must be questioned if God is a God who requires that we be "gathered."[15] Moreover, "relativism" is a far too kind description of the world which requires that God's people be gathered from the nations.

Gathered Christians greet one another in the name of the Father, Son, and Holy Spirit. Accordingly, I remind my students that any account of the Christian moral life begins and ends with the question of the God we Christians worship. The God Christians worship is known through initiation into the practices of a tradition which are necessary to know how rightly to name God—that is, Father, Son, and Holy Spirit.

That God is a name challenges the anthropological starting point so prevalent in Christian ethics. Christian ethics as a "field," particularly in America, was the child of the liberal Protestant theological presumption that theological language works primarily as a provocative account of the human condition.[16] The liberal tradition assumed Christianity names insights about "life" that should be compelling for anyone, but liberals forgot that such "insights" are empty when divorced from worship of God.

After greeting one another in the name of the Trinity, Christians confess their faith by reciting the Creeds as well as confessing their sins. The structure of such confessions is classically seen in Isaiah 6:1–13. Awed by the God that greets us as we gather and in whose name we greet one another, Christians confess their sins to one another. The confession of our sins is possible through the training we receive through worship. Sin, therefore, is a theological achievement requiring the practice of confession, reconciliation, and forgiveness. Such practices require an account of the virtues and corresponding moral psychology in order to suggest the complex relation Christians insist pertains between "acts" and "agents" for the upbuilding of the Christian community.

The practice of confession of sin, forgiveness, and reconciliation provides an appropriate context to introduce the students to the history of "Christian ethics." Drawing on Matthew 18:15 ff. I introduce the history of penitential practice in order to show the importance as well as the variety of casuistical reflection in Christian tradition. The loss of penitential practice in Protestantism helps account for the abstractness of Protestant "ethics" and why, as a result, Protestants are so tempted to sentimental portrayals of Christian existence devoid of judgment. For example, many Christians think racism is a sin because it is unjust, but they are not all sure whether they want to call adultery or abortion sin. Through the practice of confession Christians are trained to confess that racism and adultery are equally sinful, since they have learned that sin, at least for Christians, is a more determinative notion than injustice.

The centrality of scripture and preaching for worship provides a wonderful opportunity to develop the importance of authority in the church as well as for moral argument. The Christian practice of hearing the scripture read and preached as good authority challenges the presumption in liberal cultures that all authorities are authoritarian. Preaching "ethically" is not just when explicit ethical issues are addressed, but rather the very practice of preaching is an ethic to the extent preacher and congregation alike are trained to stand under the Word. Moreover, that the church is directed to preach on the same texts year after year challenges the modernist assumption characteristic of fundamentalism and historical criticism that the text of the Bible has *a* meaning.[17]

Those called to exercise authority through the ministry of the Word must have the character necessary for such ministry. Such a ministry is not just another profession in which the performance of the function can be abstracted from the person performing the function. Those called to ministry are given a power through their ordination that I as a layman do not have. The exercise of that power means, for example, the church rightly should expect them to have the virtues of constancy and patience so that the joy of the ministry will not be lost.

Exploring questions of "ministerial morality" opens up more general issues associated with an account of the virtues. Questions of the relation between the moral and intellectual virtues, how the virtues are acquired, the individuating of the virtues, whether the virtues can conflict, and in what sense they are a unity can be dealt with in a manner that make them something more than just "theoretical." For example, whether humility, a virtue unknown to Aristotle, is a virtue intrinsic to the Christian life can be investigated as well as how the naming of such a virtue requires the display of the complex relation of narrative, practice, and tradition.

Christians respond to the proclamation of the Word through the waters of baptism. I assume that just as Christian worship builds on itself, the course at this point recapitulates everything that has gone before, since baptism is the necessary presupposition for the very existence of the church. Accordingly, an account of the "sacraments" can now be given as those "summary" acts that bind the church's life to the life of Christ. Though obviously Christological themes have run through the course from the beginning, I now deal with them explicitly in the hope my students will see how questions about Christ's nature are not just "speculation" but rather required by the gift of baptism. After all, we are, only able to baptize because Jesus is our resurrected Lord.

Since in baptism we are "baptized into his death," I finally take up matters the students recognize as "ethical"—e.g., suicide, abortion, marriage, and sex. This is the crucial time in the course where students either begin to "get it" or give up on what I am trying to do. Hopefully, they will begin to appreciate why suicide and/or abortion are descriptions of practices incompatible with a community constituted through baptism. Moreover, by discussing these topics in the context of baptism the students may begin to appreciate how the Christian understanding of suicide can be quite different from that of the wider culture.

For example, given the presupposition of individual autonomy underwritten by most liberal societies, it is hard to understand what is wrong with suicide or even why you would want to continue using such a description. In contrast, for Christians the very description "suicide" is produced by our being a people formed by baptism, through which we learn that our lives are not our own. The use of this kind of example is meant to help students see that baptism is a politics just to the extent that the church in liberal society is able to maintain the practices that make the description "suicide" work. We are thus reminded that as Christians we must be willing to expose ourselves—and in particular our bodies, especially when we are in pain—to one another as a way to avoid the "necessity" of suicide. The difference such a view of the body might make for how Christians think about medicine and the development of "medical ethics" I think is quite illuminating.

It may seem odd to treat matters of marriage and sex in the context of baptism, but if baptism constitutes our true family then the question of what marriage means as well as why Christians marry must be considered. One of the most distinguishing aspects of the early church was the discovery of singleness as a necessary way of life among Christians. Christians do not "need" to marry, since their true family is the church. It is only against the background of such presumptions that marriage becomes a calling that must be tested by the community. That two people may be in love is therefore not a sufficient condition for their marriage to be witnessed by the church, since the church must be convinced that this marriage will "build up" Christ's body. Moreover, the Christian understanding of marriage as life-long monogamous fidelity only makes sense against the background of our baptismal covenant with one another. Any attempt to develop a "sexual ethic" abstracted from the church's practices of singleness and marriage cannot help but be unintelligible. Furthermore, it is only in the context of those practices that the prohibition against abortion makes sense, since there simply can be no "unwanted" child born among Christians.

Irenaeus's image of Christ "summing up" all of Israel's history is one I like to use for how the eucharist "sums up" all that we have done in praise of God that now leads to the "great thanksgiving." Without all that had gone before, eucharist could not take place, but that it takes place gives purpose that would otherwise be missing to all that we have done. The eucharist provides a wonderful opportunity to develop further Christological issues and in particular questions concerning the atonement. The attempt to develop a "doctrine of atonement" in a manner that separates Jesus' person and work is, I believe, the result of theology being separated from worship. Sacrificial doctrines of the atonement too often result in the eucharist being understood as a sacrifice God demands rather than God's sacrifice for the sake of the world in which we are graciously included.[18]

Questions of capital punishment take on quite different shape when situated in relation to the sacrifice of the eucharist. The Christian objection to capital punishment is not that it is cruel or inhumane, though such reasons are not unimportant, but because human sacrifice has been ended for all times through Christ's cross. Moreover, by discussing the question of capital punishment eucharistically, it becomes not just a question of taking life but why the church has a stake in limiting the state's power to punish. Eucharist again turns out to be a politics that reminds Christians that we are not of "this world."

Reflection on the eucharist is also a "natural" place to consider economic questions and the ethics of war. If eucharist is about the sharing of Christ's body, such a sharing should have implications for how Christians understand their relation to "ownership." We come bringing our "offerings" that challenge those capitalist practices that seem to make a distinction between what is "mine" and what is "yours" unavoidable. The Book of Acts and 1 Corinthians 11 read quite differently once they are read against our current economic practices. How the unity discovered through eucharist is not equivalent to liberal egalitarianism, insofar as the latter only reproduces capitalist practices, remains one of the most difficult but also one of the most important issues with which I deal.

The peace necessary for eucharistic celebration creates the condition necessary not only for questions of the ethics of war but for exploring the question of why war should be distinguished from murder. The peace of the eucharist is not the absence of violence or the violence that often appears as order, but rather it is the peace that comes from being made friends with God and with one another. For example, I ask the students to consider whether Christians can get up from the meal in which Jesus has been the host and begin to kill one another in name of national loyalties. The eucharist, therefore, becomes the necessary background for understanding why Christians who feel called to participate in war bear, as the just-war tradition presupposes, the burden of proof. At the very least by so situating "just-war theory" it becomes a mode of Christian casuistry rather than predetermined justification for what the state is going to do anyway.

Just as suddenly as Christians have been gathered they are sent forth with God's blessing. I again return to the Troeltsch's and Niebuhr's typologies to suggest that sending out of the church means that the church can never be a "sect." For Christians it is never a question of whether to serve the world but how they are to be of service in the world. We can never forget that worship is the way God has given us to serve the world. Historical considerations are again introduced, as here it seems important to treat Augustine's account of the two cities, Luther's understanding of the two realms, as well as the Calvinist understanding of a holy commonwealth. Too often such accounts become predetermined justifications for Christians to be loyal to a "state."[19] Rather what is needed is the kind of discriminating judgments about this or that state or society which Christians must negotiate with all the skill acquired through their worship of God. Such skills are exactly what I hope the students will discover they have acquired through the practices they have been put through in the course.

III. Ending with the Beginning

I have obviously not tried to mention every issue I take up in this course.[20] The stress I place on the narrative character of worship and ethics, the ongoing polemic with the presuppositions and practices of liberalism, the conversation with other "ethicists" obviously has more prominence in the course than is apparent from this report. Moreover, any attempt to display much less defend adequately the many claims and assertions I have made above would take at least a book, and quite a long one at that. Rather I have tried to suggest how structuring a course in Christian ethics around worship can provide the means for renarrating familiar Christian commitments in such a manner that they take on new power.

From the beginning to the end of the course I make it clear that I have no interest in teaching students about theology and/or ethics. Rather, I hope to transform my own and their lives that we all might live the life of praise more faithfully. Such transformation is an ongoing task, for our very familiarity with the language of faith becomes a mode of domestication of God. Yet it turns out that God will not be domesticated, forcing us to see what we had looked at far too long and not seen at all. So, to return to the football example, it is to be hoped that as we come out for the second half we will have learned the importance of where Christians always begin—in praise of God.

Appendix I

CHE 33   Professor Stanley Hauerwas   Fall 1993

1. REQUIRED READING

Anne Tyler, *Saint Maybe*
John Howard Yoder, *Body Politics*
Lesslie Newbigin, *Foolishness to the Greeks*
Sharon Welch, *A Feminist Ethic of Risk*
Stanley Hauerwas, *The Peaceable Kingdom*

2. COURSE STRUCTURE

Worship and Life
Gathering and Greeting
Confession and Sin: Race, Class, Gender
Scripture and Proclamation: Virtues and the Ministry
Baptism: Marriage, Sex, and the Family
Offering, Sacrifice, and Eucharist: Economic Justice, War, and Peace
Sending Forth

3. COURSE SCHEDULE

Weeks 1–2: Worship and Life
    Readings: Aug. 31–Sept. 3; Tyler, *Saint Maybe*
    Sept. 7–10; Yoder, *Body Politics*
Weeks 3–4: Gathering and Greeting
    Readings: Sept. 14–17; Newbigin, ch. 1–2
    Sept. 21–24; Newbigin, ch. 3–6
Weeks 5–6: Confession and Sin: Race, Class, Gender
    Readings: Sept. 28–Oct. 1; Welch, Parts I–II
    Oct. 5–8; Welch, Part III
Weeks 7–8: Scripture and Proclamation: Virtue and the Ministry
    Readings: Oct. 12–15; Hauerwas, ch. 1–4
    Oct. 20–22; Hauerwas, ch. 5
Weeks 9–10: Baptism: Marriage, Sex, and the Family
    Readings: Oct. 26–Nov. 5; Hauerwas, ch. 6–8
Weeks 11–13: Offering, Sacrifice, and the Eucharist: Economic Justice,
    War, and Peace
    Readings: Nov. 9–Nov. 24: Yoder, *Body Politics*
Week 14: Sending Forth

Appendix II

STANDING ON THE SHOULDERS OF MURDERS:
THE END OF SACRIFICE

Exodus 12:1–14
1 Corinthians 1:23–26
John 13:1–17, 31b–35

The idea that it would be necessary to sacrifice a lamb at Passover to save the Hebrew firstborn is offensive to us—that is, we modern people who know all unnecessary killing is offensive. Why a lamb? Wasn't there some kind of red dye that would have done just as well? However, as long as we are getting upset about the sacrifice of lambs, let us not forget the firstborn of the Egyptians. The liberation of Israel, so celebrated today as a generalized symbol of salvation, was not good news for the Egyptians, and, as events developed, it was even worse news for the Canaanites.

We Christians like to use this time, this Easter time, to differentiate ourselves from the Jews—or, perhaps better put, from all those that would sacrifice animals and even other people as part of God's economy of salvation. Foot washing is much more palatable for us. Christianity is surely about serving others to make the world better. We do not think that the idea of sacrifice is worthy of discussion, particularly nonvoluntary sacrifice, or that it might be at the heart of our worship of God.

Our abhorrence of the practice of sacrifice, moreover, comports well with the humanistic presumptions so characteristic of modernity and, in particular, the modern university. We no longer need sacrificial religions, but rather we need people who may have to sacrifice their ambition and/or pleasures, to become servants to others so we can free ourselves from our self-imposed limits. We think that the whole point of our lives is to create a world that makes sacrifice irrational. Our goal is to sacrifice sacrifice by creating a world of freedom where all limits are freely chosen. Our god, accordingly, has become a cosmic, but highly personable, bureaucrat that lovingly lures each of us to discover ourselves through our individual destinies. That one of God's creatures should be sacrificed so that it might be led to its true end can only strike us as cruelty.

The university has become the primary agent for the creation of a world free of sacrifice. Here, at universities like Duke, we produce and underwrite stories that assure us that we have now moved (or at least we are trying to move) beyond stories centered on sacrifice. That is why, of course, the contemporary university, to its credit, has become a place of multicultural turmoil. As a university we are committed to denying no one a voice in the story of progress toward a world in which no one must suffer for anyone else. We invite countervoices in the attempt to create a common story that relegates sacrifice to the past. The only problem is those countervoices seem inextricably to involve suffering that only makes sense as a story of sacrifice. Such sacrifices are relegated to the past in an attempt to create a common story that is no longer dependent on sacrifice.

Yet that project to create such a common story, the project of modernity, the university that serves it, our lives that are embedded in it—is a lie. We are not and cannot be beyond sacrifice. The stories we create to convince ourselves that we can live without sacrifice create lying stories, false memories, which require more sacrifices that are all the more destructive exactly because they cannot be acknowledged as sacrifice. That is why the Jews remain such an embarrassment for modern people—they know that they must continue to be a Passover people, a people who remember that they live by sacrifice, particularly after the destruction of the Temple.

The lie we tell is particularly apparent in our inability to deal with the horror of the past. "History," Hegel observed, "is a slaughter-bench." The university, as humane and utopian a space as exists, is built on the shoulders of murderers. America is a country constituted by slavery and genocide. Christians not only perpetrated our share of these crimes but, even more importantly, we provided the justification, or at least explanations, that ensure we will perpetuate similar crimes in the future in the name of our humanity. Duke Chapel is a monument built by Christian accommodation to that story of human progress. What is a little slavery, genocide, and rapacious economic behavior if we can all come to a place like this to worship?

I confess, I am hesitant to mention matters like slavery and genocide to people like you and me—enlightened people who dote on the guilt we think we produced by our honesty. Of course, the histories we inherit are filled with terror; we feel terrible about it, but our very recognition of the slavery and genocides of the past is surely a sign of our righteousness, that we are okay. No need to sacrifice to a righteous God in the hope of saving ourselves from God's righteous wrath. Now that we acknowledge the slaughter-bench on which we stand we just need to remember to try to be better. After all, what else can you do when what has been done is so wrong that nothing you can do can make it right? At least through the disciplines of the university we do not suppress the memory of those who have suffered—women, African Americans, Native Americans, Jews, the poor.

Of course, this in its turn creates the new righteousness of victimization, which unfortunately turns out to be the worst form of victimization. To be victimized is to be forever caught in a history created by the victimizer. Moreover, the guilt of humane victimizers like us, winners who constitute the knowledge industries called universities, become tired and bored with narcissistic delights of our guilt. Such guilt too readily can offer new reasons to victimize, to sacrifice the victim for being the victim. And so it goes. We pile murder upon murder in our desperate attempt to create a history, a space, free of murder. If you do not believe that, think about the Iraqis burned alive in the sands of Desert Storm in the name of a progressive civilization that knows it is progressive because it is not led by a "brutal ruler."

The good news of this day is that God has brought an end to such murderous sacrifice by the sacrifice of our Passover lamb. "On the same night he was betrayed he took bread, and when he had given thanks, he broke it, and said, 'This is my body which is broken for you. Do this in remembrance of me.' In the same way he took the cup also after supper, saying, 'This is the new covenant in my blood. Do this as often as you drink it, in remembrance of me,' for as often as you eat this bread and drink the cup, you proclaim the Lord's death until he comes." Here sacrifice has come to its proper end, its proper purpose, for in this sacrifice God refuses to let the history of murder determine God's life and our history. All murderous sacrifice is ended by this one mighty sacrifice of God through which we—that is, the church—have been made part of God's sacrifice, God's life, for the world.

By the creation of a people capable of remembering "on the night he was betrayed"—betrayed by us—we became a people of the new age with a history that is not based on lying. By being made part of God's sacrificial life we proclaim that God has made us an Israel-like people capable of remembering that our history is one made possible by miracle. By such a miraculous sacrifice we have been saved from the self-justifying and congratulatory lies of the world that lead only to further murder.

The great good news is that by making us participants in God's sacrifice of Jesus we become the salvation for the world. We do not sacrifice to God in eucharist, but in eucharist we are made God's sacrifice. Church names those people who are no longer tempted to sacrifice themselves and others to idols. In this sacrifice all other sacrifices come to an end because here we see the end of true sacrifice.

Only by a memory constituted by God's continuing sacrifice, moreover, can we get foot washing right. Jesus tells Peter that he cannot know what such washing entails for such washing surely anticipates a baptism into the sacrifice of the Cross. Peter cannot know for what he asks when he requests for not only his feet but for his hands and head to be submerged into the blood of the Cross. In this washing Christ makes us not generalized servants to help those in need, but rather, as he tells Peter, through such washing we share his life, his sacrifice. Servanthood abstracted from Christ's sacrifice cannot help but foster humanistic and sentimental illusions that offer us no salvation from the slaughter-bench of history. Our God, the God of Passover and crucifixion, is a bloody and bloodied God. Our salvation, our service to one another, is equally bloody. We are a church of martyrs.

Christians are not asked to wash one another because we think service will make the world less murderous. Rather, we became servants to one another as Christ served us—through sacrifice. Once we see it is the crucified Christ who kneels before us ready to wash us in a basin of blood we cannot help but be sympathetic with Peter's "You will never wash my feet." Yet through our baptisms we have been so washed, made part of God's counterhistory, counterkingdom, countercommunity that would rather die before we kill. Moreover, we believe as we are made a people of such memory we offer the world a history not destined to repeat our murderous past.

Our savior's blood is now smeared on the lintels of our bodies, the church's body, so that God will remember not to destroy the world. It is a frightening and terrible thing God has done to us by making us part of Christ's sacrifice. Yet in that doing we have been freed from the history of sacrificial vengeance and murder. By being so constituted we believe we have learned to wash one another with the truth.

Such a truth constitutes our servant ministry here at this university. We cannot fail to challenge the false histories enshrined here that deny the necessity of God's sacrifice.

Do not expect to be celebrated for such a servant witness. Expect to be reviled. Indeed, we had better learn to eat with our loins girded and the sandals on our feet. Our sacrifice, after all, is a moveable feast.

That the world may be offended by sacrifice is why we will time and time again need to rush back here—to this different time than university time—to have our bodies washed in the sacrificial memory of Passover and our Passover lamb called Jesus. Is it any wonder that we hunger and thirst for this feast of the new age through which we are made God's proclamation of Christ's death? So come, rush to the table, knowing that here we are lifted up so that we and the world are saved from the slaughter.

11

Casuistry in Context:
The Need for Tradition

I. Why Casuistry Is Not Applied Ethics

I sometimes suggest that there are some words that certain religious traditions should never be allowed to use. Anglicans should never be allowed to say "Incarnation" because they usually mean by that "God became human and said, 'Say, this is not too bad!' " In like manner, Methodists should not be allowed to use the word "experience" because they usually mean that salvation consists in having the right feelings at the right time and in the right place. Rather than our confrontation with God being an occasion for challenging our endemic narcissism, the emphasis on experience thus only underwrites our fatal narcissism.

All of which is to say that I am not all that happy with an emphasis on experience in and of itself as an end for moral reflection. I feel about experience like I do about talk about values—namely, I do not want to know what you value—tell me what you want. So do not tell me about the importance of experience, but rather name the experience you think is important. What is important is not that we attend to experience but whose experience, where they had it, and how they understand it. More important than having had an experience is knowing how to describe it or name it.

I think the same is true about casuistry. I am completely convinced that Albert Jonsen (and Stephen Toulmin) are right to remind us of the significance of casuistry.[1] Moreover, I think Jonsen is right to suggest that modern moral philosophy has tended to ignore the importance of casuistry in its attempt to secure the foundation of

169

morality *qua* morality; or perhaps more accurately, modern moral philosophy has tended to distort the nature of casuistical reasoning with a model of basic principles applied to particular cases. The "cases" discussed turn out to be cases amenable to our theories. For instance, what do you do about the fat person stuck in the mouth of the cave with the water rising on the inside threatening to drown the four companions left in the cave? Can you use the dynamite that has been conveniently found to blow the fat one out of the hole in order to save the four inside?

It is instructive that this kind of case is assumed to be crucial for almost all varieties of contemporary ethical theory—i.e., Kantian, utilitarian, contractarian, and all the various ways they can be combined. Such cases are made for such theories because, as Alasdair MacIntyre has observed, these various theories share the presumption that the role of ethics is "to specify universally binding principles or rules whose universality has the scope of humanity itself."

> Detachment from and disinterestedness towards all social particularity and positivity is thus a defining mark of morality. It follows that morality can be formulated and understood independently of any considerations which arise from highly specific forms of social structure. Ignorance of sociology and history will not be a defect in the student of morality as such. But what then of those areas of human life in which the regulation of conduct requires the framing of rules which specify how institutionalized relationships of physician, nurse and patient, of lawyer, client and judge, of elected public officials to civil servants and to the public? The answer, according to the dominant standpoint, is that the rules of morality as such have to be *applied* to this kind of socially and institutionally specific rules. The academic discipline of *ethics as such*, which enquires into the nature of morality as such, has to be supplemented by the discipline of *applied ethics*.[2]

Examples like the one above become standard cases for such a conception of "applied ethics." For what it seems needed is but the statement of ethical principle—e.g., "Never do evil that good may come" or "Always act for the greatest good for the greatest number"— and the testing of its implications in such "cases." It is to be noted that such "cases" are ideal for such ethical theories, since the variables of the cases are interchangeable with other cases. Therefore, all that is needed to make such theories relevant to medicine, for example, is to change the situation to the problem of scarce medical resources such as dialysis machines and how patient selection is to be done fairly. When those captured by this understanding of ethics and, in particular, "applied ethics" turned their attention to medicine, they were not challenged to change their conception of ethics but instead simply changed the examples so that their theories seemed relevant to issues raised in medicine.

MacIntyre argues that this understanding of "applied ethics" is incoherent in its very conception because it cannot be that we can first comprehend the rules of morality in the abstract and then ask how they are applied.

> For, were this to be the case, the rules of morality as such would be effectively contentless. On the dominant view, for example, we are first and independently to frame a rule or rules about truth-telling and honesty in general and then only secondly need to enquire how it is, or they are to be applied in such relationships as those of physician to patient or lawyer in respect to his or her client's affairs and so on. But no rule exists apart from its applications, and if, as we approach the question of whether a physician on a particular type of occasion ought to answer a question by a patient, truthfully or not, it must be in the light of previous applications of the rule. But these applications will have been to situations and relationships quite as socially specific as is the physician-patient relationship.[3]

MacIntyre's analysis of the incoherence of the very notion of "applied ethics" at first seems to share much with Jonsen's criticism of ethical theory since Henry Sedgwick. Yet I hope to show that Jonsen (and Toulmin) are actually much closer to Sedgwick than MacIntyre. For the problem is not, as Jonsen would have it, that philosophers have tried to do ethics on the model of scientific detachment, but rather they have tried to do ethics free from any concrete tradition and corresponding moral practices. In order to accomplish this they have sought to reduce morality to a few basic moral principles that are allegedly constitutive of rationality *qua* rationality. Unless ethics could be so grounded it was assumed that there could be no defense against relativism, subjectivism, and arbitrary starting points. Though Jonsen's defense of casuistry is an attempt to critique or at least supplement this kind of moral theory, I find that his account of casuistry still assumes the fundamental correctness of the account of ethics sponsored by the heirs of Sedgwick.

II. Casuistic Reasoning

In this respect it is interesting how modern accounts of Christian ethics have attempted to model the philosophical project of modernity. Thus theologians stress love, justice, or some other monistic principle as all-determining for ethical rationality and judgment. I say it is interesting because we might have expected that those from religious traditions would have resisted such monistic reductions because they would have noticed that they were working from within an ongoing tradition. I suspect, however, that because the social and political context we occupy makes the particularity of traditions something to be overcome, we perpetuate this kind of ethical reductionism. We try to use our theories to supply for reason and the self a unity that can only be forthcoming from our communities and their practices.

Against this background the call for us to attend to "experience" and/or casuistry makes great sense. For I take it that "experience" is meant to name those aspects of our moral existence that are simply ignored or distorted by our longing for the certainty and unity which our theories promise but fail to supply. Therefore, by calling our attention to a method of casuistry which is not the application of theory but the ongoing reflection about cases, Jonsen is trying to help us recover what anthropologists call a "thick description" of our moral existence. In that respect, I think we are in his and Toulmin's debt, not only for trying to rescue casuistry, but for providing us with the rich history of casuistry. In particular, I am sure that they are right to direct our attention to rhetoric as a crucial component for understanding moral reflection.

But just as I suggested that I am suspicious of any appeal to experience in itself, so I am suspicious of appeals to casuistry as a good in and of itself. Put as succinctly as I can, what bothers me about Jonsen's account of casuistry, both in his paper and in his book, is the failure to acknowledge that casuistry is only intelligible in an ongoing tradition.[4] I am well aware that with the introduction of the term "tradition," most will anticipate that I am going to begin a MacIntyrean critique of Jonsen. Such suspicion is not wrong, but I do not think it would be all that useful to spell out MacIntyre's arguments in *Whose Justice? Which Rationality?*[5] Rather, I find more than enough leverage needed to carry out this critique within Jonsen's description of casuistry. In *The Abuse of Casuistry* Jonsen and Toulmin point out that classical casuistry was not closely associated with any ethical theory,[6] but as a result I think that they fail to note how the intelligibility of casuistry depends on a tradition-formed community constituted and sustained by particular sets of virtues. Rather than rehearsing MacIntyre, I will try to suggest what I hope is a compatible account of casuistry by exposing some of the uneasy tensions in the account Jonsen provides.

Jonsen rightly emphasizes that crucial to casuistry is a "procedure of reasoning based on paradigms and analogies, leading to the formulation of expert opinion about the existence and stringency of particular moral obligations framed in terms of rules and maxims that are general but not universal or invariable." There can be no question that analogical reasoning is central for casuistral reflection. But I think it is a mistake to use the phrase reasoning "based on paradigms and analogies," because it implies that paradigms and analogies have the same status or function. That surely cannot be the case, as I illustrate by putting the matter in Kantian fashion—e.g., analogy without paradigms is empty.

Since Jonsen might well respond that he certainly understands that analogical reasoning depends in a crucial way on examples and that this is surely an insubstantial quibble. Yet I think the issue cannot be resolved so easily because of the very way he goes on to display the nature of casuistrical reflection—namely in terms of morphology, taxonomy, and kinetics. As he notes, the primary work of casuistry so construed is to determine "which maxim should rule the case and to what extent." I am tempted to make something of the fact that that maxim is Kantian language—indeed I believe everything Jonsen wants could be accounted for from within a Kantian-construed moral theory—but it would be uncharitable to attribute a philosophical position to him on the basis of a word. Rather, the problem is his assumption that it is the interplay of "circumstances and maxims" that give structure to the case."

For example, Jonsen says, "the work of casuistry is to determine which maxim should rule the case and to what extent." That sounds, however, very much like MacIntyre's account of "applied ethics"—namely, one assumes the existence of a rule or several rules or maxims and then sees if and how they fit certain kinds of cases. Thus it is assumed that the rules—"competent persons have a right to determine their own fate," "the physician should respect the wishes of the patient," "relieve pain," "thou shalt not kill," "give no deadly poison, even if requested"—exist separate from their application. Maxims are not, as Jonsen would have it, the "moral" of the story, for the story is the moral of the story.

My difficulty with Jonsen's way of putting the matter is that it overlooks the prior question of how paradigms are located in the first place, what interests determine the reason they are seen as crucial, and what determines our description of them. Paradigms do not spring from the head of Zeus unmediated but are located within an ongoing tradition in which the telling of stories suggests why certain examples are crucial. Thus, for some cultures the eating of meat is a paradigmatic issue for informing and shaping moral rationality as well as living.

I am, in this respect, particularly suspicious of Jonsen's suggestion that necessary assumptions about causality grant an invariant character to practical reasoning. Indeed, I am suspicious of the distinction between physical and moral causality when dealing with descriptions of human significance. Causality is a term that is secondary to the narrative display necessary for arriving at the appropriate description. Jonsen, in this respect, is quite right to direct our attention to detective stories, but not because detectives display "invariant patterns" of reasoning, but because by watching them we see how "solutions" depend on retrospective judgments that consistently reconfigure relations between contingent events through narrative construals.

In this respect, I think no text explores these issues in a more troubling fashion than Eco's *The Name of the Rose*.[7] For there Eco's detective, a Franciscan nominalist theologian who does not believe in necessary causation, must discover who the murderer is by painstaking narrative reasoning. The dark side of such a project is intimated by Eco as he has his detective discover the right murderer based on a false narrative—thus suggesting that all narratives are illusory constructs we impose on a random world. Of course, the only way we come to understand the irony of the detective's narrative is through Eco's narrative—i.e., the only way to discover a false or inadequate narrative is by a true one.

I want to be very careful not to attribute to Jonsen a theory about casuistry that he may not hold, but I find some of his language at least troubling. For example, he suggests that the "morphology of a case reveals the invariant structure of the particular case, whatever its contingent features, and also the invariant forms of argument relevant to any case of this sort. The first task of the casuist is to discern the structure. To modify the metaphor, the casuist must 'parse' the case, getting below the surface of the story to the grammatical structure of argument from grounds to claim through warrant and to the deeper grammar of the topics that underlie that argument." I am suggesting that language like "invariant structure" or "getting below the surface of the story" leads us away from the very nature of casuistry. For we do not reason analogically by "getting below the surface" but rather by comparing and contrasting similarities and differences between paradigmatic examples.

Jonsen tells us that we get our cases from the "moral experience of mankind," though he notes that such a simple answer sheds little light. Yet he seems to suggest that it is at least important in order to inform us why we are all drawn to cases as the heart blood of ethical reflection. I think that appeals to the "moral experience of mankind" not only fail to tell us much, but such appeals are positively misleading. They suggest that there is some universal perspective that can help us locate the "cases" or "examples" or "paradigms" that shape our reasoning.

Jonsen acknowledges that casuistry succeeds only when it is employed in a relatively coherent social and cultural community in which certain paradigms are "enshrined." While I worry a bit about the qualifier "coherent," since in our social context that word too often suggests a society without conflict rather than a community capable of having significant moral disagreement, I am still happy to see Jonsen acknowledge this point. Yet I think he has still not accepted the full implications of such an acknowledgment.

He rightly says that casuistry can only be done within a moral community but then denies that such a community can be identified with any specific "sociocultural continuities in time and space." I must admit that I simply do not know what Jonsen means by a community that is free from actual determination in time and space. He calls for the development of a "comparative casuistry" but fails to tell us from what possible perspective such "comparisons" might be made. Presumed in the call for such comparisons is the assumption that "we" stand in a community that has somehow freed itself from its particularity.

The same arguments MacIntyre makes in *Whose Justice? Which Rationality?* against the idea of translation based on the assumed internationalized languages of modernity render Jonsen's "comparison" problematic. Only when it is recognized that a language as used in and by a particular community, at a particular time and place, with particular shared beliefs and practices, can we appreciate the impossibility of thinking that we can translate Irish-as-such into English-as-such. There simply *are* no such languages, but rather only Irish-as-written-and-spoken-in-sixteenth-century-Ulster.[8] Thus the Irish "Doire Columcille" can never be the English "Londonderry." Just as the pseudo-languages of modernity carry imperialistic presumptions that any language can be translated into English, so Jonsen assumes "casuistry" to be a common practice subject to common comparison. Such a "casuistry" would be so abstracted from the practices of any community that it could not pretend to do any serious work.

I am aware that this criticism may seem deeply unfair, as Jonsen is struggling to help us recover the concreteness of moral discourse. Yet I think his machinery—morphology, taxonomy, and kinetics—gives the impression that casuistry has an invariable pattern in and of itself. I think the point of contention between us becomes clearer by attending to the quotation Jonsen uses from Aristotle's *Nichomachean Ethics*:

> Prudence apprehends the ultimate particular, which cannot be apprehended by scientific knowledge, but only by perception—not the perception of objects peculiar to one sense, but the sort by which we perceive that the ultimate figure in mathematics is a triangle; because there too there will be a halt. But this is perception rather than prudence, although it is another kind of perception. (*EN* 1142aff)

This is one of my favorite passages in Aristotle's *Ethics* because it seems as right as it is obscure.[9] Aristotle, I think, rightly sees that the crucial issue is one of perception—"this is a murder" or "this was a suicide." But is "murder" or "suicide" the same as "triangle?" I think there can be no in-principled answer to this, since the ability to answer it depends on the tradition in which one has been trained. As a Christian I want to say that "murder" or "suicide" marks when our perception should come to a halt. As Philip Devine pointed out some time ago, the word "murder" means neither "wrongful homicide" nor "killing of the innocent" but rather a homicide that is neither justified nor excused nor mitigated.[10] It is therefore a philosophical mistake to ask what is wrong with murder. If we rightly understand the grammar of the word murder, we understand that the only issue is whether this or that killing is a case of murder.

But, of course, the attempt to explain or to give a further reason why murder is wrong has been one of the besetting temptations of modern moral philosophy. Fearing that if morality is based on the "intuition" that murder is wrong then such judgments are arbitrary, it became the philosophical task to find a single principle that could "ground" such "intuitions." That is the reason, moreover, that modern moral philosophy has tended to corrupt our morality through the attempt to give reasons when no reason is required and has the effect of undercutting our true judgments.

Jonsen rightly sees that a renewed appreciation of casuistry might be a check against the endemic tendency of theory to undercut our moral perceptions and judgments. For the casuisist does not seek to get "behind" our moral perceptions, but rather to aid us through the analogical comparison of cases. Yet that process only works in the context of a community's practices, which are materially embodied in space and time. Just to the extent that Jonsen wants casuistry to create moral community "where it has ceased to exist or not yet come into being," he is coming dangerously close to assimilating casuistry to the very forms of moral "theory" for which he is trying to provide an alternative. Jonsen cannot simply commend casuistry to us; he must commend the casuistry of Catholics or Southern Baptists, very different casuistrical traditions to be sure, if we are to rightly understand his proposal.

If we are to take seriously the quote about "ultimate particulars" from Aristotle, it has to be recognized that casuistry, at least the kind of casuistry in the Catholic tradition, is not about making decisions but about getting descriptions right. Moreover, if descriptions are at the heart of the casuistrical enterprise they will be found only as part of practices that give our discourse life in the first place. For example, until we know why we use the description "abortion" rather than "termination of pregnancy," or why "suicide" is central for our moral description rather than "self-life taking," we cannot know what we are doing when we reason analogically. What must be recognized is that the description "abortion" intelligibly derives from a whole set of practices and beliefs of a community, practices and beliefs about the

place of children that can only be characterized as a tradition. Those
who use the language of abortion and/or suicide dwell in a different
world from those who use the language of termination of pregnancy
and/or self-life taking.

That does not mean that those who use the language of abortion
and those who talk of termination or pregnancy may not share some
practices in common, but it does mean they may well find that their
differences on such a significant issue create gulfs they had not anticipated. I suspect that behind antiabortion advocates' appeal to "slippery
slopes" lies an intuition about the relation of practices to description
that is not stated candidly. The problem is not whether justification for
abortions may lead to infanticide, though they may, but rather the
question is, "Once the description abortion is no longer working, how
do you sustain the ability to be open to children at all?"

It would be a mistake for us to get into this nest of problems. I only
raise them to suggest that analogical reasoning about cases—e.g.,
what difference, if any, does it make that conception occurred in a
rape—depends on the prior description. That description, moreover,
is dependent on a tradition that sustains the practices necessary for
that description to make sense. As a result, casuistry does not end
with the problem of the "perception of the ultimate particular"—it
begins there.

III. On Causitry in a Christian Context

That Jonsen does not begin there may be due to a certain understanding of his (and Toulmin's) project. Faced with our interminable
inability to resolve differences in ethical theory, they are attempting
to remind us that in spite of our theories people go on living fairly
decent, if not morally admirable, lives. This is, perhaps, manifested
particularly in times of life-crises that so often are associated with
medical practice. Confronted with our own difficulties or the crisis of
someone for whom we care, we discover moral resources and limits we
did not know we had. By drawing our attention to the actual discourse
and casuistical reflection present in such contexts, we can find ways
to get on with our lives. Jonsen and Toulmin are not suggesting that
we forget theory but they are trying to find a way not to let our
theories corrupt our lives.

I am sympathetic with this project, but I think it does not adequately account for the complexity of our situation. Because their analysis accepts an account of the relation of theory to practice that is determined by a bad theory. It is an account that has been spanned by what MacIntyre calls the liberal tradition. Liberal presuppositions have encouraged us to associate theory with the formal presuppositions or principles that allegedly underlie our moral experience. This way of construing our experience fails to see that we cannot step back from our moral traditions into theory, but rather our ability to have critical purchase on our moral practices depends on the substantive presuppositions of our traditions. The penchant for theory derived from liberal presuppositions cannot be cured by appeal to the importance of casuistry; rather we must be willing to reason about our moral lives with the confidence that we are possessed by a truth-finding tradition.

I think Jonsen is right to direct our attention to the importance of rhetoric in this respect, but I wish he had carried his analysis further. I am sure he is right that rhetoric is crucial to moral reflection, not simply because moral language is persuasive but because rhetoric makes sense only in particular communities and contexts. Rhetoric, as Jonsen points out, is the study of appropriate speech by the right person, at the right time, in the right manner. But crucial to rhetoric are assumptions of audience. Unless the rhetorician and his or her audience share fundamental assumptions, then appeals to rhetoric will be of no more help than appeals to casuistry.[11]

All of which is to say that the community in which we do casuistry makes all the difference. In that respect, I think casuistry in the Christian community is different from that done in other communities. As Jonsen and Toulmin document, casuistry in the Christian community arose against the background that it was a new community of holiness, a background that forced reflection on moral behavior that had not been anticipated.[12] Casuistry makes no sense for Christians unless it presupposes the practice of baptism. Only in view of baptism are questions about serving in the military, cooperation with pagans, observance of vows, or behavior during persecution questions at all.

Indeed, baptism provides the background for the understanding of the penitential practices that spawned the development of formal casuistical methods. The necessity of confession and repentance was the church's way of maintaining communal corrections necessary to be the kind of community capable of receiving eucharist. Confession, which required people to learn to name their sins, was necessary for the church to deal with sin after baptism. Though private penitential practice developed, interestingly enough initiated by monastic forms of spiritual direction, it was never "private" in the sense that the penitents could think of themselves as individuals. Their confession was necessary for the good of the church, so that the whole church could come to the table as a reconciled community.

No doubt casuistry could degenerate into minimalistic ethics that were concerned primarily with avoiding evil rather than doing good, but to so characterize casuistry would be a distortion. For the whole enterprise for Christians made sense only against the background of the Christian presumption that it was not sufficient to avoid evil, since Christians were called to be holy. Jonsen's and Toulmin's treatment of usury, equivocation, and insult witness to the church's attempt to understand the implications of Christian practices of sharing goods, saying the truth, and avoiding killing.[13] This does not mean I would always agree with how such matters were worked out, but one cannot help but admire the seriousness with which moral theologians addressed questions occasioned by Christian's positive commitments.

As Jonsen and Toulmin rightly argue, casuistry was not, as it is often depicted, an attempt to help Christians evade the imperatives of the Gospel in the name of worldly power. For they note "even today Christian moral theologians are troubled by the problems of linking a faith that includes moral imperatives of paradoxical sublimity with the incessant demands of a rough and mean world."[14] This statement is but a confirmation of my claim that casuistry in a Christian context makes sense only against the background of a determined set of practices shaped by a commitment to be imitators of God.

In this respect, however, I think Jonsen and Toulmin do not adequately account for the close interrelation between the flourishing of the virtues and casuistry. They note that casuistry had never been intended as a substitute for ethical theory or moral theology. It was not, in itself, a doctrine about what is the best life for man, what virtues characterize the good person, or what ideals humans should strive for. It did not even offer a general or fully elaborated doctrine about what sort of acts are right, or about how principles and rules are to be justified. It was a simple practical exercise directed toward a satisfactory resolution of particular moral problems. In this respect, it resembled philosophy or theology less than it did present-day "counseling," or, as it would have been called, "cure of souls."[15]

I think this is a bit of an overstatement. First, many of the confessional books were written for the laity with the clear intent that they should not only do the good but do it in a way that in the doing they became good.[16] But even more important, the development of casuistry presupposed that such reflection was necessary not because people were devoid of the virtues but because having the virtues forced the community to think about matters that might otherwise have been avoided. People consider questions of sexual immorality only if they first presume that those in their community are pledged to live lives of fidelity. So casuistry and virtue necessarily presuppose one another.[17]

From this perspective, casuistry is less an attempt to find the minimal requirements for the Christian life than it is the imaginative mode for the Christian community to locate the innovative aspects of our convictions. No one can anticipate what being formed virtuously may require. I may well discover that if I am to be courageous in one aspect of my life, I am required to confront matters in other areas I had not even anticipated. Casuistry is the mode of wisdom developed by a community to test past innovations as well as anticipate future challenges.

Put differently, the ultimate test of casuistry in the Christian community is how well our reasoning embodies as well as witnesses to the lives of the saints. Casuistry rightly done is meant to call Christians to attend to the innovative lives that we believe help us know better what our convictions entail. That does not mean we are called to slavishly imitate the saints, but rather they provide the paradigms to help us know better what we are to reason about.

Of course, the innovative aspect of casuistry is also occasioned because our lives confront new developments we had not anticipated. For example, when monied economies developed, Christian thinking about usury had to be rethought—I might add I am not at all sure it was rethought well. However, new developments do not necessarily mean adjustment, but rather might well mean refusal to adapt and thus occasion new duties.

But what, if anything, do these broad claims about how casuistry worked in the Christian tradition have to do with the attempt to recover the importance of experience for rethinking medical ethics and, in particular, the importance of casuistry? I fear the implications are largely negative. For I think what is missing from most discussions of "case studies" in medical ethics is exactly the kind of tradition necessary to make the discussion of cases useful. Rather than being an exercise in casuistical reasoning, too often the cases become the testing ground of ethical theories and their fundamental principles. So the "cases" are the means by which students and doctors decide whether they are more or less consequentialist or deontologists in their approach to ethics.

Jonsen's appeal to casuistry is, of course, an attempt to avoid this mode of presentation of "case." But in fact, I fear, his very way of presenting casuistry will only result in legitimating the practice of medical ethics as we currently have it. If medical ethicists heeded Jonsen's argument they might attend more to the "structure" of the cases, but to what end? For what is missing is the tradition and institutional means to make the comparison of cases serve for moral illumination.

One of the ways we might think of our current situation is an analogy with past Roman Catholic practice. "Medical ethicists" have now become the institutional figures who help the liberal tradition think through the issues raised by medical practice. Just as Roman Catholicism produced moral theologians who were charged with the task of knowing the cases from the past in order to test new developments, "medical ethicists" have become the keepers of the moral quandaries raised by trying to practice medicine in a liberal culture. The only difficulty is that these new "moral theologians" lack sufficient shared practices to give their enterprise moral coherence. In short, "medical ethicists" lack authority and as a result they must become "experts."

The situation, however, is more complicated. I think it is no accident that "ethicists" have been drawn to medicine as a particularly rich area for moral reflection. For medicine is a moral practice with a rich casuistical tradition though it was not recognized as such. The casuistry that medicine embodied was based on the everyday practice of physicians through which wisdom was acquired about how to care for this patient with this particular problem.[18] Medicine has been a rich storehouse of paradigmatic examples that have been subsequently extended and qualified in the light of new challenges.

That is why the "case-study" method works so differently in medicine than in business schools. In business schools cases are presented only as "problems" to be solved. It is assumed that what one learns from one case may not carry over to another except as one learns certain management skills in "problem solving." In this respect, medical education is much closer to legal education as the medical student is introduced to a narrative of a particular illness and given a sense of the various responses. Of course, this does not preclude the possibility of radical innovation and change—not only new illnesses but reconfigurations of past descriptions of illness and therapeutic alternatives.

So by all means let us attend to the experience of illness and those who attempt to provide care for the ill. For surely such care represents one of the last sets of practices we have left that can be characterized as a tradition. It is, of course, a tradition that is constantly threatened by institutional perversion, but in fact the actual commitment of physicians to their patients remains a moral resource that stands as impressive testimony that our culture still possesses substantive moral convictions. In a world like ours we ought to pay particular notice to that kind of "experience."

12

A Trinitarian Theology of
the Chief End of All Flesh

with *John Berkman*

I. Clearing the Swamp: Some Distinctions That Matter

This article seeks to engage the issue of the relation between "the world of humans" and "the world of animals" from a thoroughly theological perspective.[1] The task is admittedly both ambitious and fraught with difficulty, because there is painfully little precedent for this endeavor in most traditions of theological discourse. In broaching this subject we want to avoid the approach taken by the "theological mercenary," who uses theology merely to confirm what many of us have already decided on other grounds. Our task, therefore, is to try to show what difference it makes when one strives to discuss the relation between humans and animals in a way that seeks to do justice to the integrity of theological discourse.

The article proceeds in four parts. The first section outlines four hazards in the path of this project which might prevent the reader from taking seriously this challenge to rethink theologically how Christians relate to other animals. The second section presents a Trinitarian account of creation showing how this view of creation is crucial for rightly seeing and living in relation to our fellow creatures. The third section makes suggestions about what is involved in living the way of the Trinity in regard to relationships between humans and other animals. The final section posits vegetarianism as an eschatological act and shows analogies between following the call of Jesus in not doing violence to other humans and not doing violence to other animals.

The first hazard confronting our approach to this topic involves a possible misreading of the phrase "the integrity of theological discourse" in the opening paragraph. The phrase might indicate to the reader that this essay is simply trying to show how a belief system separated from concrete practices can influence how we *think* about the relationship between humans and other animals.[2] While there are, no doubt, valuable things to be learned from such an enterprise, such an understanding of the discipline of theology is severely inadequate. For our *practices* in all their diversity—including our sinful ones—exercise coercive power over us with regard to our ability to *think* about these matters.

For instance, this paper is written by one person who eats animals and one who does not. That may sound like an irrelevant biographical detail, but we are convinced of its deep significance, because our practices, more than our arguments, reveal and shape what is truly important to us. Hauerwas has argued this same point in the past with regard to pacifism:[3] that our theological commitments to that position are distorted insofar as our lives are shaped violently. Thus, Christian pacifism is not the result of holding certain beliefs, nor is pacifism even so much what it might mean to know these beliefs truthfully. Rather, living non-violently is in a sense *the very condition for even knowing what we believe about pacifism*. Likewise, if Christians are to engage seriously with the issue of their relationship to other animals, vegetarianism may well be a prerequisite.[4]

Acknowledging this first point, that our practices with regard to other animals shape our beliefs about them, it is clear that Christians' practice of consuming animals has shaped and continues to shape how Christians have thought about them. Here lies a second hazard that threatens to derail our project—a latent anthropocentrism. Returning to the analogy of war, in the same way that our engagement in war encourages a form of patriotism or ethnocentrism that leads us to depersonalize our enemies by turning them into the "Other," that is, "Gooks" or "Huns" or "madmen," our eating of animals undoubtedly encourages a form of anthropocentrism that maintains animals in the position of "Other" and justifies their use as such. We find theological warrant for neither this type of patriotism nor this type of anthropocentrism.

It is revealing that the most determinative attack on anthropocentrism in modern theology does not address theologically the issue of the relationship between humans and other animals. Given James Gustafson's general perspective in *Ethics from a Theocentric Perspective*, that is, that we are all ultimately doomed, one can conclude that neither human nor animal life has any special status vis-à-vis God.[5] To be sure, Gustafson's position is much more complex than is indicated here, but it serves to remind us that the *way* one critiques anthropocentrism makes a huge difference.[6]

Of course, this is but a way of developing the point with which this article began, that theology so often ends up underwriting classifications that are not intrinsic to its own discourse.[7] Avoiding implicitly anthropocentric assumptions is no easy task, as the authors found whenever they met to discuss what would go into this paper. For example, one question that came up was whether we have a stake in the survival of particular species that might go out of existence if we stop eating and/or experimenting on animals.[8] One of us raised the question of whether we should even retain the notion of species, and if so, what sense of the term "species." Aristotle meant one thing by "species," medieval theologians meant quite another, and modern biologists mean still something else again. What reasons, if any, do Christian theologians have for preferring one of these ways of classification over the others?

Put more radically, it is not clear that Christians have a stake in *any* kind of classification of ourselves in relation to other creatures. That is not to say that there is anything wrong with such classifications in and of themselves, but it may also be that these classifications represent interests antithetical to the convictions and practices of Christians.[9] For example, such classifications might underwrite an anthropocentrism antithetical to the Christian conviction that God, not humanity, is the end of all creation. So one must investigate who is making these classifications and why they are being made.

Classification systems aside, we are suspicious of almost all purportedly theological justifications for distinguishing humans from other animals. Of course, we as humans generally think of ourselves as "animals with a difference." Yet the account produced to elicit that difference makes all the difference in the world!

To put it most simply, we argue that the only significant theological difference between humans and animals lies in God's giving humans a unique *purpose*. Herein lies what it means for God to create humans in God's image. A part of this unique purpose is God's charge to humans to tell animals who they are, and humans continue to do this by the very way they relate to other animals. We think there is an analogous relationship here; animals need humans to tell them their story, just as we gentiles need Jews to tell us our story.[10]

Our account of what humankind as created "in the image of God" means is admittedly a minority viewpoint. The dominant view holds that "image of God" is some unique human capacity or ability, such as rational ability. Millard Schumaker argues that this stance owes far more to Cartesian presuppositions than to Christian theology.[11] There is simply no good theological reason for claiming that what it means to be human is to possess some unique *capacity* which distinguishes humankind from that which is non-human. Thus, the second part of the article will develop our "purposive" understanding of "image of God" in a Trinitarian context, our emphasis on the Trinity being in opposition to an implicit Deism[12] countenanced in much of contemporary theology. Contra Gustafson, we believe it is from within a Trinitarian context that the anthropocentrism so characteristic of our lives can best be challenged.

We are well aware that our call for a serious theological consideration of these issues can be quite tiresome. Confronted by the horrors of our cruelty toward animals, we are tempted to use any arguments we can to stop it. The temptation is made even more enticing by the fact that society gives theological language almost no status for operating in the realm of public discourse. At most, theological language is allowed credence for guiding people's so-called private lives, and more often than not it is thought to be pure mystification. Thus we find ourselves sorely tempted to use a language that has greater currency in the marketplace when addressing issues of "public concern." This leads to the third stumbling block for our discussion, for at present, be the issue that of homelessness or home ownership, of minorities or majorities, of humans or animals, arguments are almost always couched in the language of "rights." Though this is not the appropriate context to attempt a full-scale critique of the notion of rights, compelling reasons for avoiding this language require brief mention.

Our hunch is that the language of rights finds mass appeal in a society where individuals can no longer sustain their civic order on the basis of shared ends and purposes. The very idea of inalienable rights is the product of individuals who no longer trust their lives to the hands of those they live with and who thus seek to protect themselves through having "trumps" against the actions of their neighbors.[13] There are, of course, other accounts of rights besides this rather individualistic one, but this account is still quite prevalent. Moreover, we see the appeal of universal inalienable rights, as they seem so humane and enlightened when compared with particularistic and retrograde moral traditions, such as those associated with Judaism and Christianity!

Ironically though, this use of the language of rights embodies the very anthropocentrism that is antithetical to the goals of those who participate in the movement known as "Animal Rights." For the language of rights—understood as inalienable rather than as correlative of social duties—presupposes that those who are candidates for these inalienable rights are agents with the kind of rationality that is generally ascribed only to humans, and thus this view of rights is inextricably bound up with the Cartesian perspective that we criticized earlier. Most troubling from our theological perspective is that within this account animals have status only as a reflection of human interest. Furthermore, the very notion of inalienable rights presupposes a world at war with itself, which is exactly antithetical to Christian convictions about God's good end for creation.[14]

The situation is not significantly different if we understand rights from a contractarian perspective of human society, where humans come together and agree that they have certain rights that cannot be overridden. This conception of rights also precludes the possibility of the participation of animals in the social contract, except as a reflection of the interests of particular humans. As any rights theorist knows, having an interest is very different from having a right.

From this all too brief discussion we conclude that to ascribe rights to an animal may in the short run be a strategy for the animal's survival, but in the long run this language will simply maintain the current understandings of and practices in relation to other animals that continually bring about their destruction. Our reasoning is as follows.

We have already noted our suspicion that we live in a society unable to sustain—either conceptually or practically—the language of rights. This inability is demonstrated every time rights are overridden in favor of a compelling interest. If this is the situation with human rights, how successful can one be in an appeal to animal rights? To give animals rights is to radically broaden traditional uses of the term "rights" into an almost all-encompassing term. From a purely pragmatic viewpoint, rather than having to struggle against a society that is for the most part unwilling to see the language of rights used in the way animal rights activists would like, animal rights activists would be better off coming up with a new concept. Our suspicion is that many animal rights activists, like many human rights activists, do not really know what they are advocating when they call for "rights" besides saying there are certain things we really do not want to be seen done to humans or animals and the way to prevent these horrible activities is to say humans and/or animals have a "right" to protection from these horrible activities.

We think that Christians have far richer resources by which to address the question of how we should relate to other animals; any appeal to rights pales in comparison with the peace and love of Christ to which the Christian is called. Thus, while we do not wish to argue for animal rights, neither do we wish to argue for human rights. Andrew Linzey, perhaps the foremost Christian advocate of animal rights, attacks the position of those who will argue for human rights but not animal rights and claims that "the most consistent position is that . . . of Christians who *consistently* refrain from all such [rights] language."[15] Here, Linzey is perfectly correct. However, he errs when he assumes that "it is *inevitable*, however, that 'rights' language *should* have an appeal to Christians."[16] For this appeal becomes inevitable only when the Christian community can no longer articulate and sustain its own particular convictions about human relations with other animals. Contra Linzey, there simply are no good *theological* reasons why rights language should appeal to Christians. It will be the task of the second part of the paper to develop this alternative theological account.

The final hazard—one relating to our earlier remark about the power that our sinful practices exert over us—is our fear of criticizing our most impressive institutions. This is particularly the case when we realize that what are thought to be our most humane institutions—the medical profession, those dedicated to the development of food for the hungry—have routinized cruelty toward animals. However, we take these horrible truths to be reminders that good and humane people are capable of doing terrible things, as we gentiles well know from our participation in the Holocaust.

II. Why Creation Is Not "Nature"

We have outlined only briefly what we take to be some of the major obstacles impeding Christians from even raising questions about the relationship between humans and other animals. The first section challenges the presumption that the issue should be posed in terms of questions such as "How should *we* treat animals?" or "Do animals have rights?" Instead, we believe the place to begin is with God's creation of the world.

Of course, the notion of creation is not self-explanatory. In much of the literature devoted to questions concerning how Christians conceive of the environment and/or animals, the term "creation" too easily becomes synonymous with "nature" and why nature is important. In such an account, the affirmation of creation becomes simply a kind of romanticism toward nature. Though we stand in awe of our so-called natural world, we certainly do not intend to stand for this kind of romanticism.[17] We discussed earlier how the language of "inalienable rights" presupposes a world at war with itself, a view that is antithetical to the Christian understanding of creation.[18] However, advocates of inalienable rights and other analogous viewpoints may rightfully argue that the natural world is also at war with itself. We are acutely aware that animals still eat animals, even under the best of conditions. We cannot avoid the fact that hawks eat rabbits, lions eat gazelles, cats eat mice, and that, if necessary, we human animals eat all of them.

Acknowledging the tragedy of the natural world being at war with itself inevitably leads us to "survival of the fittest" conclusions, unless we realize that "nature" and "creation" *are not referring to the same world.* Those who believe that "nature" and "creation" are synonymous often buy into an implicit Deism (which sometimes also appears under the name "Theism"), believing that God functions primarily as "the first cause of it all" and thus presuming that "nature" is coextensive with what Christians mean by "creation."

This implicit Deism fails on two counts. First, it does not recognize that the world created in the Genesis accounts is radically different from our present natural world, and thus it ignores the significance of the Fall as an account of our present tragedy. Even more significantly, those who buy into this implicit Deism are oblivious to the fact that Christian convictions about creation must be correlated with christological and eschatological convictions, since Christian convictions about creation are Trinitarian convictions. On our Trinitarian view, "nature" must be understood as "creation in bondage."

The Westminster Catechism begins by asking us "What is the chief end of man?" This question—a question concerning the ultimate end for life—is the one with which Christians must begin if they are to understand themselves and other animals. So, minus the sexism and anthropocentrism of the original question, let us begin by discussing the chief end for all God's creation.

We have criticized the view that understands "nature" and "creation" as coextensive and its attendant survivalist ethic. This "survivalist ethic" is frequently underwritten by theologians, not only on the issue of human relations with animals, but also in debates concerning nuclear weaponry.[19] It is particularly important that the position being argued for in this section be distinguished from this survivalist ethic, because Christians simply do not have an overriding stake in the survival of the earth or our own survival. As God's creatures, our chief end is not to survive, but to be capable of serving one another and in doing so to serve as signs of the kingdom of God. In comparison to this service, survival is a secondary commitment.

Thus, we must not allow the Christian doctrine of creation to function as an apology for a survivalist ethic, for in the end, this ethic requires us to sacrifice not only many fellow human beings to guarantee human survival, but also any other animal that may possibly help guarantee human survival. We oppose this survivalist ethic because we believe that the Christian affirmation that we are God's creatures means that neither our lives nor the lives of other animals are at our disposal. This Christian affirmation requires a very different attitude toward the world.

These kinds of reflections are intended to help make it clear that the doctrine of creation is by no means self-explanatory. Without a theologically disciplined account of creation, one easily arrives at a survivalist ethic. When the exponent of this survivalist ethic understands God fundamentally as first cause, "creation" is thought of as the way Christians, and perhaps other religious people, explain the fact that the world had to have a beginning. On this view, creation becomes an explanation rather than a confession.

Yet, in Christian theology the last thing creation does is to serve as an explanation. Rather, creation is a christological and an eschatological affirmation derived from the Christian confession that the God who has discovered us in Jesus of Nazareth, the God who intends for us to share in God's peaceable kingdom, is a saving God from the beginning. Christians do not believe that the notion of God as creator is conceptually self-sufficient, to which one then has the option—if one so chooses—of specifying further God's nature in terms of Jesus of Nazareth. On the contrary, creation is part of a narrative of fulfillment for Christians; from our conviction that God redeems all of creation we learn that God, having created all things, wills that all things enjoy their status as God's creatures.

As for how scripture is thus to be read, a Christian understanding of creation cannot be guided first and foremost by Genesis 1 and 2. In fact, these passages must be read in the light of our redemption in Christ and our end in the kingdom of God, an end to which Christians are guided by the Holy Spirit. More specifically, Christians cannot understand creation solely in terms of Genesis 1:31— "Behold, it was very good"—but must read this passage in conjunction with Romans 8:19–21 and Isaiah 11, where the original creation is understood in relation to the present bondage of creation, and the dawning eschatology of the new creation.

In light of the scriptural witness that humans and other animals share in the ultimate end, which is God's peaceable kingdom, we thus believe that each and every creature is created to manifest God's glory. Animals will not manifest God's glory insofar as their lives are measured in terms of human interests, but insofar as their lives serve God's good pleasure. Similarly, humans manifest God's glory when we learn to see animals as God sees animals, recognizing that animals exist not to serve us, but rather for God's good pleasure.

Understanding creation in this way decisively challenges many traditional theological efforts that make a sharp distinction between our status as humans and the status of other animals. Too often the story of God's creation of humans in God's image has been read falsely as licensing humankind to dominate the animal world. Thus, the language of "dominion" in Genesis 1:28 is used to justify human manipulation of the rest of God's creation for humanity's own ends, thereby underwriting the presumption that all the world is created for the flourishing of humankind.

However, as Schumaker makes clear, this sense of dominion cannot be justified theologically. At most, the concept of "dominion" can only mean that God has chosen humanity to be an image of God's own rule in the world. In other words, God appoints humans as rulers not because humans hold any special intrinsic trait, but simply because of God's sovereign will—God simply chooses humans for the task of acting as God's deputies amidst God's good creation.[20] Thus, following Schumaker, Christians must not understand "image of God" to be based on any metaphysical or morphological difference between humans and other animals, but must reconceive "image of God" in terms of the particular purposes that God assigns to humans. Specifically, Christians need to discover what it means for a human to act as an image of God's *rule* in the world.

At this point we realize that our understanding of how Christians are to rule over animals is directly connected with how we understand God to be ruling over us. If we are to throw off the view that dominion means domination over the other animals, we must turn to a Trinitarian understanding of what it means for humans to be in the image of God.[21]

Christians cannot read "image of God" in Genesis 1 apart from what it means for them to be "image of Christ." Ultimately, true likeness to God is not found in the "image of God" of Genesis 1, nor even in the present striving to live in the image of Christ, but will only come at the end of time, when we shall see God face to face. Jürgen Moltmann puts this point very well: "The restoration for new creation of the likeness to God comes about in the fellowship of believers with Christ: since [Christ] is the messianic *imago Dei*, believers become *imago Christi*, and through this enter upon the path which will make them *gloria Dei* on earth."[22]

As a result, Christian lives are to display this purposive understanding of the image of God. In Genesis 1 the image of God is part of the vision of a peaceable creation, both between human and animal and between animal and animal, a peace where it is not necessary to sacrifice one for the other. Similarly, for Christians to live as the image of Christ means to live according to the call of the kingdom of God. In Gethsemane—in taking up the way of the Cross—Christ shows us clearly that the way of the kingdom of God is not the way of violence. In reaching the ultimate end of all our strivings, in the peaceable kingdom of God, we shall finally live in true shalom with all creatures of God.

III. Creation as an Eschatological Confession

A prime reason why Christians have such difficulty with the question of what it means to live in the image of God lies in a failure to live our lives in the faith, hope, and love of the Trinity. This is particularly true with regard to our inability to live our lives with a Trinitarian view of our history and of time, and thus of our inability to live in the light of our ultimate end and to see animals in light of their ultimate end.

To see our place in the world in such a manner is to think of our lives in community with all flesh. However, the temptation of this line of thinking is then to think that what it means to be God's creature is to see ourselves in continuity with nature and the animals. The difficulty with putting it this way is that it conveys the notion that Christians know how to classify nature and animals on grounds separate from our knowledge of God. We are not denying that such classifications are possible, as they obviously exist all around us and we constantly use them. Our challenge is to get to the roots of such classifications, to know why they are being produced and who is producing them.

We are aware that the claim that creation is a christological and eschatological affirmation will appear odd and probably unnecessary for consideration of the place of animals. However, we believe that this claim is extremely important, as the very phrase "the place of animals" illustrates. For we find problematic the very notion that we already have a standpoint that requires us to determine a place for the other animals, because this standpoint presumes a sense of power on the part of humans and a sense of separation between ourselves and our fellow creatures.

To say that creation is an eschatological notion is to say that the universe is part of the drama that is not of its own making. That is, creation is part of a story Christians learn through being initiated into a community that has learned to live appropriately to that story. Since one cannot understand "creation" apart from initiation into such a story, we do not believe that "creation" is something that all people can affirm. Rather, the confession of "creation" is something made by a group of people who are called to be the church in a world of people who do not know that they are, in fact, "creatures."

Therefore, Christians cannot separate their understanding of creation from their ecclesial stance. The church's confession of God as creator is also a confession of God in Jesus Christ and the Holy Spirit;

thus, confession of the Trinity is necessary if Christians are to affirm that God is creator of all. For the church finds in Jesus not simply the restorer of a lost creation known separately from Jesus himself, but rather in Jesus the church discovers the very nature of the created order. In short, in Christ we know that creation was not an act in and for itself but an act carried out for a purpose. This is what is meant by saying that the confession of God's creation of the world is an eschatological confession: the original creation is aimed at a new creation, the creation of a community of all flesh that glorifies God.

Thus, we believe the church is faithful when it lives out the fact that "nature" has a sacred element, not because Christians wish to uphold or preserve "nature" for its own sake, but because "nature" is creation in travail and as such has its own end to glorify God rather than to serve humans. Christians must therefore strive to live the relationship between human and animal life in terms of the common end being life in the peaceable kingdom, the kingdom of God. In addition, Christians will strive to read Jesus' parables of the kingdom as indications that our everyday actions may be signs of the power of the Christ, who will bring about the coming of that kingdom.

IV. Vegetarianism as Witness

If we have been right so far about the Trinitarian context of creation and of the church's participation in it, we think this puts the practical issues of Christians' relationship to the other animals in a different framework. In this respect, we think that there is a significant similarity between the issues of pacifism and vegetarianism. For just as we believe that Christians are not called to be non-violent because non-violence is a strategy to free the world from war, but because as Christians we cannot conceive of living other than non-violently in a world of war, so it may also be true that Christians are called to live non-violently toward animals in a world of meat-eaters. Thus, the perspective that we have presented that leads us toward vegetarianism is not one that can be for everyone; rather, it is the perspective that a particular people called to be the church must embody in their relationship to other animals, given that Christians live in God's space and time. So Christian vegetarianism might be understood as a witness to the world that God's creation is not meant to be at war with itself. Such a witness does not entail romantic conceptions of nature and/or our fallen creation but is an eschatological act, signifiying that our lives are not captured by the old order.

One person who understood the logic of our position but who would not go along with it to its practical conclusion was Karl Barth. Barth knew that the killing of animals was not part of God's vision for peaceableness, but then backed off from the inevitable conclusion by saying that to stop eating animals entirely would be "wanton anticipation" of the kingdom of God.[23] Even though we believe this response is less than faithful to the Gospel, those who take this view still at least need to accept the following; those in the Christian community that would eat animals bear the burden of proof. This can be understood in much the same way that just war reflection works in the Christian community: presupposing that non-violence is the fundamental stance of Christians. Christian just war theory is most appropriately understood as a theory of exceptions, exceptions for allowing Christians to engage in limited forms of violence in order to protect the neighbor.[24] Analogously, those Christians who cannot abstain entirely from eating animals need to develop similar criteria of "just" meat-eating.[25]

If any form of meat-eating is to be justified for Christians, it must be understood as animals making a sacrifice for us that we might live, analogous to the way soldiers are seen to be making a sacrifice of their lives for their nation-state, empire or tribe. This is but a reminder that as Christians we cannot understand the story of our lives apart from the importance of sacrifice, because God sacrificed his son Jesus that we might live.

We are aware that the language of sacrifice is dangerous language, and we have no desire to underwrite the way this language of "sacrifice" has so often been used in the past and no doubt will continue to be used, to justify all kinds of murderous deeds. However, Christians cannot give up the language of sacrifice if they are to be the kind of people that Jesus has made possible. After all, it is the great good news that in our eucharistic celebrations God has called us to walk in the way of the sacrifice of Jesus—the Way of the Cross and the Way of Resurrection Life—so that the world might know that we are meant to live at peace with God, with one another, and with the other animals. In this time between the times, the good news for the other animals is that Christians do not need to ask the other animals to be part of a sacrifice that has no purpose in God's kingdom.

13

The Kingship of Christ:
Why Freedom of "Belief" Is Not Enough

with *Michael Baxter, C.S.C.*

I. The Current Situation: The Prevalence of "Mere Belief"

In addressing matters of church and state, Christian theologians in America by and large have assumed that it is their task to justify the first amendment. We do not intend to take up that task in this paper; indeed, we intend to do quite the opposite. We intend to show that the theoretical presuppositions and concrete practices underwriting the so-called "separation" of church and state has produced a set of political arrangements (i.e., "the United States of America") that presents a deep and intractable challenge to that community whose allegiance is first and foremost to the kingship of Christ (i.e., "the one, holy, catholic, and apostolic church"). We intend to show, in other words, that the relation between church and state is marked by conflict and that Christian theologians make a profound mistake when they posit some kind of harmony between the two by means of a so-called church-state theory.

A most revealing, and disturbing, version of such church-state theory was put forth in a syndicated column by George Will.[1] The column focuses on the Supreme Court's ruling in *Employment Division, Dept. of Human Resources of the State of Oregon v. Smith and Black.* Briefly, the case involved two Oregon men, both Native Americans, who were fired from their jobs for ingesting small amounts of the hallucinogen peyote and were then denied unemployment benefits. The men argued that peyote is sacramental in the Native American church and that, on the basis of the first amendment prohibition of laws "prohibiting the free exercise" of religion, they should not be penalized for using it. The Court sent the decision back to the state with the affirmation that the Oregon Department of Human Resources has no obligation to pay benefits to the men if they had actually violated state law; the fact that they had used the peyote in religious worship was not relevant.[2]

Will commends Scalia, author of the majority brief, for upholding the lower court rulings that denied unemployment benefits to Smith and Black, but then he argues that Scalia did not go far enough. Specifically, Will adverts to a 1972 Supreme Court decision that exempted children of the Old Order Amish, on free exercise grounds, from having to comply with Wisconsin law requiring parents to send their children to school until age sixteen, and he contends that Scalia should also have struck that decision down. Scalia missed an opportunity to set the record straight, says Will; he could have reasserted the distinction that lies at the heart of the constitutional understanding of "religion": the distinction between "conduct" and "mere belief."

In elaborating on the importance of the distinction between conduct and mere belief, Will spins out a story that is at once familiar and sobering. The founders of the American republic "wished to tame and domesticate religious passions of the sort that convulsed Europe. They aimed to do so not by establishing religion, but by establishing a commercial republic—capitalism. They aimed to submerge people's turbulent energies in self-interested pursuit of material comforts." The hero of Will's story is "the patron saint of libertarians—Saint Thomas. No, not Thomas Aquinas—Thomas Jefferson." It was Jefferson who "held that 'operations of the mind' are not subject to legal coercion, but that 'acts of the body' are. Mere belief, said Jefferson, in one god or 20, neither picks one's pockets nor breaks one's legs." As Will explains it, Jefferson's distinction between conduct and mere belief "rests on Locke's principle . . . that religion can be useful or can be disruptive, but its truth cannot be established by reason. Hence Americans would not 'establish' religion. Rather, by guaranteeing free exercise of religions, they would make religions private and subordinate."

It is with this business of making "religions private and subordinate" that Will's familiar story becomes sobering. Will writes that a "central purpose of America's political arrangements is the subordination of religion to the political order, meaning the primacy of democracy." This means that "religion is to be perfectly free as long as it is perfectly private—mere belief—but it must bend to the political will (law) as regards conduct." Ingesting peyote, teaching children in the home, and any other form of religious conduct thus goes un-protected by the constitution; and Will thinks this is a good thing. Why? Because even though some religious conduct must be restricted (quoting Scalia, Will refers to this as "an unavoidable consequence of democratic government"), this is far more preferable (and here he quotes Scalia again) "to a system in which conscience is a law unto itself"; because, in other words, it avoids anarchy. Will contends that the genius of the founders was that they "favored religious tolerance because religious pluralism meant civil peace—order." So, in spite of the laxity displayed with regard to the Old Amish children, Will commends Scalia for confining the free exercise of religion to "mere belief" and for allowing the restriction of religious "conduct." "To understand the philosophic pedigree of Scalia's sensible position," Will maintains, "is to understand the cool realism and secularism of the philosophy that informed the founders." Thus he states in conclu-sion that "Scalia's position is not only sound conservatism, it is constitutionally correct: It is the intent of the founders."

It is a secondary matter to us whether or not it was "the intent of the founders" to "make religion private and subordinate," as Will suggests. We believe that, in either case, this is what has taken place, at least as regards Christianity. Christianity in America is "private and subordinate"; it has succumbed to "a central purpose of Amer-ica's political arrangements," i.e., "the subordination of religion to the political order, meaning the primacy of democracy." But whereas George Will celebrates this achievement, we think it is disastrous. Moreover, we find it ironic (to say the least) that theologians in America have entered into this conspiracy to privatize and subordi-nate Christianity. The conspiracy operates whenever theologians acquiesce in the assumption (so vividly articulated by Will) that Christianity consists of a set of beliefs (mere belief) that can be abstracted from practices and actions (conduct). Part and parcel of this assumption is the notion that in America we are "free" because we are permitted to "believe" anything we want to, just so long as we do not assume that our beliefs can be embodied. The problem with this notion is that "belief" gets confined to an asocial sphere of interiority (e.g., Jefferson's "operations of the mind") in such a way that "freedom" pertains solely to that entity of liberal subjectivity called "the individual" and never to the only body, for Christians, wherein true belief resides, the body of believers called "the church."

The usual question that theologians and others take up at this point is the interminable one concerning whether the first clause of the first amendment, "establishment," is subordinate to the second clause, "free exercise," or vice versa. But we wish to avoid this tack, for when the issue is construed in terms of the first amendment, the prior questions of the meaning of "freedom" and the meaning of "religion" are too often overlooked. We do not believe that freedom in and of itself is a good. Indeed, we do not believe that freedom *in and of itself* even exists. And the term "religion" is even more problematic in that it usually implies that the service and worship of God can be meaningfully discussed without specifying the identity of God, who God is, which god is being worshiped. In this sense, Christians are not "religious" in any general sense; rather Christians are the people who acknowledge the kingship of Christ. So we are dubious about the intelligibility of "freedom of religion," especially when it is put forth as the centerpiece of a political project such as the United States of America.

In order to make our case, we are going to bring together the most unlikely set of political and intellectual allies: Stanley Fish, John Courtney Murray, and Pope Pius XI. We advert to the work of Stanley Fish because Fish has helped us to see how all claims to "freedom" must inevitably be constrained when it comes to political practice; to John Courtney Murray, because his work was more ambiguous than is usually supposed; and to Pius XI because he reminds us that Christians must acknowledge Christ's kingship not only in belief but in practice, lest they find themselves worshiping foreign gods. By attending to this variety of perspectives on freedom and the good, we hope to show why the problem of "church-state relations" affords no real resolution.

II. How "Free Speech" Degenerates into Indifference about Speech

In an article entitled "There's No Such Thing as Free Speech and It's a Good Thing, Too," Stanley Fish delivers a simple, straightforward point: free speech cannot be a good in and of itself.[3] In introducing his argument, Fish points out that while defenders of free speech often buttress their assertions with a quote from Milton's *Aereopagitica*, where the virtues of toleration and unregulated publication are extolled, they seldom take note of the way in which Milton "catches himself up short and says, of course I didn't mean Catholics, them we exterminate."[4] Fish notes that in excluding Catholics, Milton was not stipulating the single exception to an otherwise universal principle. Rather, Milton was simply doing what any defender of free speech is compelled to do, he was pointing to possible future scenarios in which freedom of speech would have to be checked for the sake of the overriding ends of the community (which in this case would not continence seventeenth-century British notions of evil, impiety, and bad manners). Fish thus expands what he sees in Milton into a general observation:

> Speech, in short, is never and could not be an independent value, but is always asserted against a background of some assumed conception of the good to which it must yield in the event of conflict. When the pinch comes (and sooner or later it will always come) and the institution (be it church, state, or university) is confronted by behavior subversive of its core rationale, it will respond by declaring "of course we mean not tolerated——, that we extirpate"; not because of an exception to a general freedom has suddenly and contradictorily been announced but because the freedom has never been general and has always been understood against the background of an originary exclusion that gives it meaning.[5]

Hence the first half of the article's title: "There's No Such Thing as Free Speech."

Fish notes that one way we have managed not to acknowledge this plain, unavoidable reality is by creating laws which posit a distinction between speech and action, the assumption being that speech is inconsequential unless and until it translates into some form of action. And then, within this distinction, legal theorists fashion yet a further distinction: in Fish's words, "Some forms of speech are not really speech because they have a tendency to incite violence; they are, as the court declares in *Chaplinsky v. New Hampshire* (1941), 'fighting words,' words 'likely to provoke the average person to retaliation, and thereby cause a breach of the peace.' "[6] The difficulty with the "fighting words" notion, of course, is that utterances which for one group are "fighting words" are for another group quite innocuous. Thus it becomes virtually impossible to determine, in the abstract, what constitutes "fighting words." The point is this: there is no such thing as "speech" alone, speech *in and of itself*, speech separate from action (or conduct). Better it is, Fish suggests, to view the entire matter in terms of consequential and inconsequential behavior (i.e., speech and/or action).[7]

In his essay, Fish is trying to relieve us of laboring under the false notion that free speech is curtailed only in abnormal contexts. In actuality, the case is quite the opposite. Only in abnormal contexts is free speech *not* curtailed. What contexts? Fish lists two, on street corners in Hyde Park and radio talk shows. The extraordinary thing about these contexts is that they are artificially designed for people to say what they want exactly because what they say does not matter. In contrast, most of our speech does matter, does carry consequences, does make a difference. The problem with appealing to "free speech" as an absolute is that it reduces speech to the level of radio talk-show prattle. It makes speech a matter of indifference.

Fish points out how this notion that speech is inconsequential, a matter of indifference, works to the detriment of those who are on the losing end of society's political power games. It works like this. Defenders of free speech (Fish cites Benno Schmidt) maintain that the solution to racial epithets, for example, is not to restrict speech but to counter those epithets with more speech. Therefore the key task is to construct a setting in which harmful speech can be canceled out by additional speech, a marketplace of ideas where speech is freely exchanged according to its worth. But we should note, Fish insists, that among the defenders of free speech, "The idea that the effects of speech can penetrate to the core—either for good or for ill—is never entertained; everything is kept on the level of weightless verbal exchange; there is no sense of the lacerating harms that certain kinds can inflict." This could work, Fish argues, "only if the pain and humiliation caused by racial or religious epithets could be ameliorated by saying something like 'So's your old man.' "[8] Fish's point, again, is that "expression is more than a matter of proffering and receiving propositions, that words do work in the world of a kind that cannot be confined to a purely cognitive realm of 'mere' ideas."[9]

We find Fish's argument particularly helpful in showing how the constitutional principles of "freedom of speech," when fused with the notion that speech is inconsequential, that speech in and of itself consists of "mere speech," too often serves as a rhetorical cover for the most venomous of ideologies.[10] A controversy on the campus of Duke University illustrates what we mean. In the fall of 1991 the student newspaper, *The Chronicle*, ran an advertisement by a group called the Committee for Open Debate on the Holocaust. The ad declared that the Holocaust never happened and alleged that the standard historical reporting of the Holocaust has been the product of a worldwide Jewish conspiracy designed to gain support for the creation of a Jewish homeland. The ad also called for "openness" to this "revisionist" interpretation of the Holocaust. On the day the ad appeared the student editors also ran an editorial defending their decision to publish the ad in the name of "the spirit of freedom of speech." A spate of commentary and controversy ensued in the midst of which it was pointed out that the editorial policy had been inconsistent; the editors accepted the Holocaust ad in spite of its abhorrent content, whereas months before they had rejected an advertisement for *Playboy* magazine because they did not want to encourage young women to expose their bodies to soft-core pornography. The point was well-taken. What was at work in the editors' logic? The *Playboy* ad was forbidden because it promoted the degradation of bodies; the Holocaust ad was approved because it dealt in the realm of "ideas."

What was at work here was more than a matter of a terribly shallow understanding of the deleterious power of speech and ideas (though it was at least that). More troubling was the way the editors assumed an understanding of "freedom" whereby "speech" and "ideas" (as opposed to "actions" or "fighting words") are cordoned off and given a domain of their own which then, so everyone assumes, deserves protection. Theoretically, this protection is normally thought to be the job of constitutional law; but as was evident at Duke, it is a job that many, many people and organizations in American society have internalized and taken on as their own. In this sense, the constitution's rhetoric on free speech has certainly performed its pedagogical task—all too well, as we see it. For now we have a private sphere not only of speech and ideas, but also (as George Will might put it) of "*mere* speech" and "*mere* ideas," of speech and ideas understood apart from any substantive account of the good which they serve. The upshot is that our society is now marked by a pervasive form of indifferentism as regards speech.

The indifferentism which inevitably ensues when speech is considered apart from the good is the "freedom of speech" which enjoys protection in the United States. Such "speech" is subject to the arbitrary patterns of political influence and power as much as any consistent application of constitutional principles. Moreover, the rhetoric of free speech in this context can be put to dangerous purposes. Many Jews and others at Duke came to recognize this in the fall of 1991. Catherine MacKinnon and other feminist theorists have been arguing the same point for some time.[11] We suggest that this ideology can also be of great danger to Christians, not only in relation to freedom of speech, but also, in any even more destructive way, in relation to freedom of religion. For just as "freedom of speech" has paved the way for an indifferentism about speech in America, likewise "freedom of religion" has paved the way for "religious indifferentism."

III. How "Freedom of Religion" Degenerates into Religious Indifferentism

In light of this last claim about religious indifferentism, the name that often comes to mind is John Courtney Murray, the great apologist of the "American compromise." Murray is currently celebrated both by Catholic liberals and Catholic neo-conservatives as the one who single-handedly turned the church around regarding religious freedom in general and American democracy in particular. Specifically, Murray is lauded for securing a distinction between the public profession of religion of a given society and the care (or establishment) of religion by the state within that society. But there is an aspect of Murray's thought which Murrayites of virtually all persuasions (liberal, conservative, and in between) neglect to take seriously. We refer to Murray's enduring belief that any society is best which worships the true God and cleaves to the good, and his fear that when this is not done the result is religious indifferentism.

Ironically, Murray exemplified this problem as he sought to preclude the state from tending to any aspect of the care of religion while at the same time insisting that the state protect the public morality. The tension is irresolvable.

The deep ambiguity of Murray's project has been brought to light by Keith Pavlischek, who makes clear that Murray tried to have things both ways. While Murray defended the First Amendment as a necessary pragmatic accommodation in the face of America's religious pluralism, he would not *in principle* exclude the possibility that the state might be competent to speak in religious matters. Pavlischek reasons that if the citizens of a given society determine to restrict the activity of what they take to be false religion and if they do so through due process and out of concern for the well-being of the temporal order (e.g., if they want to curb the spread of religiously based polygamy), then there is nothing in Murray's argument to provide a basis for prohibiting such a development.[12] Pavlischek thus notes the arbitrariness in Murray's *a priori* claim that the state is incompetent in religious matters.[13]

The problem, Pavlischek argues, lay in the very structure of Murray's categories. Take, for instance, the distinction Murray made between direct and indirect influence of the church on the state and civil society. Murray consistently insisted that the church, as mediated through the Christian conscience, could and should wield influence in the temporal realm so as to bring it into harmony with universal moral order; thus he stipulated that the state is incompetent to speak on contentious "religious matters." And yet at the same time Murray refused to give a merely procedural or functionalist (Rawlsian) account of the state. Pavlischek explains the intractability of this dilemma:

> The crucial issue revolved around the extent to which a society should strive to bring the juridical order into harmony with the moral order, which in Catholic thought could not be totally abstracted from its own revelationally grounded truth claims. More precisely, it involved the extent to which a society should strive to bring the juridical order into harmony with the moral order if certain conditions were to hold. The traditionalists simply held that if Catholic hegemony obtained, the state ought to be confessional. Murray conceded to his traditionalist opponents that Catholic-Christian society is a good, indeed a "good of the highest order," but at the same time wanted to remove the state from positive concern for that good. Consistently carried out, this would put

the state out of the virtue-creating business altogether. The state would indeed be a purely functional state, a position that Murray, as a Thomist, could not accept.[14]

Pavlischek concludes, in other words, that try as he might, Murray could not have it both ways.

It is important to note that this was not due to any shortcoming of Murray; on the contrary, Murray's ability to perceive this dilemma and wrestle with it was but an indication of his high intellectual stature in comparison to that of his detractors, whose more blunt-edged analysis remained incognizant of it. Moreover, we want to make it crystal clear that Murray's dilemma was not simply the result of the institutionalization of the liberal (and supposedly limited) state. Rather Murray's inability to resolve the tension between Christianity and the state was due to the nature of Christian convictions. In short, inherent in Christian convictions is a substantive account of the good, and this account of the good cannot be held in abeyance while determining the moral character of a given political arrangement. Thus there is an inherent tension between the Christian account of the good and all so-called "political" accounts of the good.

This tension has been captured nicely by Charles Taylor in an essay entitled "Religion in a Free Society."[15] Taylor argues that "the Christian Church gave its members a universal allegiance, which could easily conflict with, or at least rival their political ties."[16] The political ties with which Christianity originally conflicted were associated with civic republicanism. Christianity, Taylor points out, "tended to preach against the warrior virtues, which were often central to the patriotism of early republics. The ideal citizen of an ancient republic was also a warrior." The ideal citizen of heaven was anything but a warrior, or else a warrior in a remarkably different sense. "The result," Taylor observes, "was a certain distance between Christianity and the republican tradition," and then Taylor elaborates:

> A writer like Machiavelli, who has to be seen in this light, wondered whether Christianity, as against the ancient pagan religions was not an element of potential corruption in a republic. And not only Machiavelli, who might be thought to be specially anti-Christian: Rousseau had similar doubts, although he was more embarrassed about them. From the Christian side, the insistence on some distinction between church and

state seemed to render impossible the kind of fusion between polis and religious community that was normal in the ancient world.[17]

Because it is impossible to fuse the polis and the religious community, church-state relations, says Taylor, are irremediably marked by tension and irresolution. He refers to it as a "malaise" and remarks that "[i]t is one of the legacies of Christendom that religion can neither be fully integrated in nor fully excluded from the state."[18]

Taylor observes that the United States is the one polity which has attempted to bring together Christianity and the republican tradition. The political and cultural ethos of the founding of America was marked by a unique mix of republican virtue and Christian rectitude. Granted, there were differences between orthodox Christians from New England and "the more urbane deists" from Virginia, but amid the differences, Taylor argues, there was a shared religious consciousness and a core of common values which issued forth in a political arrangement that enabled people to do two things at once: on the one hand, they were able to be part of the new republic and to share in its common values, including its religious values, while on the other hand, they were able to participate in their own particular confessional church. As Taylor describes it, "To the extent that freedom was seen as part of what God destined for humans, one could be playing a part in God's purposes as a citizen outside any denomination, even as one did as a worshiper in one's particular church. Many Americans could feel related to God in one way through the state, as much as they did to Him in a rather different way through the church congregation."[19] Thus there were two spheres in which people in America were able to be "religious," one in their own specific confessional or denominational context, the other in an expressly nonspecific national context. Taylor acknowledges that this unspecified, civically sponsored "god" was not always in the forefront of people's religious consciousness; "[b]ut it comes out in moments of crisis and high significance, as one would expect. Think of the invocations of God on the occasion of great decisions by Abraham Lincoln during the Civil War. The God invoked at these moments was a nonconfessional God, no church's property (though sometimes foreigners might feel that He belonged to the Republic)."[20]

The purpose of Taylor's article is to emphasize how the separation of church and state was not designed to preclude "God" or "religion" from public life and to make the case against the contemporary proponents of what he calls "liberal freedom" that "God" and "religion" need not, and ought not, be excluded or "sidelined" from public life, which, as Taylor has it, would erode "civic freedom." In other words, Taylor pits "liberal freedom" against "civic freedom" and contends that in these days of individualism and privatization, we have too much of the former and need more of the latter.

We think Taylor is wrong to pit "liberal" against "civic" freedom, for they are but two sides of the same coin made necessary by the kind of political arrangement we call the United States of America. Moreover, insofar as that political arrangement underwrites a "non-confessional God" and a non-ecclesial version of Christianity, it runs into profound conflict with Christianity. When "Christianity" becomes separable from the social form in which it is to be embodied, two things happen: one, Christian belief gets located in an interior, asocial sphere, "the heart" or "conscience" or some other private (i.e., non-public) space, and thus degenerates into "mere belief"; and two, in consequence of the first, a "public" space is cleared away for a counterfeit form of "religion" to emerge that is said to be "common" and thus becomes "the religion of the nation." What gets obscured in this arrangement is the possibility of a Christianity the material form of which is located neither in a private space nor in a general public space, but in the body of believers, in the church. Only within this ecclesial context, that is, only within a context in which the social landscape is imbued with the presence of Christ, can Christianity emerge as an alternative both to liberal freedom and civic freedom and, more generally, to the political project we call United States of America.

In reference to the non-confessional, non-ecclesial god-of-the-nation, Taylor points out, "The great majority of American Protestants had no difficulty accommodating the God so invoked with the one they worshiped on Sunday in their respective congregations." And then he remarks that "Catholics had greater problems, but then American Catholicism has been remade by this experience." We find this last remark to be significant. It has been precisely because Catholicism has had an ecclesially grounded understanding of Christianity that it had "greater problems" adapting to America's god-of-the-nation. Yet, insofar as "American Catholicism has been"—or *is being*—"remade by this experience," Catholicism has lost (or is losing) its strong sense of the inherently social character of Christianity.

Put differently, in their embrace of the American experiment, Catholics have learned to adapt to a political landscape marked by religious indifferentism. Furthermore, Catholics have been aided in this adaptation to indifferentism by Murray's successors, who have far too readily appropriated the kind of procedural liberalism to which Murray was so averse. Rather than defend this claim, however, we will provide an alternative vision to the political vision of America, one that is shaped by the acknowledgment that true political authority is to be found not in any republican virtues, new or ancient, nor in any set of governmental procedures, but in Jesus Christ who is our true king.

IV. Pius XI: Why Belief Is Not Enough

It is no coincidence that when Francis J. Connell opposed Murray's revision of the traditional church-state doctrine on the grounds that it would breed indifferentism among Catholics, he employed the image of Christ the King.[21] In doing so, Connell was invoking the authority of Pius XI, who had established the feast of Christ the King in 1925 with the encyclical *Quas primas*.

In *Quas primas*, Pius XI shows no use for refining abstract distinctions between "belief" and "conduct," nor for positing the "individual conscience" as the site of "religious freedom." Rather, he boldly and bluntly asserts the importance of publicly recognizing and celebrating the kingship of Christ in reconstituting the entire social order. Reflecting on the title "Christ the King," Pius XI acknowledges that it has often been interpreted metaphorically: Christ exercises reign over our minds, our wills, our hearts, and so draws us along the path of perfection. "But, if we ponder this matter more deeply," the Pope points out, "we cannot but see that the title and power of King belong to Christ as man in the strict and proper sense no less."[22] The Pope's reasoning, based on the Nicean doctrine of the consubstantiality of the Son with the Father (the church was celebrating the sixteen-hundredth anniversary of Nicea that year), was that if Christ became one of us, then he (like us) was embodied; and if Christ is king, then his kingdom is embodied as well.[23] Or to put it conversely,

Christ's kingship cannot be confined to some interior, privatized, spiritual realm; it is social, material, and (in the fullest sense of the word) political.

The political point that Pius XI wanted to drive home in instituting the feast was that the common good is to be defined by Christ. This is why the Pope writes of "the lordship of Christ" in terms of "a threefold power" coinciding with the legislative, judicial, and executive powers of government.[24] Against the effort of governments to privatize Christian discipleship or eliminate it altogether, and even against Christians and Catholics who tend toward proffering a purely "spiritual" understanding of the kingdom, Pius XI insists that the kingdom is also, in the formal sense, "civil." "It would be a grave error," he writes, "to say that Christ has no authority whatever in civil affairs, since by virtue of the absolute empire over all creatures committed to Him by the Father, all things are in His power."[25]

Elaborating on the power of Christ to pervade and influence all creation, the Pope explains,

> Nor is there any difference in this matter between the individual and the family or the state; for all men, whether collectively or individually, are under the dominion of Christ. In Him is the salvation of the individual, in Him is the salvation of society. . . . He is the author of happiness and true prosperity for every man and for every nation. "For a nation is happy when its citizens are happy. What else is a nation but a number of men living in concord?"[26]

Conceptually, this is a most remarkable assertion, for the Pope is dissolving several of the leading antinomies of modern social theory, individual/society, individual/state, and individual/family antinomies, much in the way that Augustine dissolved the antinomies that shaped antique political theory.[27] Pius XI thus arrayed himself and the church against the tendency in secular social theory to create spheres whereby Christ's kingship is confined to "the soul," "the individual," or at best "the family," and is thereby prevented from directly shaping "the political," "the social," and "the economic."

The antipathy that Pius XI held for secular theory is perhaps nowhere more clearly exhibited than in his story of the rise of the liberal (or "laicist") state. "Anticlericalism" or, to use a clearer word, "secularism"[28] has become a plague on modern politics, an "evil spirit." The Pope recalls that this evil spirit . . . has not come into being in one day; it has long lurked beneath the surface. The empire of Christ over all nations was rejected. The right which the Church has from Christ Himself, to teach mankind, to make laws, to govern peoples in all that pertains to their eternal salvation, that right was denied. Then gradually the religion of Christ came to be likened to false religions and to be placed ignominiously on the same level with them. It was then put under the power of the State and tolerated more or less at the whim of princes and rulers. Some men went further and wished to set up in the place of God's religion a natural religion consisting in some instinctive affection of the heart. There were even some nations who thought they could dispense with God, and that their religion should consist in impiety and the neglect of God.[29]

Here we have, to say the least, a different narrative than George Will's. George Will commends the founders of the new republic for exercising "cool realism and secularism" in setting up a political arrangement a "central purpose" of which is "the subordination of religion to the political order." Pius XI sees such a subordination as the undoing of any true politics. Thus he continues his narrative by noting:

The rebellion of individuals and of nations against the authority of Christ has produced deplorable consequences. We lamented them in the Encyclical *Ubi Arcano*; We lament them today. They are the seeds of discords sown far and wide; those bitter enmities and rivalries between nations which hinder so much the cause of peace; that insatiable greed which is so often hidden under a pretence of public spirit and patriotism, and gives rise to so many private quarrels; a blind and immoderate selfishness, making men seek nothing but their own comfort and advantage, and measure everything by these.

Here again, whereas George Will praises the founders for seeking to "domesticate religious passions" by directing people's efforts not toward the establishing religion but, rather, toward establishing "a commercial republic—capitalism" and for aiming "to submerge people's turbulent energies in self-interested pursuit of material comforts";[30] Pius XI condemns modern political orders for cultivating "a blind and immoderate selfishness, making men seek nothing but their own comfort and advantage, and measure everything by these," and he links this "insatiable greed" to "a pretense of public spirit and

patriotism." Interestingly, both George Will and Pius XI see acquisitiveness as central to their social analysis; but whereas Will sees it as
a social virtue, Pius XI sees it, rightly, as a social vice. His point on
this score is crucial: societies constituted on acquisitiveness cannot
help but be imprisoned within perpetual conflict and violence.

In the face of the deleterious political, economic, and social forces
of the day, Pius XI insisted, in rather startling language, that peace
among nations can only be re-established through "the restoration of
the Empire of Our Lord."[31] The kingship of Christ, for Pius XI, was
the alternative to the New World Order that was emerging in the
mid-1920s. We believe that the kingship of Christ is the alternative to
the New World Order that is emerging today.

We have quoted so profusely from *Quas primas* because Pius XI
resists the temptation to conceive of politics as a procedural arrangement which precludes any strong account of the good. Put differently,
Pius XI resists conceiving of politics in anything less than soteriological terms. Separating politics from soteriology has become the norm
among theologians today, but as we see it, this only lays the theoretical groundwork for religious indifferentism, for assuming that we can
discern political realm as something independent from Christ. This
separation, in turn, paves the way for what we Christians must regard
as a truly frightening national agenda: domesticating religious pas-
sion, submerging people's energy in the self-interested pursuit of
material comfort, constructing an arrangement in which religion is
subordinated to the political order.

V. A Call to Worship

We confess to offering little in the way of juridical steps for resolving
the problem of the relationship between church and state in America. Indeed, we are not concerned with positing any theories of "the
state" at all, for we have found that when "the state" is given abstract
theoretical status, too often the way is paved for underwriting very
concrete forms of violence. We do not seek to provide Christians with
a better theory about states but rather to help Christians discover the
habits of resistance we need in order to resist that state called the
United States, whose power remains virtually unchecked precisely
because it alleges to be a "limited" state.[32]

Toward this end, we take it that one of the more hopeful political tasks for the Catholic Church in America these days would be to make the Feast of Christ the King as attractive and important for as many as possible. The potential of the liturgy to be a formative power in people's lives should not be overlooked, for as Pius XI explained,

> people are instructed in the truths of faith and brought to appreciate the inner joys of religion far more effectually by the annual celebration of our sacred mysteries than by any pronouncements of the teaching of the Church. Such pronouncements usually reach only a few and the more learned among the faithful; feasts reach them all. The former speak but once, the latter speak every year—in fact, forever. The Church's teaching affects the mind primarily; her feasts affect both mind and heart, and have a salutary effect upon the whole of man's nature. Man is composed of body and soul, and he needs these external festivities so that the sacred rites, in all their beauty and variety, may stimulate him to drink more deeply of the fountain of God's teaching, that he make it a part of himself.[33]

We realize that such a call to worship will appear to many people, especially academics, as quaint at best. And we are well aware that our use of Pius XI in general will be judged by many to be less than "serious" because it does not tackle the complex legal issues attending church-state relations in this country.[34] To these criticisms we have two responses. First, we write not as apologists for the liberal project as does George Will, nor as theorists groping for a way to make peace with the nation-state, but as theologians of a church constituted by a politics that acknowledges Christ as King. And second, what Pius XI said of the Church's teaching could also be said of papers delivered by theologians at academic conferences: "[s]uch pronouncements usually reach only a few and the more learned among the faithful; feasts reach them all."

Finally, we are aware that some will infer from what we have written that we favor some kind of restoration of "the confessional state." We favor no such restoration. However, we do favor restoring a theoretical commitment to grounding politics in the christological claim that Christ is King. While we find Francis J. Connell's christology to have been inadequate (Murray was probably right to accuse him of being a "crypto-monarchist"[35]), we find the christologies of Murray's successors, both liberal and neo-conservative, to be inadequate as well; indeed they are nonexistent. So we have wanted to underscore that Christians are called first and foremost not to resolve the tension between church and state, but to acknowledge the kingship of Christ in their lives, which means leaving church-state relations profoundly unresolved, until the day when He comes again in glory.

Perhaps the political form this irresolution takes can be alluded to in the life of Father Max Josef Metzger (1887–1944). After serving as military chaplain in the German Army in World War I, Metzger became a tireless worker in the cause of peace. After being in contact with the International Fellowship of Reconciliation and attending many peace conferences and congresses, Metzger founded a secular institute, the Society of Christ the King, which was devoted to the lay apostolate and the works of mercy, particularly to the work of international peace. Metzger was also deeply committed to the Catholic ecumenical movement and was a founding member of *Una Sancta*. Metzger was arrested and jailed by the Gestapo three times before his final imprisonment in 1943. Metzger's "crime" was that he had contacted bishops in Allied countries in the hope that they could influence their governments to seek a negotiated peace rather than unconditional surrender. This the Nazi government considered to be treasonous, so Metzger was executed on April 17, 1944. As Thomas Merton has written, "Metzger did not believe in power, in bombs. He believed in Christ, in unity, in peace. He died as a martyr for his belief."[36]—which thankfully consisted of much more than "mere belief." Metzger's life demonstrates that "making peace" with the polities of this world is not the first task of a church that worships Christ the King. Our first task rather is to embody Christ's kingdom and thus to make good on the prayer after communion for the feast of Christ the King, "Lord, you give us Christ, the king of all creation, as food for everlasting life. Help us to live by his gospel and bring us to the joy of the kingdom, where he lives and reigns for ever and ever."

Notes

Introduction

1. If you have to explain an allusion you probably should not use it, but I could not resist alluding to *God Matters* by Herbert McCabe, O.P. (Springfield, Ill.: Templegate Publishers, 1987). Few theologians equal McCabe's great good sense, philosophical brilliance, and theological profundity. He writes matter of factly about God, but also in a way that helps us see that God matters. Just as important, God and matter turn out to have deep affinities in his work as he writes against the spiritualization of God so characteristic of capitalist social orders.

2. David James Duncan, *The Brothers K* (New York: Bantam Books, 1993).

3. The "unfairness" of Irwin being drafted was due to Brother Beal's, the pastor of the First Adventist Church of Washougal, refusal to support Irwin's request for status as a conscientious objector. He did so to spite Hugh Chance and the other brothers who lacked respect for him. During Irwin's "treatment" Hugh Chance provided some strong "arguments" that convinced Brother Beal to write in support of Irwin. Unfortunately it was too late.

4. Duncan, p. 604. "Winnie" is Irwin's nickname.

5. Duncan, pp. 606–7. I realize that it is terribly unfair to leave the story at this point, but suffice it to say that enough of the congregation were moved by Everett's sermon to join in a caravan to rescue Irwin. Particularly important was the participation of Elder Joon. The rescue was accomplished with the cooperation of high Adventist officials from the national headquarters as well as the doctors from the medical school at Loma Linda. Irwin, though rescued, was never the "same."

6. For a devastating analysis and critique of the presupposition of the church growth movement see Philip D. Kenneson, "Selling (Out) the Church in the Marketplace of Desire," *Modern Theology* 9/4 (October 1993): 319–48.

7. Rasmusson's book was originally published by the Lund University Press in Lund, Sweden in 1994. It has subsequently been published by the University of Notre Dame Press.

8. Rasmusson, p. 11.

9. I confess that I am not sure that I understand what "post-modernism" is, much less whether it is genuinely "post" or just another form of modernism. I am inclined to think the latter, however, as the kind of disillusionment characteristic of post-modernism is but a reproduction of the modernist presumption. As I have argued in *After Christendom* (Nashville: Abingdon Press, 1991), I do not wish to be associated with those who call themselves anti-foundationalist, even though I am quite sympathetic to their critique of foundationalism, because anti-foundationalism but reinforces the presumption that a theory of knowledge is necessary to know what we know.

Zygmunt Bauman puts the kind of disillusionment associated with post-modernity well by observing "contrary to the widely shared view of modernity as the first universal civilization, this is a civilization singularly unfit for universalization." *PostModern Ethics* (Oxford: Basil Blackwell, 1993), p. 215. I have found Bauman's account of post-modernity one of the more insightful, in particular his account of the importance of the creation of risk for "post-modern societies." Bauman notes, "to keep the wheels of the consumer market well-lubricated, a constant supply of new well-publicized dangers is needed. And the dangers needed must be fit to be translated into consumer demand: such dangers as are 'made to measure' for privatized risk-fighting" (pp. 204–5). Accordingly, risk-detection and risk management are seen as the most precious functions of science and technology, with the result that "science and technology feed, perversely, on the resilience and vitality of the selfsame disease they are appointed (or self-appointed) to disarm and shackle. *Objectively* and *subjectively* they are a major force in perpetuating, rather than arresting, the risk-generating propensity of the social system" (p. 207).

10. Rasmusson, pp. 187–88.

11. Rasmusson's presentation of my position is not only fair, it is done so well that I am left with the feeling, "I wish I had said that." Often he not only says better what I have said, he provides a more compelling case than I have provided. For another equally compelling account of the political character of the church, and in particular the importance of dogma, see, Reinhard Hütter, "The Church as Public: Dogma, Practice, and the Holy Spirit," *Pro Ecclesia* 3/3 (Summer, 1994): 334–61.

By dogma, Hütter is referring to the church's need for a publically recognizable binding teaching that transcends individually held beliefs. Drawing on classical political theory, Hütter argues "there is no public without clear visibility, without a defining and constituting set of binding convictions, rules, and key practices. . . . The crucial dividing line runs between a public that is constituted by dogma (as conciliar and papal decisions, of Scripture and confessions, or the Amish *Ordnung*) on the one hand and a religion—on the other hand—that is thought of as something essentially private, that 'motivates,' 'guides,' or 'directs' our ways of 'going public'—'public' being the normative political public. The latter is 'religion in the limits of the *saeculum* alone' " (p. 349). I make extensive use of Hütter's essay in the first chapter of this book. Equally important is James J. Buckley's essay in the same issue of *Pro Ecclesia*, "Liberal and Conservative—or Catholic and Evangelical?: Some Limits to the Debate over the Public Character of Theology," pp. 324–33.

12. C. L. R. James, *Beyond a Boundary*, with an Introduction by Robert Lipsyte (Durham, N.C.: Duke University Press, 1993), p. 206. I am indebted to Professor Ken Surin for first introducing me to James. I was spurred to read the book by being told by Alasdair MacIntyre that I could read it, but that I certainly could not understand it. On finishing the book, I ruefully have to admit that MacIntyre is certainly right; I do not understand cricket (and thus the book) but I better understand why I cannot understand cricket. That is no small accomplishment, due not to my abilities, but to James's extraordinary work.

13. James, p. 58.

14. James observes, "To watch cricket critically you have to be in good form, you must have had a lot of practice, you must have played it" (p. 35). I am sure James is right, particularly if you attend to what "critically" means, but I suspect it is also possible to learn to watch baseball, for example, with appreciation, even if you have never played it. "Appreciation" is a skill which does not have the same force as "critically," but is nonetheless morally significant.

15. James, p. 65. That James's politics were Marxist is surely not accidentally related to the politics of cricket.

16. Duncan, pp. 573–74. I have argued a somewhat similar thesis in my *Against the Nations: War and Survival in a Liberal Society* (Notre Dame, Ind.: University of Notre Dame Press, 1992), pp. 169–208 and in *Christian Existence Today: Essays on Church, World and Living in Between* (Durham, N.C.: Labyrinth Press, 1988), pp. 253–66.

17. J. A. Dinoia, O.P., *The Diversity of Religion: A Christian Perspective* (Washington, D.C.: Catholic University Press, 1992), p. 61. Dinoia is concerned to combat the presumption that salvation is a common goal of all "religions." Other religions may well have soteriological programs, but like the Christian understanding of salvation they are embedded in larger contexts of belief and practice from which they cannot be extracted. He points out that the Christian story does not claim that only the members of the church enjoy the final consummation. Yet it is part of the Christian story that the fulfillment of the "divine promise about history's happy ending depends in some largely obscure way on the continued existence of a particular community. The

perseverance of the Christian community in fidelity to its Lord and in persistent narration of its special story is of intrinsic significance for the salvation of the rest of humankind" (p. 80).

18. James notes that W. G. Grace finds "no place in the history of the people because the historians do not begin from what people seem to want but from what they think the people ought to want. He [Grace] had enriched the depleted lives of two generations and millions yet to be born. He had extended our conception of human capacity and in doing all this he had done no harm to anyone. He is excluded from the history books of his country. No statue of him exists. Yet he continues warm in the hearts of those who never knew him. There he is safe until the whole crumbling edifice of obeisance before Mammon, contempt for Demos and categorizing intellectualism finally falls apart" (*Beyond a Boundary*, pp. 184–85).

19. Too often "doctrine" is relegated to the world of thought and ideas. Church doctrine is one of the crucial *practices* of the church necessary to sustain the church's identity. I think George Lindbeck's "rule-theory" of doctrine at least reminds us that doctrine is meant to do some work and is therefore not "about" something in and of itself. See his *The Nature of Doctrine: Religion and Theology in a Postliberal Age* (Philadelphia: Westminster Press, 1984), pp. 73–90. In his essay, "Identity and Difference: The Ecumenical Problem," Michael Root provides an extremely useful account of Lindbeck's understanding of doctrine in service to the church's quest for unity. Root's essay is in *Theology and Dialogue: Essays in Conversation with George Lindbeck*, edited by Bruce Marshall (Notre Dame: University of Notre Dame Press, 1990), pp. 165–90.

20. Nicholas Healy provides a fascinating account of Karl Barth's understanding of this "creedal rule" in "The Logic of Karl Barth's Ecclesiology: An Analysis, Assessment and Proposed Modifications," *Modern Theology* 10/3 (July 1994): 253–70. Healy argues that Barth's understanding of the "creedal rule" results in a bifurcated church because of Barth's refusal to grant any status to the visible church as necessary for salvation. As Healy observes, the irony "is the more Barth reduces Christianity to a matter of knowledge, the more he unwittingly encourages its appropriation and domestication within a non-Christian framework. One result of the loss of sociocultural particularity could be that Christianity becomes a more or less dispensable part of an individual's private worldview. This 'neo-Protestant' outcome is clearly the last thing that Barth would want." (p. 265).

21. I am sometimes tempted to think that nowhere is the myth of the golden age more embodied than in those historical disciplines that dominate current theological curriculums. The assumption that we should if we could get back to the "original language or meaning," or discover "what the first hearers heard," sometimes implies that at one time someone got it right. History done in the objectivist mode often turns out to be the expression of mythological assump-

tions quite foreign to Christian practice. For example, consider these comments by the distinguished scholar of the Hebrew Bible Professor James Crenshaw: "After all liberal existentialism nurtured me during the formative years of my theological training. Accordingly, I have searched for authentic expressions of self-understanding, for I think at the deeper levels of Angst, modern individuals differ little from their ancient counterparts. Believing this, I have explored the rich language of describing suffering in the Bible, and I have tried to understand lonely persons of faith in a silent universe. Naturally, my concern has extended beyond what the text meant, although the latter investigation has governed most of my research. Furthermore, it has prevented me from imposing Christian readings on the Hebrew Bible for I have always asked what ancient Israelites would have heard in a given text" ("Reflections on Three Decades of Research," *Religious Studies Review* 20/2 [April 1994]: 112). Crenshaw's candor is commendable, for few today are so willing to expose such modernist sentiments.

For an extraordinary account of the implications of a "restitution" account of the history of the church see John Howard Yoder's, "Anabaptism and History" in his *The Priestly Kingdom: Social Ethics as Gospel* (Notre Dame: University of Notre Dame Press, 1984), pp. 123–34. Yoder argues that the ecclesial Anabaptist stood with the majority of Protestantism in ascribing to the Incarnation a significance that means there is no going behind or forward to discover some more fundamental meaning. But restitutionists begin with a view of the seriousness of the fall that commits them to believing that there can be no account of the indefectibility of the church based on continuity or succession. Restitutionism is therefore incompatible with an ahistorical point of view, since for the restitutionist the work of historiography is required for the display of how things go wrong. Restitutionism, therefore, does not, as is often alleged, judge the present age in the light of a timeless garden of Eden or primitive simplicity, or a speculative utopia, but rather is an attempt to read the history of the church in the light of the Incarnation. Hence, there is no fear of acknowledging discontinuities that come from our sinfulness.

22. I am thinking of the kind of work exemplified in Hans Küng's early but still quite good book *The Church* (New York: Sheed and Ward, 1967).

23. The kind of ecumenical theology I have in mind is that represented by my colleague Professor Geoffrey Wainwright, who has served the church in exemplary fashion through his ecumenical work. See in particular his book *The Ecumenical Moment: Crisis and Opportunity for the Church* (Grand Rapids: Eerdmans, 1983).

Wainwright's closing essay on Methodism's ecclesial location and ecumenical mission mirror's my own position insofar as I can be said to have a position. He quotes Albert Outler's suggestion "who should know better than we [Methodists] that denominations may be justified in their existence for this "time being" or that, but not forever? We were commissioned by the Spirit of God "for the time being" to carry out an extraordinary mission of witness and service for just so long as our life apart is effective in the economy of God's providence. We are, or ought to be, prepared to risk our life as a separate church and to face death as a denomination in the sure and lively hope of our resurrection in the true community of the whole people of God. . . . The price of true catholicity may very well be the death and resurrection of the churches that we know—in the faith that God has greater things in store for his people than we can remember or even imagine" (p. 220). The deep difficulty, as Outler and Wainwright know well, is that the ecumenical movement cannot simply be a merging of the different "riches" of the denominations. The unity of the church is "richer" than that and is, accordingly, eschatological in the most profound sense. Part of the problem, of course, is that Protestant denominationalism has become an end in itself.

I had originally used the word "idiosyncratic" rather than "homeless." Dr. James Fodor rightly pointed out that "idiosyncratic" smacks too much of the very individualism I wish to avoid.

24. I am not suggesting that these theologians agree about the character of Methodism, but they do represent the recovery of Wesley's indebtedness to the Catholic tradition. Outler was an active observer at Vatican II. He edited the volume in the Library of Protestant Thought on John Wesley (New York: Oxford University Press, 1964). Cushman, for many years the dean of the Divinity School at Duke, spent the last years of his life working on Wesley and Methodism. His reflections are found in his *John Wesley's Experimental Divinity: Studies in Methodist Doctrinal Standards* (Nashville: Kingswood Books, 1989). Langford has chronicled developments in Methodist theology in his *Practical Divinity: Theology in the Wesleyan Tradition* (Nashville: Abingdon Press, 1983) and has recently written on Methodist doctrinal standards in his *God Made Known* (Nashville: Abingdon Press, 1992).

The best article I know of on Wesley's own ecclesiology is by F. Ernest Steffler, "Tradition and Renewal in the Ecclesiology of John Wesley," in *Traditio-Krisis-Renovatio aus Theologischer Sicht*, edited by Berndt Jaspert und Rudolf Mohr (Marburg: Elwer, 1976), pp. 298–316. Steffler suggests "what we really have in Wesley's understanding of the church is the restorationism of the older, and by this time well entrenched, movement of the church-related Pietism, especially that of the early Moravians. In this view the church as an historical institution is accepted as necessary for God's purposes among men. There is much to be said even for an established church to which all Christians within a given territory normally belong by baptism. Yet, there is also the realization that such a church needs to be constantly informed and reformed from within by a community of earnest believers in whose corporate life the Spirit of God is peculiarly at work, as he is thought to have been in the primitive Christian community. It was in this light that Wesley regarded his societies. They were not to be rivals of the Church of England but fellowships of earnest Christians within it, who by their corporate effort would restore to the Church of England that apostolic witness which to the Wesleys it seemed to lack in their day" (p. 306). Of course the American Methodist Church is only tangentially related to Wesley's views on these matters—so much the pity.

25. In case anyone is interested, I am a member of Aldersgate United Methodist Church in Chapel Hill, North Carolina. Since I am a layman, my immediate ecclesiastical authority is Rev. Susan Allred. All inquires about my ecclesial life should be directed to her. I realize that it is a bit odd for theologians to declare their ecclesial commitments in public, but I increasingly believe that one of the most important questions you can ask of a theologian is "where do you go to church?"

26. Michael Cartwright thinks I am making a mistake to describe myself, as I do in chapter 4, as an "ecclesial cannibal." That description, no doubt, gives my enemies more ammunition than they need. Moreover I hope it is true that I am more consumed than I consume. The "cannibal" image is not a good one, but it is better than being a consumer.

27. There are actually quite a number of Baptists who have engaged and influenced me. Some of them are even Southern Baptists, such as Kyle Childress. Kyle is pastor of Austin Heights Baptist Church of Nacogdoches, Texas. Kyle's church newsletters are always a source of inspiration. The rediscovery of the Catholic tradition by Southern Baptists is as extraordinary as it is hopeful. See, for example, *Ties That Bind: Life Together in the Baptist Vision*, edited by Gary A. Furr and Curtis W. Freeman (Macon, Ga.: Smyth and Helwys, 1994). See in particular the essay by Curtis Freeman, "A Confession for Catholic Baptists" and by Barry Harvey, "Holy Insecurity: The Practice of Piety and the Politics of the Spirit."

28. For a more extensive investigation of the extent to which a Baptist can be a Catholic see my "Reading McClendon Takes Practice: Lessons in the Craft of Theology" (forthcoming).

29. I have borrowed this subtitle from Philip Kenneson's wonderful review of my *Christian Existence Today: Essays on Church, World and Living in Between.* See his "Taking Time for the Trivial: Reflections on Yet Another Book from Hauerwas," *Asbury Theological Journal* 45/1 (Spring 1990): 65–74.

30. Any significant craft requires the learning of a new language, or at least new ways of speaking. For example, it is not accidental that "A Note on Cricket" has been added to the front of James's *Beyond a Boundary*, pp. xvii–xx. I develop the relationship between craft and language in my *After Christendom?* (Nashville: Abingdon, 1991), pp. 93–111.

31. The claim that repetition is never the same requires more analysis than I can provide in this context, but I have in mind the kind of reflection Stanley Fish provides in his wonderful article called "Change" in his *Doing What Comes*

Naturally: Change, Rhetoric, and the Practice of Theory in Literary and Legal Studies (Durham, N.C.: Duke University Press, 1989), pp. 141-62.

32. I think my good friend Professor Michael Cartwright was the first to describe my position as "contrarian." I think it is an accurate description which no doubt has some basis in my personality. Yet more importantly, or at least I hope it is more important, my "contrarian" style is necessitated by my polemic against theological and political liberalism. The liberal, of both kinds, is committed to "englobing" all positions into liberalism. To resist being "explained" or, worse, "appreciated" by liberals you have to resist their categorizations. That is why I often have to resist friendly overtures—"Aren't you really simply trying to remind us of . . ."—because such overtures too often turn out to be attempts to domesticate Christian convictions.

33. My first book, *Vision and Virtue: Essays in Christian Ethical Reflection*, was published in 1974 by Fides/Clarention Press of Notre Dame, Indiana. It was reprinted by the University of Notre Dame Press in 1981.

34. I learned from David Burrell, C.S.C., the importance of exercises for intellectual work. See in particular his wonderful book *Exercises in Religious Understanding* (Notre Dame: University of Notre Dame Press, 1974). I love the first sentence of his "Introduction" to the book: "Each essay in this work is designed to be a workout" (p. 1).

35. Karl Barth is the great exemplar of writing that is "incomplete." Such a judgment may seem surprising given the massive character of the *Dogmatics*. But they were massive not because Barth was trying to be "complete" in the way, for example, Tillich tried to create a system. Accordingly, I have no ambition to write the final big book on Christian ethics, though I do hope someday to write a book shaped by the suggestions in chapter 10. I cannot deny that my work is "incomplete" and deficient in a way quite different from Barth's. But as a friend suggested I should simply say, "at a time when what we call American Protestantism totters at the brink of extinction, I cannot afford the care I would like. The silence in academic theology is deafening. Someone must speak, and quickly."

36. Hauerwas and Willimon, *Resident Aliens: Life in the Christian Colony* (Nashville: Abingdon Press, 1989). I have no idea how much the popularity of this book is due to the title, but it obviously has attracted a good deal of attention both positively and negatively. The original title Will had tentatively given the book was "The Colony." I did not like that title, but had no better alternative. The title was suggested by Dr. Paula Gilbert, my wife, after she had read the book. Will and I immediately thought that that was perfect. When we sent the manuscript to the publishers, however, they did not like it. They said it sounded like a book on illegal aliens. We said, "perfect."

37. The criticism I make of Catholic moral theology in "The Importance of Being Catholic" does not need to be updated but only applied to the steady

stream of books that want to argue for a compatibility between Catholicism and America. In particular, see the quite good essays in *Catholicism and Liberalism: Contributions to American Public Philosophy*, edited by R. Bruce Douglass and David Hollenbach (Cambridge: Cambridge University Press, 1994).

38. Miroslav Volf writes much more appreciatively of the encyclical, but still criticizes John Paul II for failing to give an appropriate account of the purpose of work. See his "On Human Work: An Evaluation of the Key Ideas of the Encyclical *Laborem Exercens*," *Scottish Journal of Theology* 37/1 (March 1984), 65–79. For a full account of Volf's understanding of work from a theological perspective see his *Work in the Spirit: Toward a Theology of Work* (New York: Oxford University Press, 1991). To his credit Volf is one of the few who deal with the alienating character of work characteristic of capitalism.

For a more recent collection of essays on *Laborem Exercens* see *Readings in Moral Theology, No. 5: Official Catholic Social Teaching*, edited by Charles Curran and Richard McCormick, S.J. (New York: Paulist Press, 1986), pp. 188–286. Peter Hebblethwaite's "The Popes and Politics: Shifting Patterns in Catholic Social Doctrine" (pp. 264–84) is particularly interesting by his calling attention to Paul VI's letter in 1971 to Cardinal Roy. Paul VI argued that given the varied situations in which the church found herself, it is impossible to give one teaching to cover them all—an argument not unlike the one I make concerning *Laborem Exercens*.

39. The copy of the speech I am using appeared in the *Durham Herald-Sun*, Sunday, July 17, 1994, p. A15. The title in the *Herald-Sun* was "Toward a New Democratic Faith."

40. Havel's speeches and essays are often if not usually reprinted in the *New York Review of Books*, yet this speech has not appeared. While there may well be other explanations for the nonpublication of this speech, I cannot help but wonder if Havel's theology, sparse and thin as it is, is too much for the *New York Review of Books*.

41. This essay is also written for a festschrift honoring Rev. Dan Hardy.

42. This essay was part of a symposium sponsored by the DePaul Law School on the separation of church and state in America. There were a number of respondents to the paper which appear, along with this essay, in the *DePaul Law Review* 42/1 (Fall, 1992): 107–90. I call attention in particular to the response by Professor Michael Eric Dyson, entitled "God Almighty Has Spoken from Washington, D.C.: American Society and the Christian Faith," pp. 129–59. His response can also be found in his book, *Reflecting Black: African-American Cultural Criticism* (Minneapolis: University of Minnesota Press, 1993), pp. 286–318. Rev. Michael Baxter, C.S.C., my co-author of "The Kingship of Christ," has written a response to Dyson's critique that is so good I can only wish I had written it. It is humbling to have students who are so much smarter than I am. Baxter's essay is entitled " 'Overall, the First Amendment Has Been Very

Good for Christians'—*Not!*: A Response to Dyson's Rebuke," *DePaul Law Review* 43/2 (Winter, 1994): 425–48.

James Fodor observes that there is a danger that I could be read as another ethicist producing works for "consumption" in America. He thus suggests: "No doubt, America presents its own distinctive challenges and possibilities, but perhaps more could be said about how the church in America is not only a *polis* but an *oikos* as well. In this regard, a little playing with the title of the book, a little pun, might provide a slightly different inflection. Considering 'In Good Company' more along economic rather than political lines brings to mind the notion of a goods company; namely, Hauerwas's Dry Goods Co. Drawing upon our capitalist, consumer ethos, this conjures up something analogous to an old-fashioned theological general store in which there is a wide assortment of items, none of which are present in any great quantity but sufficient nonetheless for daily Christian living. The metaphor of a general-store-type theology to describe Hauerwas's approach is a useful contrast to the Wal-Mart orientation of present-day consumer-obsessed society, because it rightly stresses the day-to-day needs of Christian dependency; i.e., the need to regularly, rhythmically, approach God in prayer to ask for our daily bread rather than to stockpile great hoards of goods, to rely on our own resources to see us through difficult times. This comparison may be more clever than it is revealing, but it intended to underscore the need to balance the economic and political aspects that the phrase 'in good company' conveys." To which I can only say—"I wish I had said that."

1. What Could It Mean
for the Church to Be Christ's Body?

1. I am indebted to Professor Reinhard Hütter for suggesting the subheadings for this paper as well as his reflections about what a rethinking of ecclesiology might look like. In particular see his wonderful article "The Church as Public: Dogma, Practice, and the Holy Spirit," *Pro Ecclesia* 3/3 (Summer, 1994): 334–61.

2. I cannot resist contrasting this account of Sneem with the description offered in *Newsweek* (Dec. 17, 1990, pp. 50–56) of the Church Growth Movement (CGM). "A group known as the CGM has sprung up, advocating an unsentimental, businesslike approach for clergy. 'The marketplace is now the most widely used system of evaluation by younger churchgoers,' says Lyle Schaller, a leading figure in CGM. In practice that means polling, marketing and advertising. Evangelical Protestants, who have always been entrepreneurial, take those teachings as their own. 'The No. 1 rule of church growth is that a church will never get bigger than its parking lot,' says the Rev. Gerald

Mann, pastor of the 3,000-member Riverbend Baptist Church in Austin, Texas. On Sundays, therefore, Mann employs a squad of off-duty police officers to direct traffic around the church's 51-acre complex.

"CGM experts judge a minister's accountability not by his faithfulness to the Gospel but whether, as Schaller puts it, 'the people keep coming and giving.' By that measure, the most successful churches are those that most resemble a suburban shopping mall. What works best, according to the CGM, is a one-stop church complex that offers an array of *affinity groups* where individuals can satisfy their need for intimacy yet identify with a large successful enterprise. The ideal advocated by the CGM is the megachurch, a total environment under a single canopy.

"Second Baptist of Houston, which claims a membership of 17,000, tries to be all a megachurch can be. It supports 64 softball teams and 48 basketball teams and fields an additional 84 teams in volleyball, soccer and flag football. There are also periodic golf tournaments and a year-round snack bar called Second Helping. The hub of this activity is the church's Family Life Center, which is equipped with six bowling lanes, two basketball courts, an indoor jogging track, racquetball courts, weight and aerobics rooms, and separate areas for crafts and games—plus a music wing for its orchestra and 500-member choir. 'Second Baptist is a place where I can go with my family to worship, where my wife can play and teach music and where I can play and coach basketball,' says Phil Elders. 'It meets all my needs, both spiritual and physical.' Elders, 31, is a former college player who joined the church in 1988 after going through bankruptcy. He recently ran Second Baptist's conditioning programs for congregants, including members of the San Antonio Spurs and the Houston Rockets basketball teams." I am grateful to Dr. Philip Kenneson for calling my attention to this quote in his "The Reappearance of the Visible Church: An Analysis of the Production and Reproduction of Christian Identity" (Ph.D. diss., Duke University, 1991), pp. 408–9.

It is interesting to ask, "Why is Sneem appealing and Second Baptist of Houston so appalling?" Of course most people who go to Second Baptist wouldn't even know what the feast of the Ascension means, but is that sufficient to suggest their difference? I think it is sufficient, yet both are clearly forms of "cultural Christianity." Sneem is a culture shaped by monasticism and skills necessary to survive a "foreign" government; Second Baptist is the product of a commercial civilization in which the "body" is "privatized." The hard practical question is "How can bodies shaped by a Sneemlike Christendom ever be reclaimed in a culture that produces Second Baptist Church of Houston, Texas?"

I obviously prefer a Sneem because of the "obligatory" nature of what goes on in Sneem. As we shall see, the crucial issue is whether a Sneem can be sustained as church practice without a state. I am indebted to Mr. William Cavanaugh, a good Roman Catholic graduate student, for pressing the issue.

John Howard Yoder in a memo to me challenges my use of Sneem as an example of "Constantine." He suggests Sneem is a celebration of primitive pagan (i.e., village) religiosity, covered with a Catholic veneer by St. Patrick. He thinks we need to somehow honor the elemental human dignity which is in such rites but to also distinguish them from the Gospel. More important, according to Yoder, is to see that Sneem is not Constantine, "who burns dissenters at the stake, having done so literally in the foundational generation of all mainstream forms of 'responsible' Christendom, and still does so with a good conscience in derived forms (from Baghdad to Waco.)" There is no doubt something right about Yoder's objection, though I am not convinced he is rightly narrating Sneem, but the strategy of choosing a Sneem-like example is to try to show a way of disciplining the body that is not a choice between bureaucratic stratification and "individual choice." I am looking for traditioned practices or disciplines where imposed will and total freedom are not assumed to be the only alternatives.

3. This is the characterization of my teacher James Gustafson in his "The Sectarian Temptation: Reflections on Theology, the Church, and the University," *Proceedings of the Catholic Theological Society* 40 (1985): 83–94. For my response see the "Introduction" of my book *Christian Existence Today: Essays on Church, World, and Living in Between* (Durham, N.C.: Labyrinth Press, 1988), pp. 1–24. Hunsinger and Placher do not mean to underwrite Gustafson's characterization.

4. Hans W. Frei, *Theology and Narrative: Selected Essays*, edited by George Hunsinger and William C. Placher (New York: Oxford University Press, 1993), pp. 213–14. There is no question that Hunsinger and Placher are right to suggest that there may be some difference between Frei (and Lindbeck?) and me on these matters. Just to the extent that Frei (and Lindbeck?) have tried to reclaim an intratextual account of Christian doctrine abstracted from ecclesial context, they continue, I fear, to reproduce the presumptions of liberal political practice and thus liberal Protestant theology. Though Frei (and Lindbeck?) are not, I think, the clear targets of John Milbank's suggestion that some sorts of neo-orthodox theology are but variants of liberal Protestantism, insofar as the revealed word of God speaks only of itself without penetrating human construction, how they avoid his critique will make an interesting story. See John Milbank, *Theology and Social Theory: Beyond Secular Reason* (Cambridge, Mass.: Basil Blackwell, 1990), p. 101. For Milbank's explicit worries about Frei and Lindbeck, see pages 385–86. I suspect that at least part of the story involves the difference being an American theologian makes. American "exceptionalism" is a hard habit to break.

5. This quote came to my attention in an article by Michael Hollerich that deals with correspondence between Erik Peterson and Adolf von Harnack. His article is particularly important as he helps us see that the issues raised by

Bonhoeffer were clearly seen by Peterson. He notes that Peterson understood well that the "modern church movement," as represented by Dibelius and Barth as an alternative to Harnack, "was doomed because no amount of activity could possibly demonstrate the church's public character if it didn't already have it." Hollerich, "Retrieving a Neglected Critique of Church, Theology and Secularization in Weimar Germany," *Pro Ecclesia* 2/3 (Summer, 1993): 325. The Bonhoeffer quote is from page 305. The article by Reinhard Hütter to which I refer in note 1 above is a response to Hollerich's article. In the same issue of *Pro Ecclesia* 3/3, David Cunningham and James J. Buckley also have responses to Hollerich's article.

6. I owe this way of putting the question to Phil Kenneson in his "The Reappearance of the Visible Church" (note 2, above). In contrast to theologians who do not believe that it is possible for the church *not* to be the church, Kenneson argues, "but if the church is the community of the Holy Spirit, and the Holy Spirit can be quenched (at least Paul thought this was a danger, and therefore, presumably, a possibility), then it must remain at least thinkable that a community which considers itself 'church' could fail to be a community of the Holy Spirit. If this is so, then there is good reason to allow some place for those forms of social analysis that help make more visible obstacles to the Holy Spirit's work" (p. 309). For an argument quite similar to Kenneson's see Nicholas Lash's book, *A Matter of Hope* (Notre Dame: University of Notre Dame Press, 1982).

7. Of course, one of the deep problems is specifying how different we as moderns have become, given what Anthony Giddens calls the "disembedding" process characteristic of modernity. See his *The Consequences of Modernity* (Stanford: Stanford University Press, 1990), pp. 21–29. Giddens suggests that money is "a means of bracketing time and so of lifting transactions out of particular milieux of exchange." More accurately put, "money is a means of time-space distanciation" (p. 24). That such a process cannot be avoided is exemplified by my "use" of Sneem—e.g., I may have turned Sneem into a commodity through my use of it as an "example."

The "timeliness" of modernity, the subsequent reshaping of the university as well as what counts for knowledge, and the church's accommodation to these developments for theology are nicely suggested by Peterson. If Protestant theology followed a Harnack-like position, Peterson argued, one of three things would happen: "to preserve its academic integrity, theology would be subsumed into history, in which case the field would survive only so long as there was an audience of those interested in the subjects whose history was under investigation; or theology would be reduced to nothing more than the personal opinions of its professors; or it would become mere catechetical instruction" (Hollerich, p. 322). As a result, "theology" has begun to look the "same" everywhere as theologians seek to become good academic cosmopolitans.

8. George Lindbeck treats these matters in his account of Vatican II, *The Future of Roman Catholic Theology* (Philadelphia: Fortress Press, 1970).

9. Paul Minear, *Images of the Church in the New Testament* (Philadelphia: Westminster Press, 1960).

10. Minear observes: " 'The body of Christ' is not a single expression with an unchanging meaning. Paul's thought remains extremely flexible and elastic. Here the term 'body' has one meaning; there it has quite another. Here the term 'members' signifies one thing, there another. In some passages the church is explicitly identified with Christ's body, but in other passages this identification becomes very tenuous indeed. This variety of usage should warn us against seeking to produce a single inclusive definition of the image, and against importing into each occurrence of the analogy the range of meanings which it bears in other passages" (pp. 173-74).

11. *The Documents of Vatican II*, edited by Walter Abbott, S.J., and translated by Joseph Gallagher (New York: Guild Press, 1966), p. 22, from sections 7 and 8 of *Lumen Gentium*.

12. See, for example, Elaine Scarry's, *The Body in Pain: the Making and Unmaking of the World* (Oxford: Oxford University Press, 1985) for an extraordinary account of the relation of medicine and torture.

13. In *The Corinthian Body* (New Haven: Yale University Press, forthcoming) Dale Martin helps us see that Paul's understanding of the body has little relation to the modern assumption of duality between spirit and matter. *Pneuma* was for Paul incorporeal, but that did not make it any less material. The body, moreover, is not circumscribed by being an "individual," but our bodies are literally made up of the body of Christ. Thus the concern for pollution. As Martin puts it "for Paul, firm boundaries must be drawn between church and world precisely because firm boundaries do not exist between flesh and spirit, body and spirit, divine spirit and human spirit" (p. 276).

14. David Matzko has developed this point in his *Hazarding Theology: Theological Descriptions and Particular Lives* (Ph.D diss., Duke University, 1992). As Matzko puts the matter, "for Christian theology, sainthood and the naming of particular saints are intelligible only when set within a network of relationships, a common memory, and a history of interpretive practice, all of which make God present to the world. I propose that saints are the inhabitants of this common memory and network of relationships, and I make the stronger assertion that 'naming saints' is the means by which this common life is created. I assert not only that saints are a *means* of naming a continuing history of God's presence to the world but also that they *are* this continuing presence" (p. 4).

I confess that I first began to reflect on these matters when considering the place of the profoundly mentally handicapped in the church. What they give us is their presence as through the body of Christ they become constitutive of our bodies and we of theirs. The implications for how we understand the place of those who suffer from Alzheimer's disease is obvious. They may no longer "know" who they are, but the church knows who they are.

15. At this point I need to clarify the suggestion made above that Sneem represents a form of Constantinianism. Obvious "Constantinianism" is as various as "church," though I assume only Christian presumptions can produce Constantinianism. For Constantinianism denotes the "identification of the church's mission and the meaning of history with the function of the state in organizing sinful society. This preference is so deeply anchored and so unquestioned that it seems scandalously irresponsible of the 'sectarians' to dare to question it. This is why the American churches as a whole are embarrassed to be asked to talk of eschatology. Yet it is clear in the New Testament that the meaning of history is not what the state will achieve in the way of progressively more tolerable ordering of society, but what the church achieves through evangelism and through the leavening process." John Howard Yoder, *The Original Revolution* (Scottdale, Pa.: Herald Press, 1971), p. 83. "Constantinianism" is, therefore, no more a "given" than "church." What at one time may have been practices associated with a form of Constantinianism may later prove to be sources for resistance to those that would rule in the name of God. I suspect that when all is said and done charges and countercharges of whether one is or is not "Constantinian," given the condition of the church in modernity, are largely beside the point. Our situation as Christians is at once too desperate and too hopeful for such games.

This is a partial, but not sufficient answer to Yoder's challenge mentioned above. Sneem is, of course, part of the lingering Constantinianism of the Irish nation-state. Yet insofar as the practice of first communion at Sneem only makes sense as narrated from Rome the "Constantinianism" of Sneem is qualified.

16. For a more extended account concerning these matters see my book *Dispatches from the Front: Theological Engagements with the Secular* (Durham, N.C.: Duke University Press, 1994). Ronald Beiner in his *What's the Matter with Liberalism* (Berkeley: University of California Press, 1992) argues that communitarianism is but the other side of liberalism. As he puts it, "at the moment, there are millions of North Americans passionately committed to a shared vision of a Christian evangelical community. Is their communitarian commitment in itself an answer to the ills of liberal individualism, or is it rather an expression of those ills? Surely, communitarianism of this sort is the consequence, not the cure, of the moral emptiness of liberal culture. If this is what the situated self looks like, then, as liberal countercritics argue, by all means give us back the 'disencumbered self'! This is the standard liberal rebuttal of community, and to be sure there is much truth in the liberal's case that there is nothing intrinsically good in the experience of community as such. But the liberal rebuttal fails to recognize how deeply implicated the liberal and the communitarian are in each other's dilemmas" (p. 29).

A quite different account of community is offered by Wendell Berry, a Kentucky farmer, poet, novelist, and essayist, who observes that we cannot talk simply of community but of healthy communities. But to speak of a *"healthy* community, we cannot be speaking of a community that is merely human. We are talking about a neighborhood of humans in a place, plus the place itself: its water, its air, and all the families and tribes of the nonhuman creatures that belong to it. If the place is well preserved, if its entire membership, natural and human, is present in it, and if the human economy is in practical harmony with the nature of the place, then the community is healthy," *Sex, Economy, Freedom, and Community* (New York: Pantheon Books, 1992), p. 14. Later Berry argues that the concepts of "public" and "community" are radically, though not necessarily conflictually, different notions. He suggests, however, that the "public" we confront in the modern state, that thrives by trying to create an economic and technological monoculture, cannot but be the enemy of community.

17. Alasdair MacIntyre, "A Partial Response to My Critics," in *After MacIntyre: Essays on the Recent Work of Alasdair MacIntyre*, edited by John Horton and Susan Mendus (Notre Dame: University of Notre Dame Press, 1994), p. 302. Vice President Albert Gore often speaks of the need for government to give a good return on the "consumer's" tax dollar. I find such candor admirable, acknowledging as it does that we are no longer citizens but consumers of government services.

18. Ibid., p. 303.

19. Wendell Berry, in *Sex, Economy, Freedom, and Community*, observes, "Despite its protests to the contrary, modern Christianity has become willy-nilly the religion of the state and the economic status quo. Because it has been so exclusively dedicated to incanting anemic souls into Heaven, it has been made the tool of much earthly villainy. It has, for the most part, stood silently by while a predatory economy has ravaged the world, destroyed its natural beauty and health, divided and plundered its human communities and households. It has flown the flag and chanted the slogans of empire. It has assumed with the economists that "economic forces" automatically work for good and has assumed with the industrialists and militarists that technology determines history. It has assumed with almost everybody that "progress" is good, that it is good to be modern and up with the times. It has admired Caesar and comforted him in his depredations and defaults. But in its de facto alliance with Caesar, Christianity connives directly in the murder of Creation. For in these days, Caesar is no longer a mere destroyer of armies, cities, and nations. He is a contradicter of the fundamental miracle of life. A part of the normal practice of his power is his willingness to destroy the world. He prays, he says, and churches everywhere compliantly pray with him. But he is praying to a God whose works he is prepared at any moment to destroy. What could be more wicked than that, or more mad?" (pp. 114–15).

20. Karl Barth, *Church Dogmatics*, I/1, trans. G. T. Thomson (Edinburgh: T. and T. Clark, 1936), p. 36.

21. Reinhard Hütter, "The Church as Public: Dogma, Practice, and the Holy Spirit," *Pro Ecclesia*. Hütter argues that Barth's account of dogma provides an alternative to Rome and Harnack. As he puts it, "The key issue is how we understand this eschatological 'novus ordo seclorum,' this assembling of an *ekklesia* of the eschatological *polis* that took place at Pentecost. Does not this *civitas* explode the understanding of 'politics' of any *civitas terrena* by constituting another distinct 'public,' a *public sui generis?* And if the dogma is the prolongation of the body of Christ in any significant pneumatological and eschatological sense does that not have precise consequences on how we understand dogma and church law, and even ministry—*jure divino*—but that means precisely christologically as forms of the Gospel in the 'upside down kingdom' with the consequence that the dogma is not 'defended' at the body of the heretic through burning, drowning, etc., but that it is precisely the life and death of the martyrs and the confessors that defend the church's dogma. Thus from the perspective of a theology of the cross it needs to be maintained that if the dogma is truly the prolongation of the body of Christ in this world then it is not the body of the heretic who should feel that; this would be false *theologia gloriae* and would only copy the power-logic of how the *saeculum or civitas terrena* maintains itself as public—namely, by sheer force. Rather it is precisely the martyr and the confessor who rightly give witness to the fact that the dogma is the prolongation of *Christ's* body—and we get to feel it bodily *sub contrario specie*." (Ibid. I have taken the quote from Hütter's original manuscript.)

22. The Very Rev. Georges Florovsky, "Empire and Desert: Antinomies of Christian History," *Greek Orthodox Theological Review*, 1957, p. 133.

23. John Milbank, "Enclaves, or Where Is the Church?" *New Blackfriars* 73/861 (June 1992): 341–42.

24. Ibid., p. 342. Milbank's account of the eucharist is quite similar to Barth's account of proclamation, which makes one wonder what difference it makes whether one concentrates on word or sacrament.

25. Reinhard Hütter, "Ecclesial Ethics, the Church's Vocation, and Paraclesis," *Pro Ecclesia* 2/4 (Fall, 1993): 433–34. For Hütter's more developed critique of my work see his *Evangelische Ethik als kinchliches Zeugnis* (Erlangen: Neukirchener, 1993). For a wonderful account of the problems and potential of Barth's doctrine of the Holy Spirit see James J. Buckley, "A Field of Living Fire: Karl Barth on the Spirit and the Church," *Modern Theology* 10/1 (January 1994): 81–102. Nicholas Healy provides an insightful critique of Barth's ecclesiology in his, "The Logic of Karl Barth Ecclesiology: Analysis, Assessment, and Proposed Modifications," *Modern Theology* 10/3 (July 1994), pp. 253–70. Healy argues that almost in spite of himself Barth reduced Christianity to a matter of knowledge and as a result his ecclesiology borders on being docetic.

26. Hütter, "Ecclesial Ethics," p. 435.

27. In contrast to Milbank, I am more than ready to recommend "pacifism" as a necessary stance for the church to be the church. Milbank is certainly correct to argue that no prescriptive criteria are sufficient to distinguish violence from non-violence in principle, but I take it that that is why practices of reconciliation are intrinsic to the church's life. See his "Enclaves, or Where Is the Church?" p. 349.

28. Michael Wyschogrod, *The Body of Faith: God in the People Israel* (San Francisco: Harper and Row, 1983), p. 26.

29. Wyschogrod, p. 28. Gordan Lafer, in his wonderful essay "Universalism and Particularism in Jewish Law: Making Sense of Political Loyalties," observes that the Jewish "understanding of social solidarity helps make sense of the concept of a 'chosen people,' which will be a 'light unto the nations.' The example Jewish law seeks to set is one aimed not at individuals but specifically at other 'nations.' The institutions of solidarity that mark off Jews' commitments to one another from their more minimal obligation to outsiders are not designed to be applied as universal law governing all people, but rather to be reiterated within each particular nation. This, then, is the universalistic mission of Judaism: not to be 'a light unto all individuals,' not to establish an international system of justice, but rather to teach specific nations how to live *as* a nation," in *Jewish Identity*, edited by David Goldberg and Michael Krausy (Philadelphia: Trinity University Press, 1993), p. 196. I am indebted to Rodney Clapp, of InterVarsity Press, for calling my attention to Lafer's article. Lafer put quotes around "nation," I hope, because he rightly understands that "nation" in "the light unto the nations" does not entail any theory about "nations."

30. Throughout the writing of this paper I have thought of the challenge of John H. S. Kent's, *The End of the Line? The Development of Christian Theology in the Last Two Centuries* (Philadelphia: Fortress Press, 1982). In the "Introduction" to that book Kent observes: "One senses the end of a line of growth, an end which neither Marxism nor Christianity can prevent, not even when they combine in 'liberation theology,' which would like to see itself as legitimating an ecclesiastical take-over of a post-revolutionary situation, but which may be more correctly interpreted as a theology of nostalgia—the characteristic theology of the twentieth century—a harking back to the style of the *ancient regime*, however paradoxical this may sound, to a society in which the churches regarded themselves as the spiritual form of a material community. If the politics of the present century simply reflect human appetite—and I don't believe for a moment that they do more—no human interest of survival will be served by committing what remains of the Christian tradition to politics in any of its twentieth-century forms. A theology of survival would be more to the point than a theology of liberation. Survival, however, is a political issue, and we shall depend much more upon diplomacy than on ideological crusades" (p. viii).

It was with this quote in mind that I ended with the appeal to the practices that have provided the basis for the survival of Jewish bodies, in the hope that Christians might begin to learn that our task is in surviving and not ruling. Kent, moreover, seems to me right to suggest, as the Jews have long known, that the trick is diplomacy. In a holocaust century such a suggestion may appear naive. Perhaps even more troubling is the creation of the state of Israel. One can hardly blame Jews for imitating Christians, though I hope they learn from us, the pre-eminent builders of nation-states, that such a "state" may not be the best survival strategy.

I am indebted to Bill Cavanaugh, David Toole, and, of course, John Howard Yoder for their criticisms of this paper. I am also grateful to the response of those at the SST meeting for their attention and criticisms.

2. The Church's One Foundation Is Jesus Christ Her Lord

1. James W. McClendon, Jr., and James M. Smith, *Understanding Religious Convictions* (Notre Dame: University of Notre Dame Press, 1975); rpt. Valley Forge, Pa.: Trinity Press International, 1994). McClendon's and Smith's account of convictions has never been exploited sufficiently in recent theology. In particular, if their account of justification were followed the way theological convictions could interact with other convictional communities would be enriched. Nancey Murphy's, *Theology in the Age of Scientific Reasoning* (Ithaca: Cornell University Press, 1990) is an example of the kind of work McClendon's and Smith's analysis should encourage.

2. For McClendon's account of that tradition see his *Systematic Theology*, vol. 1: *Ethics* (Nashville: Abingdon Press, 1986), pp. 27–35. In my "Reading McClendon Takes Practice," (forthcoming) I raise the question of whether a baptist can be, as McClendon's claiming of Dorothy Day might suggest, a Catholic. Of course, McClendon claims her as part of the baptist tradition.

3. I confess that I find the "humility" of much of current Christian theology and practice humiliating. In a time like ours the church's task is to celebrate the triumph of our Lord. God is providing the church with that possibility by freeing us from our secular power. Our new-found weakness can become a source of renewed power. As John Milbank observes, "the pathos of modern theology is its false humility," *Theology and Social Theory: Beyond Secular Reason* (Oxford: Basil Blackwell, 1990), p. 1. Milbank counters the totalizing narratives of modernity with what he takes to be the totalizing narrative of the church. I have no doubt that we Christians, particularly when confronted by liberalism, cannot help but appear imperialistic, but I am not sure our story is well told if we try to replace the totalizing narratives of modernity. Christians must live by witness.

4. My frequent claim that the first task of the church is not to make the world just, but to make the world the world must be understood in this light. There is no world unless there is a church, nor can the world have a history without the church. That is why the church knows the world better than the world can know itself.

5. Though McClendon develops the notion of practice in the section of the *Ethics* dealing with the social strand, he certainly does not restrict practices to that strand. See the *Ethics*, pp. 162–84.

6. McClendon, *Ethics*, p. 66.

7. Methodist clergy do not belong to the local churches they serve. They are members of their respective annual conferences.

8. Robert Wilken rightly argues that the Christian adherence to Palestine is a correlative to our faith in Jesus as God incarnate. He notes, "The development of stational liturgies, that is, rituals celebrated at particular places or stations, is the most visible evidence of the primacy of place in the spiritual outlook of Christians living in Palestine. From the beginning Christian worship had been orientated to time, to the 'end time,' the eschatological hope that was foreshadowed in the liturgy, and to 'ritual time,' the representing of the historical events of Christ's life, the suffering, death, resurrection within the context of liturgical celebration. Further, the narrative character of the gospels (recording Jesus' life from birth through death) indelibly imprinted on the minds of Christians the sanctity of time. For Christians in Jerusalem, however, the proximity of the holy places made possible a sanctification of space. The liturgy could now be celebrated not only according to the rhythm of Christ's life, birth, suffering, death, resurrection, but also *at* the Eleona (Mount of Olives), or the Imbonan ('little hillock,' place of the Ascension), Golgotha, or the Anastasis (tomb): at the places where the events had taken place." *The Land Called Holy: Palestine in Christian History and Thought* (New Haven: Yale University Press, 1992), p. 113. Leo, the bishop of Rome, observed that without the witness of the "places where Christ lived, Christian memory loses its anchorage in history," p. 123.

9. James W. McClendon, *Systematic Theology*, vol. 2: *Doctrine* (Nashville: Abingdon Press, 1994), Part II.

10. For a more extended reflection on Broadway United Methodist Church, see the chapter "The Ministry of a Congregation: Rethinking Christian Ethics for a Church-Centered Seminary" in my *Christian Existence Today: Essays on Church, World, and Living in Between* (Durham, N.C.: Labyrinth Press, 1988), pp. 111–32.

11. David and Barbara Koehler joined Broadway at the same time I was received. David wrote the letter that appears in my "Ministry of a Congregation" in my *Christian Existence Today*.

12. This is a paraphrase of Cardinal Suhard's wonderful suggestion, "To be a witness does not consist in engaging in propaganda, nor even in stirring people

up, but in being a living mystery. It means to live in such a way that one's life would not make sense if God did not exist." I do not know where Cardinal Suhard said or wrote this. I have it on the 1985 ordination announcement of Rev. Michael Baxter, C.S.C.

13. The Rev. John Smith was the pastor at Broadway from 1974 to 1984. He labored for years to help us see the importance of the eucharist for the constitution of our common life. I tell the story in the "Ministry of a Congregation."

14. Sarah Webb-Phillips became the minister to Broadway two years after John Smith. She was wonderfully diligent about those, like me, who had moved but had not transferred their memberships.

15. Gary Camp was mildly mentally handicapped. He attended with his mother for many years. At his mother's death, Gary, who was in his late twenties, was devastated. But the church remained his home.

16. James W. McClendon, Jr., *Biography as Theology* (Valley Forge, Pa.: Trinity Press International, 2nd ed., 1990). The first edition was published in 1974.

17. The first four lives are those that shape McClendon's account in *Biography*, the latter three are the heart of the *Ethics*.

3. Why *Resident Aliens* Struck a Chord

1. Hauerwas was first reminded of this by a feminist theologian who pointed out the competitive presumptions behind most theological work. She noted that men simply cannot avoid having their name on their work. In contrast women, who often learned to make quilts which were not signed, did not feel so compelled to think of theology in a competitive mode. In an odd way science embodies a sense of community stronger than theology, as scientists recognize their dependence on one another through their designating the many authors of an article. Current university practice makes it quite difficult to note our dependence on one another. For example, any article that is co-authored often is difficult to use for questions of tenure, since we do not know who has made what kind of contribution. This is but an indication that the university may be very dangerous for theology's health.

We hope that the reader will forgive us for the way we have footnoted this article. We do not pretend that this is "a scholarly" article. Rather it is written in the same spirit in which we wrote *Resident Aliens* (Nashville: Abingdon Press, 1989). We have made generalizations that would require careful qualification if we were trying to be "scholarly." However, broad generalizations have their truth and we hope that our readers will not think we have been terribly unfair.

2. We are indebted to Professor Ken Surin of Duke University for calling our attention to this quote. Edward Said, in his book *The World, the Text, and the*

Critic (Cambridge, Mass.: Harvard University Press, 1983), p. 7, quotes Eric Auerbach quoting Hugo—i.e., one "outsider" quoting other "outsiders."

3. We are indebted to Rev. Jim Burtchaell, C.S.C., for calling our attention to this prayer.

4. Bellah, of course, has long disavowed the notion of civil religion. So our very characterization of him in this manner is an exaggeration. There is so much in his work with which we sympathize and admire. We think it fair to say, however, that he remains more deeply committed to the project called America than we are.

5. We refer to the Gladys example from *Resident Aliens* because we have discovered that readers of the book often center on Gladys as the primary character in the book. We do not mind that, as she is obviously a powerful representative of the kind of church we care about. In many of the lay responses to our book, we have met Gladys everywhere.

6. For a particularly powerful account of the call for theology to return to ecclesiology as its first business, see John Milbank, *Theology and Social Theory: Beyond Secular Reason* (Oxford: Basil Blackwell, 1990).

7. In a recent Duke commencement address, conservative columnist George Will embraced Luther's Ninety-Five Theses as "a marvelous blow for the freedom of the individual conscience." Luther provides no ammunition for Will's project; rather his theses were his contribution to an argument over church discipline, an argument Will does not understand.

8. For a wonderful account of the forces that produced our current notion of religion as an unavoidable universal of the human condition see Talal Asad, *Genealogies of Religion: Discipline and Reasons of Power in Christianity and Islam* (Baltimore: Johns Hopkins University Press, 1993), pp. 27–54. Asad observes that even though the "cognitivist notion of religion" is theoretically incoherent, "it is socially quite compatible with the privatized idea of religion in modern society," p. 48. This strategy of making religion an "essence" distinguishable from politics, law, and science serves the secular liberals desire to confine Christianity and the liberal Christians desire to defend some generalized "religion."

9. "Restitutionism," at least as John Howard Yoder understands that mode of historical rationality, is unavoidable. See his "Anabaptism and History" in *The Priestly Kingdom: Social Ethics as Gospel* (Notre Dame: University of Notre Dame Press, 1984), pp. 123–34.

4. Whose Church? Which Future?
Whither the Anabaptist Vision?

1. Arne Rasmusson, *The Church as Polis: From Political Theology to Theological Politics as Exemplified by Jürgen Moltmann and Stanley Hauerwas* (Lund: Lund

University Press, 1994), p. 23. For another example of the kind of ambiguous ecclesial position in which many of us find ourselves, see Frederick N. Norris, *The Apostolic Faith: Protestants and Roman Catholics* (Collegeville, Minn.: Liturgical Press, 1992). As an "evangelical Catholic" he observes "whether as Roman Catholic or Evangelical Protestants, we belong to the more basic community of those that seek to be catholic Christians," p. xv. Norris has the advantage of deep erudition in the Church fathers and spiritual writers that provides a depth to his position which I can only hope to reflect in a pale fashion.

2. Walter Klaassen, *Anabaptism: Neither Catholic nor Protestant* (Waterloo, Ontario: Conrad Grebel Press, 1973), p. 77.

3. I am using the text of "The Anabaptist Vision" that was printed in pamphlet form from the 1944 *Mennonite Quarterly Review*. Pagination will appear in the text.

4. I am indebted to Albert N. Keim's, "History of the Anabaptist Vision," *Mennonite Historical Bulletin* 54 (October 1993): 1–5 for the account of Bender's writing and the background for his essay.

5. I may be overestimating the influence of Bender's essay or confusing the influence of his essay with the influence of his life. As one who "was not present at the creation" or been a player in subsequent Anabaptist life, it is hard for me to have a sense of such matters. I have relied on Levi Miller's, " 'The Anabaptist Vision' and How It Has Changed the Mennonite Church," *Gospel Herald*, Apr. 26, 1994, and Albert Keim, " 'The Anabaptist Vision': Reassurance and a Rallying Point for the Church," *Gospel Herald*, Apr. 19, 1994, pp. 1–3, 8, for the impression I have of the influence of Bender's essay.

6. I mention Tillich's *The Protestant Era* (Chicago: University of Chicago Press, 1957), not because I think Tillich provides the definitive account of Protestantism, but because he thought of Protestantism as "a special historical embodiment of a universally significant principle. This principle, in which one side of the divine-human relationship is expressed, is effective in all periods of history; it is indicated in the great religions of mankind; it has been powerfully pronounced by the Jewish prophets; it is manifest in the picture of Jesus as the Christ; it has been rediscovered time and again in the life of the church and was established as the sole foundation of the churches of the Reformation; and it will challenge these churches whenever they leave their foundation," pp. vii–viii. By suggesting we are at the end of the "Protestant era" I mean we are also at the end of the time when their kind of universalistic claim makes sense.

7. Robert Wuthnow observes that "the church of the twenty-first century, like that of previous centuries, will probably remain vibrant as long as it can provide people with a strong sense of community. The congregation, therefore, remains at the heart of the church and in turn, at the heart of Christianity. Historical analysis shows clearly that for centuries the Christian church has been the mainstay of community life in Western society. In the

Middle Ages people lived within walking distance of the church, woke to its bells, took their animals to it to be blessed, and followed its calendar. After the Reformation people formed their own churches and called pastors who lived as they did. But now our society seems to be at a loss for community. The question that faces us, then, is whether the church can still be a vital source of community, or whether it too is beginning to succumb to the impersonal forces that fragment our society." Wuthnow, *Christianity in the Twenty-First Century: Reflections on the Challenges Ahead* (New York: Oxford University Press, 1993), pp. 32–33.

Wuthnowlike proposals are legion and a deep temptation, particularly for Anabaptists, who seem to be able to say, "You want community. Have we got a community for you!" Yet the kind of community the church is, I think, must resist the "need for community" produced by liberal cultures for no other reason than that such communities are far too "voluntary." See, for example, my critique of contemporary communitarianism in *Dispatches from the Front: Theological Engagements with the Secular* (Durham, N.C.: Duke University Press, 1994), pp. 156–63.

8. Stephen F. Dintaman, "The Spiritual Poverty of the Anabaptist Vision," *Gospel Herald*, Feb. 23, 1993, pp. 1–3.

9. Robert Friedmann, "The Doctrine of the Two Worlds," in *The Recovery of the Anabaptist Vision: A Sixtieth Anniversary Tribute to Harold S. Bender*, edited by Guy F. Hershberger (Scottdale, Pa.: Herald Press, 1957), p. 112.

10. There are signs that even some Lutherans, of all people, are beginning to appreciate the witness of Anabaptists. For example in an article in the *Lutheran Forum* 28/2 (May 1994) called "Twenty Five Theses Concerning Cultural Christianity," Mark Worthing suggests: "The elevation of Christianity to the status of favored religion of the state by the emperor Constantine should be viewed not only as the 'final victory' of the early Christians against their persecutors but also as an action which helped to undermine a correct understanding of the nature of the Church and also of the essence of Christianity itself," p. 45. Worthing goes on to suggest in a subsequent thesis that the church should welcome the dissolution of the bond with Western culture, since the true nature of Christianity is countercultural. There is little anyone from an Anabaptist tradition would add to Worthing's thesis.

11. John Milbank, *Theology and Social Theory: Beyond Secular Reason* (Oxford: Basil Blackwell, 1990), p. 387.

12. The "us" in this sentence is problematic. Who is the "us" and what ecclesial community could be envisioned by that "us?" I fear I have no good answer to such a query, but even more importantly, I suspect my inability to answer is an indication of a general ambiguity many of us feel about the church.

13. Nicholas Lash, *Theology on the Way to Emmaus* (London: S.C.M. Press, 1986), pp. 91–92.

14. I write this during the celebration of "D-Day." It is against stories such as this that the challenge of articulating the "Anabaptist vision" must be conceived. Only when the church is constituted by practices as powerful as the celebration of the sacrifices in WWII will we begin to understand the challenge before us.

6. The Importance of Being Catholic

1. The issue I was asked to address was "Ethics and Ecumenism: Can Christians Divided by Moral Issues Be United?" I was honored to be asked to deliver the Wattson Lecture, since I admire the Society of the Atonement's tireless work in service to the prayer, "That all may be one."

2. I have often discovered that when I am introduced, a paragraph from the Introduction of A Community of Character (Notre Dame: University of Notre Dame Press, 1981) in which I describe myself as a high-church Mennonite is used. Though such a designation is meant to be amusing, I am serious about it as I understand that to be a way of understanding Methodism—namely, we are a free church with a Catholic ecclesiology.

3. If you ever wonder where Protestant liberalism has gone to die, you will discover it in the soul of many Roman Catholic theologians.

4. Richard Neuhaus, The Catholic Moment: The Paradox of the Church in the Post-Modern World (San Francisco: Harper & Row, 1987), pp. 66–67. I do not share Neuhaus's sense that this is "the moment in which the Roman Catholic Church in the United States assumes its rightful role in the culture-forming task of constructing a religiously informed public philosophy for the American experiment in ordered liberty" (p. 283). I do not because I do not think it is the church's task, Protestant or Catholic, to generate such a "public philosophy," and I am particularly distrustful of what "ordered liberty" means. Nonetheless, I share his strong claim that the essential crisis for our time and the church is unbelief. I read his book basically as a call for the church to recover its theological integrity—a recovery that surely has, as Neuhaus rightly suggests, extraordinary social implications. Of course Neuhaus has now become a Roman Catholic as well as a priest.

5. For an attempt to affirm the importance of the papacy from a Protestant point of view, see Robert Wilken's and my article, "Protestants and the Pope," Commonweal 107/3 (February 1980): 80–85.

6. I do not mean to obscure the different accounts of natural law within Roman Catholic moral theology. Indeed, it is my own view that the position I have just characterized—i.e., that natural law could be divorced from theological claims has little to do with the kind of natural law position represented by Aquinas. However, this account of natural law ironically was accepted by both "conservative" and "liberal" Catholic moral theologians. For an excellent

critique of this turn in natural law theory, see Russell Hittinger, *A Critique of the New Natural Law Theory* (Notre Dame: University of Notre Dame Press, 1987), and his essay "Varieties of Minimalist Natural Law Theory," *American Journal of Jurisprudence* 34 (1989): 133–70.

7. Robert Wuthnow, *The Restructuring of American Religions* (Princeton: Princeton University Press, 1988).

8. Ibid., p. 58.

9. Ibid., p. 279.

10. James Gustafson, *The Church as Moral Decision Maker* (Philadelphia: Pilgrim Press, 1970), p. 110.

11. Curran, *American Catholic Social Ethics: Twentieth-Century Approaches* (Notre Dame: University of Notre Dame Press, 1982).

12. Coleman, *An American Strategic Theology* (New York: Paulist Press, 1982).

13. Hollenbach, *Justise, Peace, and Human Rights* (New York: Crossroads, 1988).

14. McCann, *New Experiment in Democracy: The Challenge of American Catholicism* (Kansas City: Sheed & Ward, 1987).

15. Joe Holland and Anne Barsanti, eds., *American and Catholic: The New Debate* (South Orange, N.J.: 1988).

16. Weigel, *Catholicism and the Renewal of American Democracy* (New York: Paulist Press, 1989). Weigel says "Catholic incarnational humanism is a more attractive vehicle of evangelization in America than the various dialectical approaches found in fundamentalist and evangelical Protestant worlds—and far more adequate than the apologetic accommodationism that has characterized the Protestant mainline for over a generation. Catholic liturgical sensibilities are proving attractive to those who find the lecture-as-worship model a bit aesthetically thin after a while. Catholicism's classic natural law approach to moral reasoning could make an enormous contribution to a pluralistic democracy trying to determine the right role of religiously-based values in public policy discourse. The ideal of the 'communitarian individual' in American democratic capitalism coheres nicely with Catholicism's central social-ethical principles of personalism, the common good and subsidiarity" (p. 25).

In the light of such a quote, I am tempted to simply say, "I rest my case." At the very least, we must ask Weigel to show what form of the "classical natural law" reasoning is so helpful for a "pluralist democracy." Not only do I think appeals to "pluralism" are empty in the face of the fragmentation of American society, but I do not think Weigel appreciates how controverted questions about practical reason are today. It is interesting that in this respect Weigel appeals to "common human experience" as the basis of natural law in such thinkers as Simon, Maritain, and Murray (p. 197), but seems innocent of the problematics of such an appeal. Even stranger, Weigel fails to understand that the same appeal to "common human experience" is what underwrites the program of liberal Catholic theologians of whom Weigel is so critical. In this respect Weigel manifests the same difficulties of his great hero, John Courtney Murray, who wanted to provide historical placing of Leo XIII's *Rerum Novarum*, but still wanted to make the precepts of natural law ahistorical. Like being pregnant, it is hard to be only partly "historical."

17. McCann, *New Experiment in Democracy*, p. 13.

18. The appeal to John Courtney Murray among those wishing to find a role for Catholicism in America is a book in itself. One constantly wishes that the "real John Courtney Murray would stand up." I cannot see how he can be the same person who inhabits the pages of McCann, Curran, and Weigel. I think this is partly due to the incoherence of Murray's own position. Murray tried to combine Catholic social thought, which shares much with what is being called "communitarian" today, with liberal social theory. In the last chapter of *We Hold These Truths*, Murray rightly noted that the liberal social theory of Hobbes was ultimately incoherent and, as an alternative to Hobbes, offered Catholic natural law. But his "natural law theory" certainly cannot be seen as originating the sustaining ethos behind American constitutional practice. Even if it were, his natural law remains far too rationalistic to sustain the kind of duties characteristic of the early encyclicals.

19. McCann, *New Experiment in Democracy*, p. 27.

20. Ibid., p. 56.

21. Ibid., p. 176.

22. John Murray Cuddihy, *The Ordeal of Civility: Freud, Marx, Levi-Strauss, and the Jewish Struggle with Modernity* (Boston: Beacon Press, 1974), pp. 13–14.

23. Ibid., p. 13.

24. Hollenbach, pp. 78–79.

25. Coleman, pp. 146–147. For an equally, if not more powerful analysis of this dilemma, see Gustafson's essay noted above.

26. Ibid., p. 147.

27. Schwartz, "The Restorationist Perspective: Catholic Challenge to Modern Secular America," in *American and Catholic*, edited by Holland and Barsanti, p. 90.

28. Ibid., pp. 88–89.

29. Ibid., p. 90.

30. Ibid., p. 91.

31. Ibid., pp. 95–96.

7. Work as Co-Creation: A Critique of a Remarkably Bad Idea

1. All references to *Laborem Exercens* will give the paragraph number in the text of the paper. I am using the translation provided by the United States Catholic Conference: Publication No. 825, Office of Publishing Services.

2. I am indebted to Dr. Phil Foubert for this point.

3. Gerhard Von Rad, *Genesis: A Commentary*, trans. John H. Marks (Philadelphia: Westminster, 1961), pp. 57–58.

4. Ibid., p. 58.

5. Ibid., p. 59.

6. James Gustafson, *Ethics from a Theocentric Perspective*, I (Chicago: University of Chicago Press, 1981). For my evaluation of Gustafson's critique of "anthropocentricism" see my "God the Measurer," *Journal of Religion* 62/4 (October 1982): 402–11.

7. One has the feeling that if John Paul II had read Studs Terkel's *Working* (New York: Avon Books, 1972) before he had written, he might have produced a much more realistic work. In particular, he might have been more impressed by the quiet heroism of many workers who need no grand explanations to sustain their work.

8. John Howard Yoder, *The Politics of Jesus* (Grand Rapids, Mich.: Eerdmans, 1972), pp. 97, 132.

9. For example C. B. Macpherson argues that "liberal-democratic theory must treat a man's power, in the developmental sense, as a quantity, and must measure it in terms of external impediments to the exercise of his human capacities, that is, impediments to the maximum attainable in principle at any given level of social productivity and knowledge. One impediment, namely, lack of access to the means of labour, has been shown to diminish a man's power in three respects. First, it sets up a continuous net transfer of the material value of the productive power of the non-owner to the owner of the means of labour, the amount of which transfer, in each of the repeated transactions, is the excess of the value added by the work over the wage paid. Second, it diminishes each non-owner's productive power beyond that market-measured amount, by denying him the essentially human satisfaction of controlling the use of his own productive capacities: This value is lost, not transferred. Third, it diminishes his control over his extra-productive life. Of these three deficiencies in a man's power, the first is numerically measurable and is in fact measured by the market. The other two are not so measurable." *Democratic Theory: Essays in Retrieval* (Oxford: Calendon Press, 1973), pp. 69–70.

10. For a Protestant equivalent see Robert Benne, *The Ethic of Democratic Capitalism: A Moral Reassessment* (Philadelphia: Fortress Press, 1981).

11. Though disagreeing with the specifics of some of the alternatives, my criticism in this respect is very similar to Paul Ramsey's critique of some of the social statements of the World Council of Churches. See Ramsey's *Who Speaks for the Church?* (Nashville: Abingdon Press, 1967).

12. P. T. Bauer even suggests that the Pope's recent encyclicals, which insist on large-scale aid, land reform, debt cancellation, commodity agreements have so little to do with economic realities they are not just incompetent, but they are

"immoral because they are incompetent." "An Economist Replies: Ecclesiastical Economics Is Envy Exalted," *This World* 1 (Winter–Spring, 1982), p. 69.

13. John Noonan, Jr., *The Scholastic Analysis of Usury* (Cambridge: Harvard University Press, 1957). Noonan rightly notes the importance of the shift from treating usury as a sin of uncharitableness or avarice to treating it as a sin of injustice. For when that shift occurs it is necessary to try to base the church's prohibition on "natural law" that in many ways distorts exactly the practices that made the condemnation of usury intelligible as an ethic among and for Christians.

8. In Praise of *Centesimus Annus*

1. Stanley Hauerwas, "Work as Co-Creation: A Critique of a Remarkably Bad Idea," in *Co-Creation and Capitalism: John Paul II's Laborem Exercens*, edited by John Houck and Oliver Williams (Washington, D.C.: University Press of America, 1983), p. 42. Reprinted as chapter 7 above.

2. Hauerwas, "The Future of Christian Social Ethics," in *That They May Live: Theological Reflection on the Quality of Life*, ed. George Devine (Staten Island, N.Y.: Alba House, 1972), pp. 123–31.

3. John Coleman, S.J., drawing on the work of Michael Schuck, notes that it is a mistake to begin the history of modern Catholic social pronouncements with *Rerum Novarum*. Rather, one should begin with Gregory XVI's *Mirari Vos* and Pius IX's *Quanta Cura* and *The Syllabus of Errors*. In other words, the social encyclicals are really a response to the "French Revolution and the rise of the new bourgeois liberties with the doctrine of separation of church and state. According to Coleman, Schuck argues that there is a coherence to the social encyclical tradition from 1740 to the present that is constituted by the popes' construal of "the world as a medium of God's ubiquity. Whether pictured as a positive, a cosmos, or unmarked path, the world is imbued with God's presence. Monica Hellwig [Schuck notes] discusses this characteristically Roman Catholic perspective when she says: 'There is no realm whatsoever outside the dimensions of that God.' She continues, 'Neither politics or economics, neither national interests nor international affairs, neither technology nor commerce, neither aesthetics nor productivity, can ultimately be a law unto itself.' As a result, the Popes uniformly criticize world views inspired by atheistic naturalism and dialectical materialism." (John Coleman, S.J. "A Tradition Celebrated, Reevaluated, and Applied," in *One Hundred Years of Catholic Social Thought*, ed. John Coleman [Maryknoll, N.Y.: Orbis Books, 1991], pp. 3–4.) The quote is from Schuck's dissertation, "The Context and Coherence of Roman Catholic Encyclical Social Teaching: 1740–1987," written at the Divinity School, University of Chicago, 1987.

I am sure that Schuck is right to contend that the tradition begins earlier than *Rerum Novarum*. In effect, the social encyclicals are the product of the rise of papal supremacy that went hand in hand with the rise of the new nation-state system. Those who criticize the development of "papal absolutism" often fail to appreciate that the increase of papal power, perhaps unconsciously, was necessary to counter the rise of nation-state absolutism. Schuck's important dissertation has recently been published as *That They Be One: The Social Teachings of the Papal Encyclicals, 1740–1989* (Washington, D.C.: Georgetown University Press, 1991).

4. This translation of *Centesimus Annus* is found in *Origins* 21/1 (May 16, 1991). Paragraph numbers of the encyclical will appear in the text. For a less favorable reading of *Centesimus Annus* see Russell Hittinger, "The Problem of the State in *Centesimus Annus*," *Fordham International Law Journal*, 15, 4 (1991–1992), pp. 952–96. Hittinger argues that *Centesimus Annus* "tips the scales" toward a liberal account of the state, as the Pope wants to shift toward a liberal model of economics and politics and at the same time hold a traditional understanding of culture which results in an incoherent position.

5. Václav Havel, *Living in Truth* (London: Faber and Faber, 1986), pp. 82–83.

6. "Spiritually empty" is the way some neo-conservatives defend capitalism as entailing no moral implications.

7. "The obligation to earn one's bread by the sweat of one's brow also presumes the right to do so. A society in which this right is systematically denied, in which economic policies do not allow workers to reach satisfactory levels of employment, cannot be justified from an ethical point of view nor can that society attain social peace." (43)

8. It is certainly the case John Paul II uses the language of "inalienable rights," (7) but such rights are always meant to suggest that "persons" have existence prior to the state. I am aware that such "rights" can lead to a form of liberal individualism, and there are certainly hints in this encyclical in that direction, but I think that God, not the person, stands more determinatively at the center of the Pope's vision.

9. I love the fact that *Centesimus Annus* has been published in Ireland and England by the *Catholic Truth Society*. I assume it is significant that this society rightly understands that truth is appropriately qualified by Catholic.

The quotes from *Rerum Novarum* are from *Five Great Encyclicals* (New York: Paulist, 1939). I particularly value the "Discussion Club Outlines" by Rev. Gerald Treacy, S.J. Also to be treasured is the Foreword by John B. Harvey, then the superior general of the Paulist Fathers.

10. Pius XI, *Costi Connubii* in *Five Great Encyclicals* (New York: Paulist Press, 1939), paragraph 34.

11. Havel, pp. 115–116.

12. Havel, pp. 153-154.

13. In several places in *Centesimus* John Paul II makes clear that "there are collective and qualitative needs which cannot be satisfied by market mechanisms. There are important human needs which escape its logic. There are goods which by their very nature cannot and must not be bought or sold" (40). Yet the encyclical does not provide much help for discerning what should be excluded from the market.

14. John Milbank, *Theology and Social Theory: Beyond Secular Reason* (Oxford: Basil Blackwell, 1990).

15. Havel develops this example on pages 41-42 of *Living in Truth*.

16. In commenting on the 1989 struggle John Paul II notes "it was a struggle born of prayer, and it would have been unthinkable without immense trust in God, the Lord of history, who carries the human heart in his hands. It is by uniting his own sufferings for the sake of truth and freedom to the suffering of Christ on the cross that man is able to accomplish the miracle of peace and is in a position to discern the often narrow path between the cowardice which gives in to evil and the violence which under the illusion of fighting evil only makes it worse" (25).

17. *The Rosary: A Social Remedy*, ed. Thomas Schwertner, O.P. (Milwaukee: Bruce, 1934).

18. I am indebted to Rev. Michael J. Baxter, C.S.C., for his critique and constructive suggestions for revising this paper. It is much better because of him.

9. Living in Truth: Moral Theology as Pilgrimage

1. The importance of this point is easily overlooked in the polemics surrounding the encyclical. John Paul II rightly locates moral theology within the tradition of the virtues, correlately requiring an account of practical rationality and human and action. Only in such a context is it intelligible to argue, as John Paul II does, that certain action-descriptions cannot be overridden by more general principles. For a wonderful analysis of this point see Martin Rhonheimer, " 'Intrinsically Evil Acts' and the Moral Viewpoint: Clarifying a Central Teaching of *Veritatis Splendor*," *The Thomist* 58/1 (January 1994): 1–39.

10. The Liturgical Shape of the Christian Life

1. This is documented in H. G. Bissinger's, *Friday Night Lights: A Town, a Team, and a Dream* (New York: Harper Perennial, 1991). Bissinger's wonderful book is about one football season of the Odessa Permian High School—the winningest high school football team in Texas history. Bissinger wrote what he thought was

a appreciative, if not loving, portrayal of the young men who play and the townspeople who support this rather bizarre practice. He was shocked to discover that the town was, as we say in Texas, "none too pleased" with his account. In fact, some town members threatened to kill him. They take their high school football seriously in Texas! "Friday night lights" refers to the lights that illumine the football fields on Friday nights that can be seen literally for miles in Texas.

2. Daniel Hardy and David Ford, *Jubilate: Theology in Praise* (London: Darton, Longman, and Todd, 1984). The significance of Hardy's and Ford's argument concerning the significance of praise for the grammar of Christian theology, I believe, has not been appropriately appreciated. This book is a goldmine of suggestions not yet fully exploited in contemporary theology. One of my favorite insights in the book is their claim that "Dante can set his own autobiography in a story which embraces the whole of the known universe. The modern predicament is typically that of a dichotomy between contemplating the universe and one's own life in it" (p. 50).

I sometimes observe that there must be some correlation between a dying church and the production of interesting theologians—witness the Church of England and people like Rowan Williams and John Milbank. Among those are David Ford, now Regius Professor of Divinity at Cambridge, and Dan Hardy. Of course Hardy is an American, currently Director of the Center for Theological Inquiry at Princeton but for many years Professor of Theology at the University of Durham in England.

3. See, for example, Hardy's and Ford's extraordinary account of the threat of "stoicism" as the most appealing alternative to Christianity in the past as well as today. They suggest that the problem is not simply that "stoicism" threatens Christianity, but that we now have largely a "stoicized Christianity." "The nation state is delighted to welcome a religion that is so timid and orderly, leaving the passions free for economics, war and collective sport. In Britain today the civic religion might be described as stoicism with Christian influence. It is full of rectitude, good patterns and principles, but it is being challenged by more exciting and extreme creeds to which it seems at present to have neither the daring nor the moral, intellectual and political creativity to respond" (*Jubilate*, p. 144). They quite rightly suggest that the joyful Christian worship has prophetic importance as an alternative to stoicism.

4. *Liturgy in Greek* simply meant *the work that the church*, or any community, *does for the public good*. The church impoverishes itself when it excludes from its liturgical action business meetings to consider whether the church building needs a new roof. How such business is conducted, however, finds its *telos* in the praise offered by the community gathered in word and sacrament. For a powerful account of how the "business" of the church in such matters as "binding and loosing" as well as how authority works in the church is integral to

the church's worship as well as her politics, see John Howard Yoder, *Body Politics: Five Practices of the Christian Community before the Watching World* (Nashville: Discipleship Resources, 1992).

The recognition of the political character of worship is extremely important in order that worship not become "aesthetics" in the modern sense. Terry Eagleton has rightly reminded us that the construction of the very category of the aesthetic reproduces the class presuppositions of modernity. "Art" was "depoliticized" to serve the politics of a commercial class. Eagleton argues, however, that the "aesthetic" can now provide a powerful challenge to current dominant ideological forms. My argument entails something similar to Eagleton's, but given my ecclesiological presuppositions my politics are obviously different. For Eagleton's argument see his *The Ideology of the Aesthetic* (Oxford: Basil Blackwell, 1990).

5. At stake here is the very question of how theology is to be done today as well as its most appropriate genre. I do not pretend to have great insight about such matters, though I am sure that when theology becomes "academic" in a manner that theologians write mainly for other theologians something has profoundly gone wrong.

6. The Divinity School at Duke is predominately Methodist, though we have a wide range of Protestants from other denominations in our classes.

7. Professor Smith is an Episcopal priest, but since Duke Seminary is predominately Methodist we followed the Methodist order of worship. We taught the course together the first three years, but due to the retirement of one of our colleagues we had to begin offering the course independently. Yet much of what I do in the course as well as the way I report on the course remains indebted to Professor Smith. I have included a syllabus of the course as an appendix to this chapter.

8. One of our difficulties in developing the course is that no readings exist that fit the structure of the course. This is not surprising since the very disciplinary divisions that the course is meant to challenge insure that such a literature does not exist. There are a few books that deal in general with the theme of worship and ethics, but the very existence of the "and" reproduces the presupposition we wished to challenge. We used Karl Barth's *Church Dogmatics* III/4 in some of the first offerings of the course. We have each continued to change our readings often since nothing seems quite "right."

9. Hardy and Ford, *Jubilate*, p. 21.

10. Fergus Kerr, *Theology after Wittgenstein* (Oxford: Basil Blackwell, 1986), p. 183.

11. Hardy and Ford, *Jubilate*, p. 113.

12. I therefore refuse to privilege the distinction between "personal" and "social ethics," since I assume that distinction derives from practices foreign to the church's narrative. If the church's first task is to make the world the world

that is its fundamental social and political task. Such a claim is often resisted because it sounds so intolerant, which of course it is, but it is an intolerance based on charity that would have the world saved by knowing that it is the world. If the church does not worship rightly, how can the world know that it is the world exactly to the extent it does not willingly glorify God. As Yoder puts the matter in *Body Politics*, "stated very formally, the pattern we shall discover is that the will of God for human socialness as a whole is prefigured by the shape to which the Body of Christ is called. Church and world are not two compartments under separate legislation or two institutions with contradictory assignments, but two levels of the pertinence of the same Lordship. The people of God is called to be today what the world is called to be ultimately. . . . The phrase found in the title, *body politics*, is of course partly redundant. Yet each term does say more than the other would alone. "Politics" affirms an unblinking recognition that we deal with matters of power, of rank and of money, of costly decisions and dirty hands, of memories and feelings. The difference between church and state or between a faithful and an unfaithful church is not that one is political and the other not, but that they are political in different ways" (p. ix).

13. The emphasis on the relation between church and world is a correlative of the strong eschatological theme running through the course. I argue that the attempt to display Christian ethics in terms of nature/grace or creation/redemption often results in a failure to appreciate the eschatological character of Christian convictions. For example, it is interesting to note that ethics based nature/grace and creation/redemption schemes often only refer to the church as an afterthought. That such is the case, I suspect, betrays the ahistorical character of such theologies. For example, I think it is telling that such theologies, while appearing Christologically orthodox, in fact leave Jesus behind once they begin to "work out the practical implications."

14. Alasdair MacIntyre, *After Virtue*, 2nd ed. (Notre Dame: University of Notre Dame Press, 1984), p. 23. The "twist" on MacIntyre's suggestion obviously owes much to John Milbank's arguments in *Theology and Social Theory* (Oxford: Basil Blackwell, 1990).

15. I often draw on the work of MacIntyre in order to help the students understand the philosophical issues intrinsic to the Christian ethics I am developing. In particular, I try to help them see that, once one recognizes the traditioned character of rationality, then the difficult question is not how to defeat something called "the problem of 'relativism,'" but, rather, in what position must one be standing even to know how to characterize relativism. Too often the so-called "relativist challenge" presumes a standpoint outside all tradition. MacIntyre rightly suggests that the "sociology" that seems to make "relativism" such a challenge is the creation of cosmopolitan cultures that give certain individuals the presumption they are standing in different traditions at the same time. That many are so positioned today is without

question. Nor should it be surprising that many of us who count ourselves Christians are so located. What is crucial for Christians to recognize is that any response to relativism cannot come from a theory of rationality, but must be found in practices, such as the eucharist, which embody a unity that makes it possible for our different positions to become more than the sum of our parts. For MacIntyre's reflections on perspectivism and relativism see his *Whose Justice? Which Rationality?* (Notre Dame: University of Notre Dame Press, 1988), pp. 349–69.

16. Hardy and Ford, in their appreciative account of liberalism, put the matter just right, I believe, when they note "the only safe forms of Christian liberalism are those which live a basic existence of praising and knowing God within the other three streams of Christianity. Without this praise and knowledge liberals lose Christian credibility, and distort the very content of the freedom which they champion. As soon as freedom is seen as not primarily something given by God to be fulfilled in free praise and love of God, then the whole ecology of life is polluted. When liberalism of this sort refers to God it tends to become agnostic and vague, and loses the ability to know or proclaim much that is definite about him" (*Jubilate*, pp. 143–44).

17. For a more developed account of this position see my *Unleashing the Scripture: Freeing the Bible from Captivity to America* (Nashville: Abingdon Press, 1993).

18. I have appended to this chapter a sermon, "Standing on the Shoulders of Murderers: The End of Sacrifice," to display this theme.

19. I spend at least a lecture on the church and the Third Reich in this context. The example of the church under Nazi Germany can be too comforting for American Christians, because they think they live in a political system that makes fascism impossible. Such a presumption, however, makes it particularly important to challenge the assumption that "democracy" is the form of government and society most congenial to, if not required by, Christian worship.

20. I have not, for example, dealt with the importance of hymns and music as well as prayer as intrinsic to Christian worship. Such themes are not only underdeveloped in this essay, but in the course. It is tempting to defend their absence by claiming that one simply cannot be expected to do everything in one course, but I do not think such a defense adequate. The truth of the matter is that I think the importance of music and prayer have been undervalued in much of contemporary theology, mine included, apart from the outstanding example of von Balthasar. Nor should Patrick Sherry's *Spirit and Beauty: An Introduction to Theological Aesthetics* (Oxford: Clarendon Press, 1992) be overlooked. Sherry makes the striking suggestion that "the transfiguration of the cosmos is being anticipated now in the Spirit's work of creating beauty is similar to the claim that the Spirit's present work of sanctification is an anticipation of our future glorification and life of holiness" p. 165. This strikes me as an extremely

suggestive claim that could help us understand the relation between eschatology and sanctification in worship.

11. Casuistry in Context: The Need for Tradition

1. This essay was written in response to an essay by Al Jonsen on the relation of casuistry and experience for a conference planned by Warren Reich on the importance of experience for medical ethics. I took the liberty of also responding to Jonsen and Toulmin's book, *The Abuse of Casuistry: A History of Moral Reasoning* (Berkeley: University of California Press, 1988). I think those unacquainted with the book will be able to follow the argument with little difficulty.

2. Alasdair MacIntyre, "Does Applied Ethics Rest on a Mistake?" *The Monist* 67/4 (October 1984): 499. See also my *Christian Existence Today: Essays on Church, World and Living in Between* (Durham, N.C.: Labyrinth Press, 1988), pp. 67–88.

3. MacIntyre, p. 502.

4. In a revision of his original paper Jonsen acknowledges that casuistry presupposes "a relatively coherent social and cultural community." However, I continue to think that he wants to have the "universal morality" and the concreteness of casuistry at the same time. In other words, I am suggesting that casuistry still looks too much like "applied ethics" rather than how in a tradition rules are extended, limited, or reformulated.

5. Alasdair MacIntyre, *Whose Justice? Which Rationality?* (Notre Dame, Ind.: University of Notre Dame Press, 1988).

6. In his essay Jonsen notes that in their book he and Toulmin argued that classical casuistry was not closely associated with any ethical theory even though the practitioners worked within the framework of "natural law." Yet he maintains that the methods of reasoning and principles of casuistry were equally compatible with any "modern ethical theory." But that simply cannot be the case if, as MacIntyre argues, no rule exists apart from its application—exists, that is, as a working rule in a moral tradition. It would be unfair to attribute Jonsen and Toulmin's account of casuistry entirely to their experience on the National Commission for the Protection of Human Subjects of Biomedical and Behavioral Research, but one cannot help but think, as they testify in their book (pp. 16–19), that their appreciation as well as understanding of casuistry derives from that experience. For as Toulmin reports, as a staff member for that commission, the commissioners found it relatively easy to reach agreement on particular concrete issues raised by difficult types of cases, even though they continued to disagree about matters of moral principles or about what the basic rules of morality actually were. (Stephen Toulmin, "The Tyranny of Principles," *The Hastings Center Report* 11/6 [December 1981], pp. 31–32.) Their experience

in this commission seems to have led Jonsen and Toulmin to conclude that concentrating on "cases" while leaving "theory" behind might be a way to "do" ethics—that is, a way to get on with the task of building consensus in and for our society about the good. Yet MacIntyre argues, and I think correctly, that Toulmin fails to appreciate that such agreements are not a testimony to rational and moral achievement, but rather a "nonrational social transaction" ("Does Applied Ethics Rest on a Mistake?" p. 501). According to MacIntyre, that agreement is reached in situations celebrated by Toulmin is but an indication of the ideological function of the very idea of "applied ethics." For even though the liberal presumption that morality is constituted by a set of principles to which any rational agent would assent has proved to be unfounded, that does not mean this conception of morality is without social influence. Rather, such a view of morality is designed to hide the conflicts that would otherwise make "business as usual" impossible.

7. Umberto Eco, *The Name of the Rose* (Hollywood, Calif.: Script City, 1984).

8. MacIntyre, *Whose Justice? Which Rationality?*, pp. 370–78.

9. For extensive discussions of Aristotle's account of practical reason, see MacIntyre, *Whose Justice? Which Rationality?*, pp. 124–45; Norman Dahl, *Practical Reason, Aristotle, and Weakness of Will* (Minneapolis: University of Minnesota Press, 1984); and Irven Engberg-Pedersen, *Aristotle's Theory of Moral Insight* (Oxford: Clarendon Press, 1983).

10. Philip Devine, *The Ethics of Homicide* (Ithaca: Cornell University Press, 1978; rpt. Notre Dame: University of Notre Dame Press, 1990), pp. 44–45.

11. Rhetorically rhetoric is making a comeback in many intellectual disciplines. There can be no question that this is a good, as it may help us recover the political dimension of all accounts of rationality. For a rhetorically strong defense of rhetoric see Stanley Fish, *Doing What Comes Naturally* (Durham, N.C.: Duke University Press, 1990), pp. 471–502.

12. Jonsen and Toulmin, pp. 91–136.

13. These are the examples Jonsen and Toulmin treat in chapters 9, 10, and 11 of their book. We are in their debt for their discussion of these extremely interesting issues. I do find it odd, however, that in their discussion of pride they state that Augustine incorporated into his just-war doctrine a reluctant acceptance of self-defense. They may be right about this, but Paul Ramsey spent a lifetime arguing that Augustine's defense of just war derived entirely from Augustine's understanding of the Christian's responsibility to defend the innocent.

There is an interesting issue not immediately relevant to the subject of this article but I think worth mentioning—namely, it is not at all clear to me what is the relationship between the historical account of casuistry Jonsen and Toulmin provide and their theoretical argument. I am not sure how the first and last chapter of their book are related to the history they give. Jonsen and Toulmin tell the story of casuistry with the hope of rescuing casuistry from the reputation Pascal gave it in *The Provincial Letters* and thus casuistry is identified as informal moral reasoning. As a result, their history appears a little too coherent as casuistry; as they present it, it has more continuity across the centuries than in fact it had. For other accounts of the history of moral theology see John Mahoney, *The Making of Moral Theology* (Oxford: Clarendon Press, 1987) and John Gallagher, *Time Past, Time Future: A Historical Study of Catholic Moral Theology* (New York: Paulist Press, 1990). For a good critique of these histories see John Berkman, "The Politics of Moral Theology: Historicizing Neo-Thomist Moral Theology, with Social Reference to the Work of Germain Grisez" (Ph.D. diss., Duke University, 1994).

14. Jonsen and Toulmin, p. 23. However, I think this claim is put in a far too negative fashion. Casuistry was not in the Christian tradition required to help Christians avoid the hard sayings of the Gospel but rather was an imaginative attempt to help Christians attend the world on that basis. No doubt casuistry could become a means of compromise, but that was a clear perversion.

15. Jonsen and Toulmin, p. 242.

16. For example, David Steinmetz observes, "Roughly speaking, there were two penitential traditions which lived side by side in the later middle ages, sometimes in harmony, more often in a fragile and uneasy truce. The first tradition stressed the importance of the disposition of the penitent in the confession, the sincerity and completeness of the penitent's confession, and the necessity for finding a competent and sensitive spiritual advisor. The other tradition stressed the authority of the Church and its sacraments, the power of priestly absolution, and the consolation which the faithful can find when they turn their attention away from themselves and focus on the efficacious rites and ceremonies of the Church. It was not impossible to want to stress both the necessity of a proper disposition and the power of priestly absolution, but almost all theologies of penance tended to tilt in one direction or the other" (*Luther in Context* [Bloomington: Indiana University Press, 1986], pp. 2–3).

Steinmetz points out that Dietrich Kolde's *Mirror for Christians*, written in 1480, went through forty-six editions—a book that was intended for laity to help them be genuinely contrite. It can hardly be thought that the confessional practice and casuistic reflection is easily characterized as "legalistic" if by that is meant a slavish following of rules with no concern for how the rules are obeyed.

17. I find it odd that Jonsen says so little about the virtues and their relation to casuistry in the light of his appreciation of Aristotle's account of prudence and its perception of the ultimate particular. For persons of practical reason in Aristotle are such only as they possess all the virtues. Admittedly this creates some interesting puzzles about the circularity of Aristotle's account, but I think

it is clear that Aristotle never thought it possible to see rightly without being rightly formed by the virtues.

18. Eric Cassell, *Talking with Patients*, vols. 1 and 2 (Cambridge, Mass.: MIT Press, 1985).

12. A Trinitarian Theology of the Chief End of All Flesh

1. This article was originally presented at the conference "Good News for Animals? Contemporary Christian Approaches to Animal Well-Being" in Durham, N.C., on Oct. 5, 1990. Thanks to Len Baglow, Gary Comstock, and Brent Laytham for helpful criticism and to Alice Poffinberger for her excellent editorial work.

2. In writing this essay we have struggled with the very issue of how to describe the relationship between humans and other animals. We soon found ourselves resisting phrases like "our relationship with animals," because we found that this implicitly underwrites a cozy distance between humans and animals. We continue to struggle with the lack of a language to articulate better these relationships.

3. See Stanley Hauerwas, *The Peaceable Kingdom: a Primer in Christian Ethics* (Notre Dame: University of Notre Dame Press, 1983).

4. Can one seriously discuss these questions with someone who is in the midst of eating a hamburger? We take this to be a serious question.

5. See James M. Gustafson, *Ethics from a Theocentric Perspective*, (Chicago: University of Chicago Press, 1981), pp. 281–93. Although Gustafson follows Mary Midgley in arguing for an increased appreciation of the continuity between humans and other animals, he does not appeal to any traditional theological categories for understanding this relation.

6. On the issue of the relationship between humans and other animals, Gustafson's critique employs broadly scientific criteria. This is shown by the types of appeals made (see n. 5 above) and, more generally, by his view that scientific criteria may lead to the doing away altogether with Christianity in the future (*Theology and Ethics*, p. 324). Gustafson has subsequently addressed "environmental issues" in his *A Sense of the Divine: The Natural Environment from a Theocentric Perspective* (Cleveland: Pilgrim Press, 1994).

7. As to the question of what constitutes theological discourse, no universal agreement is expected, but it would be a big improvement if we could get this to be an important issue!

8. We thank Oliver O'Donovan for originally bringing this question to our attention. If we do have a stake in their survival, it would be along the lines of an argument by James Rimbach, who argues that Noah took all the kinds of animals into the Ark, even those that were unclean (which Rimbach says means

unfit for human consumption) "to keep their kind alive upon the face of the earth" (Gen. 8:17). See James Rimbach, " 'All Creation Groans': Theology/ Ecology in St. Paul," in Wesley Granberg-Michaelson, ed., *Ecology and Life* (Waco, Tex.: Word Books, 1988), pp. 161–77. Charles Pinches has provided the most adequate defense of "speciesism" in his, "Each According to Its Kind: A Defense of Theological Speciesism," *Good News for Animals: Christian Approaches to Animal Well-Being*, edited by Charles Pinches and Jay McDaniel (Maryknoll: Orbis Books, 1993), pp. 187–205.

9. For powerful examples of the way particular enlightenment theories of biology and their attendant classifications have been used for wicked ends, see Cornel West's "A Geneology of Modern Racism" in *Prophesy Deliverance!: An Afro-American Revolutionary Christianity*, (Philadelphia: Westminster Press, 1982). West strongly argues that enlightenment biologists, anthropologists and naturalists were primarily responsible for producing a new and peculiarly modern form of racism, where "racial differences are often grounded in nature, that is, ontology and later biology" (p. 64).

For a fascinating study of the science of primatology as a form of "simian orientalism" see Donna Jeanne Haraway, *Primate Visions: Gender, Race, and Nature in the World of Modern Science* (New York: Routledge, 1989).

10. Indeed, if there is a reason for giving special attention to humankind, it is because Jesus is the second person of the Trinity, because salvation for all comes through one made human. In the same way that animals are privileged through One who became human, so we gentiles are privileged through One who became a Jew.

11. Schumaker describes Cartesianism as follows: "Descartes was a convinced disciple of the then newly-articulated mechanical philosophy, and he believed that all of physical reality (*res extensa*) was mechanical in nature; . . . After much consideration, Descartes came to believe that all animal behaviour could be understood purely in physical and mechanical terms. . . . But according to Descartes, people are not like animals. People possess both a body and a soul; that is, their existence includes both a physical substance (*res extensa*) and a spiritual substance (*res cogitans*). . . . People, then, are utterly unlike the brutes" (Millard Schumaker, *Appreciating Our Good Earth: Towards a Pertinent Theology of Nature* [Kingston, Ont.: Queen's Theological College and Bay of Quinte Conference, The United Church of Canada, 1980], pp. 9–10).

Though some might accuse Aquinas and other medieval theologians of holding a similar view with their discussion of "rational souls," we find much more determinative Aquinas's view of a human as "an animal that laughs." This, however, is not the kind of peculiar capacity that Cartesians have in mind when trying to distinguish humans from other animals! See Aquinas, *Summa Theologiae* (New York: Benziger Bros., 1947), 1a, 3, art. 4; 1a, 44, art. 1; 1a2ae, 51, art. 1.

12. By "implicit Deism," we have in mind the view in which God is basically understood as "first cause," which results in a faulty view that understands creation solely in terms of the accounts of Genesis 1 and 2. This error is further exacerbated by reading the Genesis 1 and 2 accounts as being the creation of a world which is more or less the same as the world in which we presently dwell.

13. See, for example, Robert Nozick, *Anarchy, State and Utopia* (New York: Basic Books, 1974).

14. This claim may be confusing to those who think of "creation" as synonymous with "nature," for it often appears that nature too is at war with itself. In the second part of the paper we will argue that "creation" must be understood as something both radically different and more widely encompassing than "nature."

15. Andrew Linzey, *Christianity and the Rights of Animals* (New York: Crossroad, 1987), p. 72.

16. Ibid. Linzey has continued to refine his position in quite a remarkable way. For example, see his wonderful new book, *Animal Theology* (London: S.C.M. Press, 1994).

17. As we will try to show, it is profoundly important that creation does not become just another way of praising the importance of "Mother Earth." Much has been written already about how Christians need to learn more from Native-American attitudes about the earth, the sky, and the water. While we admire much that native peoples know about the nature of their world and how they should live in it, we are not sure how, if at all, these insights can be related to what should inform Christians on this matter.

18. For a massive critique of theories which assume an ontology of violence, see John Milbank, *Theology and Social Theory: Beyond Secular Reason* (Oxford: Basil Blackwell, 1991).

19. For a defense of a "survivalist ethic" on the issue of nuclear weapons, see the United Methodist Church (U.S.A.) Council of Bishops' *In Defense of Creation: The Nuclear Crisis and a Just Peace* (Nashville: Graded Press, 1986). See also Paul Ramsey's critique of this document in his *Speak up for Just War or Pacifism: a Critique of the United Methodist Bishops' Pastoral Letter "In Defense of Creation"* (University Park: Pennsylvania State University Press, 1988).

20. Schumaker gives this purposive understanding of the *imago Dei* a historical base by arguing, following Mendenhall, that the Genesis story is to be read as patterned after treaties of Mesopotamian feudal empires. According to such a reading, "Eden is to be considered as like a vassal state in the empire of the Great King, God: Adam is to be seen as . . . a governor appointed by God to manage Eden" (Schumaker, *Appreciating Our Good Earth*, p. 12). Schumaker goes on to argue that this idea in itself is very difficult for us to accept; because we are very suspicious of any kind of monarch or hierarchy, we cannot distinguish between the dominion of a monarch and the domination of a tyrant, or more basically,

the leadership of anyone we have not elected. Christians, too, forget to make this distinction when they forget that what they long for is the Kingdom of God, a kingdom of love and peace, rather than one of tyranny and oppression.

21. For a critique of the view of dominion as domination see Janet Martin Soskice, "Creation as Revelation," *Theology* 94 (January/February 1991).

22. Jürgen Moltmann, *God in Creation: A New Theology of Creation and the Spirit of God* (San Francisco: Harper and Row, 1985), p. 226.

23. Karl Barth, *Church Dogmatics*, III, 4 (Edinburgh: T. and T. Clark, 1961), pp. 355–56.

24. On this issue, we might ask how the possibility of human starvation might make a difference in how we understand our relationship with other animals.

25. We also think it important to mention the heightened significance of saying "grace" before meals for those who continue to eat animals, particularly that element of thanking God for the sacrifice animals made so that meat-eaters might eat them.

13. The Kingship of Christ: Why Freedom of "Belief" Is Not Enough

1. George Will, "Scalia Missed Point But Made Right Argument on Separation of Religion," *Durham Morning Herald*, Apr. 22, 1990, p. F5.

2. The citation for this case is as follows: 485 US 660, 99 L Ed 2d 753, 108 S Ct 1444. A complicating factor in this case was that the men were employed as counselors at a drug and alcohol abuse center called ADAPT (the Douglas County Council on Alcohol and Drug Abuse Prevention and Treatment), whose rules explicitly proscribe the use of illegal drugs by employees.

3. Stanley Fish, "There's No Such Thing as Free Speech and It's a Good Thing, Too," from *Debating P.C.*, Paul Berman, editor (New York: Dell Publishing, 1992), p. 231. The article, in a revised form, now appears in his book *There's No Such Thing as Free Speech . . . and It's a Good Thing Too* (New York: Oxford Press, 1994), pp. 102–19.

4. Milton's qualifier reads: "I mean not tolerated popery, and open superstition, which as it extirpates all religious supremacies, so itself should be extirpated . . . that also which is impious or evil absolutely against faith or manners no law can possibly permit that intends not to unlaw itself. . . ." (Ibid., pp. 231–32.)

5. Ibid., p. 233.

6. Ibid., p. 236.

7. Ibid., p. 235.

8. Ibid., p. 240.

9. Ibid., p. 240–41.

10. In an earlier draft of this essay, Fish presses his case by exposing the remarkable inconsistency of those who currently criticize "political correctness" on the basis of free speech. He calls attention to the way *Time* magazine covers matters of free speech in a way that is contradictory, if not downright duplicitous. In the April 1, 1991, issue, *Time* asks its readers to imagine a place "where it is considered racist to speak of the rights of the individual when they conflict with the communities' prevailing opinion"; and then launches into a familiar, by now well-worn, critique of anti-harassment codes. Fish then notes, with irony, that it is something of a surprise when in the same issue one reads a report of a French anti-Semite who, after having characterized the Nazi gas chambers as a mere "detail of history," was sued by a group of Holocaust survivors and ordered to pay a fine of $180,000. *Time* commends this decision, accuses him of circulating "inflammatory rhetoric," and gives the story the headline "Comeuppance Bigot." Now what's the difference, Fish asks, between putting a muzzle on an anti-Semite in France and putting a stop to racist rhetoric on college campuses? And then he gives this answer: "What appears to be a contradiction in logical terms makes perfect sense once the issue is reconceived as one involving the different values attached to the infliction of different harms: Holocaust survivors are harmed by the trivialization of their experience; women, blacks, gays, and other minorities are harmed by the epithets and insults directed at them on many campuses. It is just that as *Time* sees it, the potential harm to Holocaust survivors is more worthy of concern than the potential harm to the sensibilities of minority students; and that is why statements demeaning to Holocaust survivors are categorized as 'inflammatory rhetoric' while language demeaning to women, blacks, etc., is categorized as the protected exercise of freedom of expression. The moral is unmistakable; whether or not an assaultive form of speech is tolerated or regulated will depend on whether or not the group it harms is in a position to command either the affection or the respect of the society." From this moral, Fish draws the appropriate conclusion: "if you wish to enjoy the protection of society against the verbal harms others may inflict on you, you must become a group the society takes seriously, either because it loves you or fears you."

11. Catherine A. MacKinnon, *Feminism Unmodified* (Cambridge, Mass.: Harvard University Press, 1987).

12. Keith Pavlischek, "The Dilemma of Religious Toleration As Exemplified in the Work of John Courtney Murray, S.J.," (Ph.D. diss., University of Pittsburgh, 1990), p. 217. A revision of his dissertation has recently been published under the title *John Courtney Murray and the Dilemma of Religious Toleration* (Kirksville, Mo.: Thomas Jefferson Press, 1994). This quote can be found on p. 191 of Pavlischek's book.

13. Pavlischek, "The Dilemma . . . ," p. 216.

14. Ibid., p. 218.

15. The essay can be found in James Davison Hunter & Os Guinness, eds., *Articles of Faith, Articles of Peace* (Washington, D.C.: Brookings, 1990), pp. 93–113.

16. Ibid., p. 100.

17. Ibid.

18. Ibid.

19. Ibid., p. 102.

20. Ibid.

21. See Francis J. Connell, C.SS.R., "Christ the King of Civil Rulers," *The American Ecclesiastical Review* 119 (October 1948): 244–53; and "The Theory of the Lay State," *The American Ecclesiastical Review* 125 (July 1951): 7–18.

22. *Quas primas*, n. 4., from *Social Wellsprings*, Joseph Husslein, S.J., ed. (Milwaukee: Bruce, 1943), pp. 30–46. Portions of these reflections on the feast of Christ the King and on *Quas primas* appeared in Michael J. Baxter, C.S.C., "Dominion Over All," *Markings*, Nov. 24, 1991 (Chicago: The Thomas More Association).

23. Ibid., n. 21.

24. Ibid., n. 7.

25. Ibid., n. 8.

26. Ibid.

27. For an account of Augustine's dissolution of the antinomies of antique theory, see John Milbank, *Theology and Social Theory: Beyond Secular Reasoning* (Cambridge, Mass.: Basil Blackwell, 1990), pp. 403–6.

28. Husslein's translation uses the word "anticlericalism." In another translation, the word "secularism" is used (cf. *Selected Papal Encyclicals and Letters*, vol. 1: *1896–1931*, New and Enlarged Edition, with a foreword by Rt. Rev. Msgr. T. E. Hallett, London: Catholic Truth Society, 1939, pp. 3–23). We think "secularism" is the better word here because it is clear that Pius XI is referring to certain theoretical trends and not just the church hierarchy, which is what the word "anti-clericalism" usually implies today.

29. Ibid., n. 12.

30. Will, "Scalia Missed Point," p. F5.

31. *Quas primas*, n. 1.

32. Such "limited states" are almost impossible to control in times of war, as the war in the Persian Gulf clearly exemplified. Americans are dying to have something that seems worth dying for.

33. Ibid., n. 10.

34. In a letter responding to this paper our friend Tom Shaffer observed, "It is no surprise to me that the lawyers at DePaul did not like your freedom-of-religion paper. I did, and that gives you one midwestern lawyer to claim as a fan. I think the dissonance has to do with perception; there is something about looking at religion through constitutional-law lens that makes even a faithful

believer define the issues as the government defines them, as if the church were an intruder on the governmental enterprise. That is really astounding when you consider that the believer-lawyer goes right on being a churchperson and, in other ways, proclaiming the Kingdom."

35. John Courtney Murray, S.J., "For the Freedom and Transcendence of the Church," *American Ecclesiastical Review* 126 (January 1952): 43.

36. Thomas Merton, *The Non-Violent Alternative* (New York: Farrar, Straus, Giroux, 1980), p. 141.

Index

263

INTRO   1   3   6   10 – 13